FROM
OX CARTS
TO JETS

Roy C. Ingersoll.

FROM
OX CARTS
TO JETS

ROY INGERSOLL

and the BORG-WARNER STORY

A Biography by

Will Oursler

PRENTICE-HALL, INC.

Englewood Cliffs, N. J.

Library of Congress Catalog Card Number 59-15137

Printed in the United States of America

33161

Preface

ON THE SURFACE, Borg-Warner might appear to be like any other large American company, doing over six hundred million dollars worth of business a year and reaching for a billion, and Roy Ingersoll, in his seventy-fifth year, might seem like many another chairman of many another board of directors.

Yet of neither is this true. Borg-Warner, because of its unique diversity and its organization of many companies into a kind of decentralized federation yet with proper central control, has been so successful that leading industrialists of other corporations have come to study this organization and its structure, to see how its pattern might be applied to their companies.

And Ingersoll himself is a mixture of the pioneer and the modern man of industry. His life is a bridge between two centuries—and two ages, from the ox cart era to the era of missiles and jet planes carrying passengers across the country at hundreds of miles an hour and man-made satellites thrust into space at speeds measured in thousands of miles an hour.

This is a book also about the rugged, indomitable men with whom Roy Ingersoll worked, a uniquely American group who blazed their own trails—and built great industries. They were men of the automotive industry, farm equipment manufacturers, auto parts makers and men of aviation, experts in jets and rockets and outer space.

It is the story of one man who built his life as if he were shaping a mural of the time: Roy C. Ingersoll, chairman of the board of Borg-Warner, an American corporation with headquarters in Chicago and more than half a hundred factories and plants scattered across America and the world.

Most of all, it is the story of change as seen through the life of this man, the change from primitive to modern ways in many aspects of our lives; in communication, transportation, production methods; in agriculture; in the personal lives, in fact, of all people.

For all those who have helped me in bringing together the many facets and facts of this complex adventure I give my thanks. For all that I have left out that should have been included, I can plead only the limitations of space and the almost limitless horizons of the story itself.

—WILL OURSLER

Contents

1

A man, a boy and a road

THERE ARE some individuals who fit no pattern and do not follow well-worn paths. They rise to heights of achievement in art, education, music, business and industry. They are, in fact, rare leaders who believe in themselves, and the right to scale to the summits.

This is a story of one such man.

As Roy Ingersoll enters swiftly and purposefully into an executive committee meeting on the top floor of the silver and blue Borg-Warner Building on Chicago's lake-front, you immediately are impressed by the man's intensity, by a sense of the dramatic in the deep brown eyes and white hair, and by the drive behind the surface.

His dynamic energy reaches out to those around him. It is an electric energy that others catch. There is an awareness that in this man, now in his seventy-fifth year, the need to accomplish is still strong. His associates not only recognize this force but react to it with harder work and greater effort—and achievement.

At this executive committee meeting, far from sitting back in austere routine concurrence, Chairman of the Board Ingersoll in effect goads the others on, stirs them up to action on some particular matter when, as sometimes happens, they have not realized the immediate importance of action.

1

"When he comes into such a meeting," one company executive said, "he brings a kind of force with him. You can't relax. But you aren't there to relax. You can't sluff off answers because he insists on facts. So you get the facts."

Few excel him in handling men. He has a hundred techniques to fit a hundred individuals. More quickly than any man in the company, he can catch an error, for which a Borg-Warner worker may well find a note on his desk in the morning, signed by R. C. Ingersoll. He has an almost uncanny knack of spotting a wrong figure in a long financial report. He can run his eye over the page and comment casually, "The tenth figure down is an error. It should be $1,500,256.00." And be right.

He can reprimand, and he can also praise, cajole or challenge. He makes himself a part of each man with whom he deals, becoming a kind of conscience and spur and goad, all at once; and becoming, also, a friend. An individual himself, he thinks of other people, not in terms of great masses, but as human beings, and he cares about them, their work, their families and their doing their best.

In a world of many changes and many retreats from past standards, particularly in human relationships on the individual level, Ingersoll has retreated not at all. He always has worked, he has striven and he has achieved, he has won or lost—all within the framework of the individual relationship. He builds men in this way. He praises them for their achievements and points out their shortcomings, but does neither to excess because he wants them to do better. And he gets the best out of them as a result.

He is still young in spirit, interested in everything. If he sees a new model or type of car parked on the street, he will stop to examine it, to see if it has any Borg-Warner parts.

He has lost none of his spirit, his zest, his need to win—or, his sense of humor. He enjoyed telling of a time when he and Gibson Cary, President of Yale & Towne, were together in At-

lantic City. As they came out of the Claridge Hotel the other
man, ten years younger than Mr. Ingersoll, and a lover of
sports, challenged Ingersoll. "I'll race you to the boardwalk for
a dollar."

Roy accepted, and the two executives ran all the way to the
ramp and up to the boardwalk itself. Roy won, but as he reached
the finish line, he slipped and skidded on his knees halfway
across the promenade. His trousers were torn and the skin was
off both knees as well. Just at that moment his friend Senator
Byrd of Virginia happened along, saw Roy and helped him to
his feet. Ingersoll, out of breath, tried to explain to the Senator
how important the race was, for it involved the wager of a
dollar.

On his return to Chicago, Ingersoll arrived the morning his
wife was giving their annual lawn party, held each year at tulip
time on the lovely grounds of their home in Winnetka, Illinois.
As he was showing some of the ladies through the gardens one
of them asked him how he kept the lawn so free of dandelions.
"There's only one way," he told them. "You have to get down
on your knees and pull them out one at a time. That's the way
I do it. Every morning I mark off a square of lawn and dig out
every dandelion in it. Next morning I start in on the next
square. It's slow and hard work and it's terribly hard on the
knees." He thereupon pulled up the bottoms of his trousers,
displaying his badly skinned knees. The ladies were startled—
but extremely sympathetic.

Yet along with his humor and his unquenchable vitality he
is also a man of remarkable perspective. He has lived through
and played an important role in bringing about vast changes
that have affected the lives of literally hundreds of millions of
human beings.

"We have seen many things that have profoundly changed
this world," Ingersoll told the Industrial Economics Conference
sponsored by the Stanford Research Institute in San Francisco

in 1957. "We have seen our cities expand into suburban areas because of the transportation the automobile has given. We find more than 21 million women who are helping to produce in our offices and factories. Why? Because they have been relieved of the drudgery of housework by the products which our household appliance industries have offered to the public.

"We see the farmer who, instead of being able to farm a maximum of 120 acres as was true a few years ago, now is farming 300 acres and doing it easily, without all the back-breaking work of yesterday, and producing more per acre. In our steel mills, where men used to work ten or twelve hours a day handling with tongs the hot metal, pushing it back and forth into the mill, we have seen that scene change to a point where the men operating the mill sit in cushioned chairs, while they control by pushbutton the rolling of the steel which travels through the mills at speeds exceeding 1,000 feet a minute.

". . . We try constantly to remind Borg-Warner's divisional presidents that many of the products which have made their own divisions prosperous may not be in existence ten years from now. We ask them whether they have thoroughly studied the future of every product, whether they are developing new products that are going to take the place or perform the functions of old ones."

Ingersoll himself works harder and longer hours than most of the younger people around him; he arrives at his office by 8:15 and usually stays until about 6 P.M. at his desk, going over reports and letters to be signed. It is not unusual for him to be the last man out of the Borg-Warner offices.

There are times when he, too, finds that he does grow tired, but this is usually after weeks of work to all hours. On these occasions Ingersoll may sleep for virtually an entire week end, then arrive early Monday morning ready for a new week of action.

If the years of struggles, victories as well as occasional setbacks, have left their marks, they have not destroyed his resiliency, his physical strength, his certainty that a job can be done if everybody puts enough effort and team work into doing it. He is impatient with excuses, and persistent in getting a thing corrected, however vast or small it may seem.

But the outsider looking on would have found also a tremendous admiration for Roy Ingersoll among those who work with him. No mere token admiration because this is the boss for whom they work, but rather a recognition of the warmth of the man, combined with his unassailable high standards for everything that he attempts for himself and his business—recognition of the unique qualities of his leadership. His day, and theirs, as a result, is often hard and long. Yet the odd fact the newcomer learns, in talking to them, is that they do not mind.

He stays young in many ways. His interests range wide. For example, he finds modern art and abstract painting difficult to understand. But Ingersoll permitted an exhibit of the most modern work of Chicago's younger artists to be shown at the new Borg-Warner offices.

To newcomers, and a few old-timers also, who did not comprehend his purpose in this exhibit, Ingersoll explained, "If we don't understand the tastes of our times, how can we serve its needs and demands?"

In his seventy-fifth year he is still a man who swims, golfs, goes on hunting trips in the Canadian woods and travels constantly all over America on business trips. And, as many young men across from him at a conference table have discovered, he remains also Borg-Warner's toughest and most tireless negotiator.

Ingersoll has led or participated in negotiations on all major deals and purchases.

Many stories are told of his persistence and skill in handling negotiations, his seemingly instinctive knowledge of when to

yield or what sudden, unexpected tack to take. One story is of
a man who had been arguing for weeks over some patent he
held. Meetings were held at a conference table in Ingersoll's
office. Finally, after lengthy discussions at one session, Ingersoll
stood up with the simple statement: "Sir, our men have spent
weeks and weeks of time debating with you and I cannot waste
any more time in this discussion. I have a very crowded desk
and I must get back to my work. My last offer is entirely proper
and fair—and final."

Before Ingersoll could get back to his desk, the offer was
accepted.

The drive which characterized Roy Ingersoll as a boy and a
youth is still there. A story is told of a time when he was negotiating for a large plant. The discussions had gone on for some
hours; most of the main points were settled and it was obvious
that it was only a matter of time before all of the details could
be resolved.

One of the negotiators on the other side of the table finally
said, "Mr. Ingersoll, I'm hungry. I haven't eaten all day.
Couldn't we stop now for dinner?"

Ingersoll, in the middle of a discussion, turned and said, "Oh,
yes. In just a little while."

"But I need something to eat," the man said. "I've got a terrible headache."

"Oh, I'm sorry." Ingersoll, obviously sincere, called in his
secretary and asked for aspirin and a glass of water for the other
man. The negotiations continued until 11:30 P.M., when all
the questions were finally settled and the deal was closed. By
that time, everyone was dead tired and wanted to go home.

It was too late for dinner.

An unusual man, people have called him. A great American
industrialist, and yet unusual in many ways. Difficult sometimes, hard to understand, impossible to keep up with. And yet
also a man of courage, some of them will add. Courage in that

he recognizes no pussy-footing on basic issues; he refuses to be afraid to speak out. He wants no "yes" men around him, and will not be one himself.

Above all, he is not afraid of the future.

The American frontier was still a reality when Roy Ingersoll was born in the town of Sandoval, Illinois, on October 24, 1884. Over the ruts and mud of the National Pike that went by the white picket fence of their yard, America rode past—in Conestoga wagons, drawn by horse or mule or oxen, loaded down with all the family possessions, furniture and clothes and baby crib, with a hand plow roped on the back. They were en route from what to these travelers were the worked-out, over-populated areas of the East, in New England, Pennsylvania, New York and Ohio, to the free land and homesteading opportunities in Kansas and Nebraska and the still unfolding world of the West.

It was a unique moment in many ways—a brief interim at the threshold of a new age. The Indian wars were almost but not quite over. Custer's last stand at the Little Big Horn had occurred a mere eight years before; it would be another two years before Geronimo, the predatory Apache, would surrender to General Crook.

The Brooklyn Bridge had been opened the year before; the Statue of Liberty was still in the process of construction. The great farms of the far Midwest were only beginning to take shape; Sandoval, Illinois, in fact, was a coal mining community surrounded by wheat fields and apple orchards.

To the boy named Roy, the wagons that rolled past the picket fence were far more than mere wagons; they were exploration and adventure and the future, just as rockets and space satellites became the adventure and the future for youngsters in the second half of the twentieth century. At six years he would peer through the pickets as horses and oxen trudged past. As the high wheels creaked and the harness strained and the driver's whip hissed and cracked, the boy would wave and call a greeting.

For hours sometimes he would watch, as he grew older. This was the world, America going by, with all its belongings, a mile or two an hour. Sometimes these pioneers would stop to fill their jugs with water at the Ingersoll well, and he would have a chance to talk with them, and ask them where they were from and where they were heading.

Indian stories were still rife in these days and some of the more sensational dime novels in the local stores showed pictures of bloody massacres and scalpings, and he would ask the wagon people if they weren't frightened about Indian attacks out on the western plains to which they were migrating.

On one occasion, at a time when there were stories of Indian uprisings in the Dakotas, the six-year-old solemnly asked one group, as he helped them fill the jugs from the well, "Where you are going will the Indians kill you, too?"

The man filling the jug was a towering giant in a weather-beaten felt hat. "We're going to Nebraska to start a farm twelve times as big as the one we had back in Pennsylvania. And my guess is they've taken care of the Indians in Nebraska."

But the boy shook his head doubtfully as their wagon drove off.

They came from everywhere—heading for everywhere. One family was going all the way to California where they would mine for gold and raise western ponies. Another was going out to Montana cattle country. A third was going to Kansas.

They were strong, serious, unfrightened, these later-day pioneers. Men who did not believe in welfare states but in their own hands and strength, and were grateful for the opportunity of land on which to build a new life. The tide of America rolling by the front yard was a symbol of life itself, forever striving to reach beyond itself, beyond the rim of wheat fields and apple orchards sprawled across the Sandoval countryside.

They were a symbol to him of life and movement and the future. Once when very young he had a terrible fever and in his delirium the boy imagined that he was lying on the pike and the wagons and horses and oxen plodded toward him and he could not move and they were about to crush him to death. He woke up in his bed screaming in terror.

But when he was well the fear was not that he would be crushed under the iron-rimmed wagon wheels, but that he would not be a part of the surging pageant. The driving need to be part of it was uppermost in his thoughts even then; the need to run forward, to be ahead of all the others.

He was a boy of ten but on Saturdays and during summer vacations he would work in his father's factory, for a few pennies an hour, and he learned how to run the machines as well as any of the older men in the plant.

The machines were a symbol to him, the promise of tomorrow. He could not conceive, of course, the vast changes that lay ahead. Yet he would listen as his father, back from a selling trip to the farm-equipment companies, would tell him of new ideas that important leaders were discussing. There were some who said that soon there would be horseless carriages that would do away with buggies and wagons, and that horses or oxen would be replaced by machines that pulled the plows. It would be a new world, built by men with new ideas and new machines.

The thoughts that danced in the boy's mind were a strange mixture—wagons and horses and mules and oxen pulling together through muddy ruts into the mechanized tomorrow.

Such was a youngster's dream, as he gazed up at blue Illinois skies, on a midwestern summer's day.

Three-quarters of a century later, in the year 1959, the pike

had become US Route 50, a high speed transcontinental high-
way where the latest motor cars raced by at fifty and sixty miles
an hour, and the reckless pushed their vehicles to eighty and
one hundred.

Perhaps nothing in history could more sharply depict the
changes that had come in this extraordinary seventy-five years
than these two highways: the unpaved road of the wagons and
the highspeed route of modern adventurers, heading for vacations to Texas, Colorado, Arizona, Mexico or California.

No period in all history had ever witnessed such great
changes in the patterns of our culture or civilization. Not one
age, but half a dozen had been born: the age of light and elec-
tricity, and the automobile, the age of flight, the age of radio
and then television, the age of movies and then talking pictures,
the age of electronics, the age of the atom and its unleashed
powers, the jet age and the age of space and its exploration.

Certainly the youngster on the grass could not have guessed
these marvels that were to come or that he would have a part
in; the machines and methods, discoveries and inventions, concepts that would change our entire way of living, even our
thinking about the structure of the universe.

Nor could the boy have foreseen the structure of a company
such as Borg-Warner, a corporation of world-wide impact, a
merging of many ideas and plants and products into a dynamic
organization, serving the needs of literally tens of millions of
customers throughout the world.

He could not have guessed of some of the products such a
company might turn out, for most were unknown. Air-conditioning equipment that could purify, heat and cool the air of
skyscrapers and great ocean liners and cars speeding over the
highways, and make living much more comfortable in hundreds
of thousands of homes across America. Machines that could
search electronically for oil in the earth; mechanisms to help
run giant airliners; many important automobile parts—clutches,

radiators, universal joints, standard and automatic transmissions, and overdrives; home appliances that would include refrigerators, freezers, automatic washing machines and dryers; chemicals and plastics—a hundred or more products that would help to change the living patterns of our times.

Whatever changes the future had in store, he would be part of it all, the boy on the grass was sure; he would help to shape it and direct it and make it go.

2

A town and a man

THE SOIL was the lifeblood of Stephen Ingersoll. The soil he loved, not only as the business by which his family earned their daily bread, but particularly as an avocation, a way of life, a philosophy, almost a religion. The earth gave and the earth demanded; you tendered it love and care and it brought forth grass and grain and fruit.

The Ingersolls had come to Illinois from Port Jervis, N. Y., in 1870 when Stephen Ingersoll was twelve. They had been seeking rich farm soil and had settled on a farm near Winona. The rail-splitting days of Abraham Lincoln were not too many decades past; the countryside was still a sparsely populated land of new farms staked out on these Illinois prairies. School had been two miles distant and Stephen had walked the distance there and back in the winter months, through the deep snows, and finished his school assignments besides, and the farm chores.

When he was finished with school in Winona he went to normal college in Valparaiso, Indiana, taught school on the side to pay expenses, and rented farm land on which he tended his crops in his spare time. He was still in his late teens when he began this operation: a few years after he had finished college he had been able to save from his earnings as teacher and farmer the fantastic sum of nearly ten thousand dollars.

The sum purchased for him a grain elevator in the town of

Sandoval, where he began operations buying, selling and stor-
ing wheat for the farmers. As soon as he bought wheat—and
particularly when he contracted for crops not yet harvested—
he would immediately sell a like amount on the Chicago market
for delivery at a definite specified date and price.

On one occasion he arranged to purchase wheat for delivery
in the Chicago market at a certain price and immediately sold
the same amount on the futures market. However, after he had
made the contract for the farmers' wheat, the price had risen
rapidly and the farmers failed to deliver the wheat as agreed.
They made many excuses for this; they could not get it thrashed,
or the horses were sick; in any case they would not deliver it.

If he had to buy the wheat on the open market to cover his
commitments he faced ruin. He hastened to Chicago to meet
with the grain brokerage firm to whom he had sold the wheat
and told them his plight. These grain experts advised him to
wait a little and the price would break.

Stephen waited. The last day for the delivery of the wheat was
only three days off, then it was two, then one; still they told him
to wait. On the following day pandemonium broke loose on the
floor of the exchange, as the prices collapsed and Stephen was
able to fulfill his commitments by buying wheat in the open
market.

A week later, after finishing his business in Chicago, he got
back to Sandoval, flushed with victory, and found disaster waiting for him on his doorstep. As soon as the price break began
the farmers had poured in their wheat to the grain elevator.
And with Stephen in Chicago, his assistant had bought the
grain in at the price for which it had been contracted, although
the wheat market price had receded far below the contract
price.

So again he faced ruin. But the grain people told him to buy
oat futures; there was a big shortage in oats, they advised, and
the price should rise sharply a little later. They were right. The

following year he made enough to pay off the losses he had suffered on the wheat and still show a profit.

In 1883, he became part owner of a lumber yard in Sandoval. That same year two unrelated events occurred that were to shape his entire future: he met and fell in love with Cordelia Gaylord who had recently moved to Sandoval from Hoyleton, Illinois. And a Pittsburgh steel expert moved into Sandoval with a plan to build a factory to produce coulter discs.

These coulter discs, or coulter blades as they were called, were fastened to the beam in front of the moldboard of the old-fashioned horse-drawn plow, and cut the sod and weeds, making it possible for the moldboard to turn over the soil into a clean furrow.

The steelman from Pittsburgh purchased building materials on credit from the lumber yard, but before the building was completed his funds were exhausted and he was forced to abandon his project. The lumber yard had a lien on this factory. Stephen was able, by buying out the interests of his two partners, to take it over.

On Thanksgiving day of that year, Stephen and Cordelia were married. It was quite an event in the small world of Sandoval. The Gaylords had come originally from the town of Skaneatales, in New York State, by way of the Erie Canal and the Ohio and Mississippi rivers, a journey that took more than a month.

Following their marriage, they began plans to build their home along side of the National Pike. The following year, 1884, the Sandoval Manufacturing Company, starting with a staff of less than twenty men, entered competition with the major steel firms of the East, as the only plant in the Midwest turning out coulter discs for farm plows—in the heart of America's farmland.

On October 24, 1884 their first son, Roy, was born.

The obscure midwestern wheatland town of Sandoval, in this

last decade and a half of the nineteenth century, was a small
and by later standards a harsh and often a bleak world. For the
Ingersolls, success was a varying condition; there were moments of high triumph and moments of desperation, when
Stephen Ingersoll did not see how he could keep on against the
competition of the big companies, when there appeared no way
to get funds to support his wife and three sons and two daughters; times when he was almost ready to quit—alone in the
small hours of the morning, gazing through the window of the
house into the darkness of the deserted Pike and the stars beyond, almost ready to say he had given this business its try.

Yet he could not turn away from it; he knew this even in such
moments. It was more than a promise of profit from the shining
sharp-edged discs that came out of his plant for sale to the farm
implement companies in cities to the north and east of Sandoval.
It was more than a piece of metal. The soil these coulters cut
into was the sustenance of the world—and of Stephen Ingersoll.

There were a few things that mattered deeply to him: his
family, his faith in God and in work, his plant and his home,
the piece of farmland he owned now on the edge of town. There
was the lawn he cultivated with his own hands, with the aid and
occasional suggestions of his eldest son Roy, and his horses, in
the care and grooming of which he took great pride, and his
consummate skill at croquet.

It was an era of beards and handlebar mustaches, of barber
shop quartets and bustles and bowler hats. If Sandoval's fash-
ions did not quite match the *fin de siècle* styles of Paris or Bos-
ton or New York they were still close to cities large enough to
offer the latest styles. The Ingersolls lived often on short supplies and last year's styles because most of the earnings went
right back into the business. But on occasions when there was
a little extra cash that could be spared from the business,
Stephen would give Cordelia fifty dollars and she would take
the children, Roy and Harold and Winifred and Jennie and

Stephen Lawrence, on a shopping tour to Centralia, six miles south. The money would be divided up so that each obtained something he needed, perhaps a suit or other piece of clothing for one of the boys, a dress or bonnet for Winifred or Jennie. And perhaps, but rarely, a new dress for Cordelia herself.

Stephen's father, ninety-three-year-old Grandfather Abraham Ingersoll, came to live with them in this house on the Pike, and Stephen built on an addition to his house, a living room and bedroom. Grandfather Ingersoll was a positive-minded individualist who could still read the newspapers without glasses, right up to the day he died—at ninety-six. His one great failing was chewing tobacco. He was always announcing that he was about to give up this dreadful habit and would throw away all the tobacco in his possession to prove it. Unfortunately, this made him so crotchety that the household would be thrown into turmoil. Stephen would buy a new plug of tobacco and slip it into his father's coat pocket, and all would shortly be peaceful again.

Central heating of homes, and inside plumbing as well, were still nonexistent in Sandoval. There was a large hard-coal stove in the living room, and on winter mornings the youngsters would grab their clothes and run from chilly bedrooms to dress by the warmth of the stove. On Saturday nights Cordelia Ingersoll would heat large kettles of water so that everybody would be clean and fresh for Sunday school and church the following morning. They had one maid to help with the cooking and housework; they paid her $1.75 a week.

The family had a surrey, as well as a runabout with red wheels and rubber tires, and a handsome pair of driving horses. None of the nearly 30 workers at the Sandoval Manufacturing Company had a surrey or buggy of his own, and when they or their families were going to Centralia for shopping, they would always ask Mr. Ingersoll if they could borrow the surrey, and he would always let them take it.

Between Stephen and his eldest son, Roy, there developed a special relationship. It was not that he loved the girls or his other sons less; it was that the oldest boy was such a complete reflection of himself, particularly in the boy's desire to be a part of the business his father was building. They shared a love of work and machines, of farming, of play, of nature. On the farm at the edge of town, the father raised corn and timothy. He enjoyed getting out there and running the cultivator himself and sometimes on a frost-tinged Saturday morning he would slip away from the factory, and he and Roy would be out there husking corn. The horse-drawn cultivators designed to break up the soil and keep it porous could work only one row at a time; in 1959, on a modern farm, a cultivator worked the soil of as many as four rows at once at three times the speed. There was much to do together on this tract of farm land; an orchard of apple trees to spray, fields to tend and keep clean of weeds, to plant and harvest.

To Mother Cordelia all the family were the same; she would help them equally in the evenings with their school work; scold them for lack of proper study or preparation, for dirty faces or failure to wear warm enough clothing. Before they went to bed she would read them passages from the Bible.

But it was Roy whom the father took with him on trips to St. Louis and, no matter how busy he was, there was always time in the summer afternoon for the ball game of the St. Louis Browns or Cardinals. It was to Roy that the father would pour out stories of what had happened, and where the coulter discs had sold and where he had failed, on his return from selling trips to the farm implement companies in Janesville and Rockford, Moline and Kankakee, Racine, Wisconsin; South Bend, Indiana; or Louisville, Kentucky.

The Janesville Machine Company was directed by one of the great men in the farm implement business—J. A. Craig. The purchasing agent was a Mr. Cobb, a Civil War veteran with a beard that reached down almost to his waist. Mr. Cobb always greeted Stephen Ingersoll effusively, always sent a messenger to tell Mrs. Cobb, and later, when phones arrived, would call to announce that Mr. Ingersoll had arrived, for he always invited him to his home for one of Mrs. Cobb's fine dinners.

Back from one such trip, he told Roy, "This time I turned that dinner invitation down."

"Why?" To the boy it sounded almost unbelievable.

"As soon as I reached the office, Mr. Cobb started to send a message to his wife and tell her I would be there for dinner, but I stopped him. I told him I'd been coming there for years and nowhere had I received greater hospitality and no one was a better cook than Mrs. Cobb."

His father paused for effect. "But I pointed out that the purpose of my visit was to try to secure a contract for coulter discs, and this I had not been able to do. I informed him that much as I would hate to do it, I would gladly pass up one of Mrs. Cobb's delicious pies if I could secure a contract from Mr. Cobb."

Again the pause, as the boy waited. Then the climax: "Mr. Cobb told me he had not thought of it that way. He gave me a contract for what amounts to 20 per cent of their needs for this year."

In the future that figure would climb steadily until it was 100 per cent. But at that moment Stephen was thinking only of this triumph, as he clasped his arm around his son's shoulder and added a confidential postscript, "And I had dinner with the Cobbs anyway—and a piece of Mrs. Cobb's delicious pie."

Often he and his father talked of business and what the leading men of the farm industry were like, the good and bad, the kind and cruel. Some of these men became his father's good friends, and to Roy, even as a youth, they were his friends too, a part of the fabric of steel and its products.

This factory was still a one-man company, with Stephen

Ingersoll filling all positions: he was general manager, sales manager, bookkeeper, comptroller, and factory manager. It was not until 1898, fourteen years after starting the factory, that he was able to buy a typewriter and hire a secretary—at eight dollars a week. Previous to that he wrote all the letters by hand and made out the invoices.

It was only a block out of the way coming from school for Roy to stop in the office where he would take care of the letters and invoices his father had written to customers, along with letters to suppliers, often with a request for a little more time to meet a payment. To make carbon copies in those days, Roy would put the letters in a "copy book" which was a book of transparent tissue paper. The copying process involved putting each letter under a carbon sheet in the book. A wet cloth run through the wringer was applied to the other side. There might be half a dozen such sheets, depending upon the number of letters. When all were properly in the copying book, it was put in a press, the upper plates screwed down and the copy letter was made on the transfer paper in five or ten minutes.

While there was a foreman to help run the operations of the plant, when some machine broke down it was usually Stephen Ingersoll, with his knowledge of each machine, who would make the adjustment to get it back into operation promptly. Often he would come home clothes covered with grease.

On Saturdays and over summers and holiday periods, almost as soon as he was tall enough to reach the machines, Roy was working in the plant, side-by-side with the men. His wages were five cents an hour—fifty cents for a ten-hour, steaming summer day.

This was considerably less than the regular employees received since a base rate in the factory for all employees was twelve and a half cents per hour, or $1.25 for a ten-hour day, shortened to nine hours on Saturday. However, there were incentives or piecework which enabled the men to make up to twenty-five cents an hour, or $2.50 per day, on some of the disc-rolling as well as the grinding and polishing machines. This was a considerably better wage he recalled than was paid to the section men on the railroad that passed the factory's door; these men, who had to work outside in all kinds of weather, received ten cents an hour. At that time the coal miners had been recently unionized into what was to become the United Mine Workers Division of the American Federation of Labor. They were earning a little more per hour, perhaps as much as twenty-five to thirty cents, but employment was very unsteady. Sometimes they would go to the mine and work for only two or three hours and run out of coal cars and their day's work would be over, along with any further income for that day. The only other industry in town was the Sandoval Zinc Company; wages there were $1.10 per day for ten hours, or eleven cents an hour.

The small companies had recognized a community of interest created by the existence of the giant steel firms and their ability to drive the small companies out of business should they choose to sell at unreasonably low prices or to force customers to buy a "package" of various products. Recognition by the small companies of this community interest led to exchange of information regarding various market forces affecting their business and any attempts by the steel firms to put the pressure on one of the smaller companies.

Disputes, charges and countercharges among the bigger companies in this combine finally smashed the whole idea. Young Roy came in from school one afternoon in the panic year of 1893 to find his mother in tears.

His father had come home to tell her of the disaster, she said.

Cooperation among the smaller companies was finished; from now on small companies would be less able to compete with the big companies on favorable terms. Sandoval was a pigmy compared to the big firms, and without a lot of luck, grit, and inspired leadership it might be snowed under in a competitive battle. Competition has been a basic premise of American public policy, it has distinguished America from some other countries and it has benefited all Americans. But survival in a competitive economy demanded of both men and firms the highest measure of courage, ingenuity, perseverance in the face of tremendous odds.

By then Stephen Ingersoll had become one of the chief employers in town and he felt an obligation to his workers. But in the months that followed, his firm, caught in a whirlwind of overwhelming competition, had to backtrack and eventually the plant was operating only three or four days a week.

The Pittsburgh firms were taking no chances: his shipments of raw steel arrived with sight drafts that had to be paid in full before the steel could be unloaded. One man who several times saved him from the very edge of disaster was his friend and former partner in the lumber yard, Fred Reinhardt, who was also president and owner of the Sandoval bank.

Stephen Ingersoll would spill out his troubles and Reinhardt would lean back in his chair behind his cluttered desk and tell him, "Stephen, Stephen, you don't need collateral with me. How much is it they want this time? Sign the note."

The money would be there—and the firm would go on.

But the battle of the pigmy against the titans grew even more grim; there were times when the plant had to shut down entirely, and the men were out of work and could not find other jobs, and some of them and their families were in want.

Ingersoll felt his obligation to these men: there had to be jobs. If he could not keep the disc plant going full time, he could do something else. The result was a first step in the theory of diversification: he started the Sandoval Canning Company, to can apples, beans and tomatoes, main products in the area. Located in a frame building which he built a few blocks from the disc plant, this factory gave work not only to the men but also to their wives, who mainly did peeling of the tomatoes and apples.

The canning plant was an immediate success. Ingersoll would contract for all the tomato crops in the area, as many as 200 to 225 acres of tomatoes. It was a tremendous production. The price was eighteen cents a bushel—later twenty.

One memorable season, the spring was very cold, summer came late and the tomatoes didn't ripen but kept growing larger and larger. Then the weather changed suddenly and the sun shone bright and hot and the tomatoes ripened overnight. The farmers picked them by the thousands of bushels and brought them in to the cannery all at once. The canning plant was operating day and night. Wagons were lined up for half a mile or more, waiting to unload, and everyone agreed there had never been so many tomatoes before.

Ingersoll had contracted to buy the entire crop, and he was obligated to take all they brought, but after the storage bins were full and the rest of the plant and several sheds besides, there was simply no more room for tomatoes. The farmers were paid off and told to get rid of the tomatoes at the town dump.

Some of the farmers would get back at the end of the line and sell the same load of tomatoes to the cannery all over again. A few sold the same load several times over before the plant manager caught on. After that the wagon loads of displaced tomatoes went to the dump in escorted convoys.

Young Roy, eager to be a part of everything, pleaded for a chance to work in that canning factory and finally obtained the permission of his reluctant parents. His job was to salt the tomato cans as they went by on the belt line. He later stated that he learned one unforgettable truth from this job: that a level teaspoon of salt is the exact amount required properly to salt a three-pound can of tomatoes.

One adventure in the cannery did teach him, however, the occasional wisdom of swift retreat.

He had been reprimanded unjustly by a corpulent lady worker whose job was to operate the machine which filled the empty but salted cans by means of an automatic plunger. Roy saw the lady standing by the machine and temptation overcame him. He turned one of the cans on the belt line upside down, so that when it reached the machine the plunger would strike against the closed end. He reasoned that the tomatoes pushed against the can by the plunger would have to go somewhere— and they did!

Screaming in outrage and wiping off tomatoes splattered from her face to her feet, the corpulent lady worker started up the stairs after him.

But the young tomato-can salter had suddenly jumped out of the second-story window, about twelve feet high, landed without any broken bones, and could not be found the rest of that afternoon.

Not long after setting up the canning company, Ingersoll launched a third enterprise, a barrel factory, largely to handle the apple crop. In addition they made crates and boxes for strawberries. Roy Ingersoll worked in the barrel factory too, as well as in the plant making strawberry boxes.

This was no colossus of industry, the companies that Stephen Ingersoll had built. There were no world-wide implications in a corrugated steel factory building turning out coulter discs for plows, or a frame structure where they canned local crops of tomatoes and beans, or an apple barrel factory to serve orchard growers of the area.

All of the vast implications lay in the unguessed future.

But Stephen Ingersoll had great pride in these ventures of his, and many of the families in this roadside metropolis called Sandoval had come to depend upon them for their work and livelihood.

3

Portrait: Father and son

SHADES WERE DRAWN to keep out the glare of sun one early fall afternoon in 1900. The man in the bed lay motionless on his back, pale, his eyes wide and glittering with fever. Typhoid, the doctor had pronounced. The word had spread in the town: Steve Ingersoll was sick with fever.

By the door, Roy and his brothers, Harold and Stephen, and his sisters Winifred and Jennie, stood watching. The hush was broken suddenly. Someone was coming in the front door. Uncle Arthur Gaylord, plant manager at the factory and Stephen Ingersoll's brother-in-law, pushed past the children into the sick room.

"Steve—listen!" Gaylord said. "There's labor trouble at the plant. You've got to——"

He halted, as if realizing for the first time how ill Stephen was. The man in the bed pushed himself up. "What's happening?" the sick man asked.

"They're all stirred up. They're down there standing around, thirty or forty of them. Nobody's working."

Perhaps, if he said a word to the workers, the sick man murmured. Perhaps if he could go to them, if he could talk to the men himself, he could show them how they were being misadvised, misled into this kind of action.

There was no reason for trouble unless someone went in to

24

foment it. The men were better paid than in factories for miles around. None of his workers needed to worry about coming to him in any difficulty. It was a small plant in a small midwestern town, trying, in fact, to compete against the giant firms.

Steve Ingersoll believed in his men. In fifty years, following this abortive trouble, there was never a strike or labor difficulty in an Ingersoll plant, even when they were employing not a handful, but thousands of men.

Ingersoll asked his brother-in-law to help him up. "I'm going over there," he told Gaylord.

Moments later, he was dressed and starting out to the street, heedless of the protests of Cordelia and his children, who could only watch as the two men drove off to the plant.

Despite his efforts, the instigators of this trouble succeeded for a brief time in getting the men to walk out on their jobs.

One strike organizer told Ingersoll and Gaylord, "I know you pay wages equal or more than average in this community. What does that matter? We've got the power to make you do what we want."

It was only a short time before the men, disillusioned by unfulfilled promises, began to return. But the strike dragged on and was not officially over for more than a year.

There were moments of grave concern, especially in the first days, with Steve Ingersoll ill and unable to assume full command.

Relatives of the Ingersolls and the Gaylords agreed to help keep the plant going if they could. One afternoon a few of them were due to arrive on the train. Waiting at the Sandoval station to meet them was Stephen Ingersoll, his seventeen-year-old son, Roy, and Arthur Gaylord.

Also on the platform was a tight little knot of surly-looking coal miners. When the relatives arrived this small band followed the two men and the boy and the relatives up the street, shouting and waving ropes and crying out, "Let's hang them. Hang them."

It was a time of terror for the family.

The company kept a dray wagon to deliver coal to the plant boilers and furnaces and also to make deliveries of steel. Because of the strike, Roy gave up high school that year to drive the wagon and keep his father's company from closing down for good.

For Roy it meant getting up shortly after 5:00 each morning to feed the horses before he had his own breakfast, so that he could have them harnessed and ready to start the day's work by 7:00 o'clock.

There were some who would shout at him as he drove his father's wagon on the streets of this town where he lived and where most everyone was their friend. "Scab!" would be heard out of the shadows.

And the seventeen-year-old would shake his head and often, alone in the darkness of his room at night, think of this terror that stalked him and his wagon, of the injustice of what was happening. Many of the workers themselves told him in secret that they did not want this strike, and said, "We want to come back to work but we can't—we're afraid."

To Roy this thing was like living in the midst of nightmare, contorted and senseless and unreal.

But it was real and already it had cost him months of school, and alone there in the dark the boy would wonder if it would ever end.

At long last it was over and the men returned to their jobs, the driver returned to his job delivering coal and steel on the wagon, and the boy returned to his schoolwork.

But that earlier afternoon as his father, ill and feverish and determined, had gone out of the house, nothing had seemed so important as the man himself. To the teen-age Roy, it was like a scene in a drama, something out of a saga in his schoolbooks—

Mr. and Mrs. Stephen A. Ingersoll and family, Sandoval, Ill. Roy is holding the pony, "Katy." Winifred Ingersoll Zetterberg is on the bicycle. Steve, Harold, and Jennie are in the cart. About 1893.

Mr. and Mrs. S. A. Ingersoll, Sandoval, Ill. About 1900.

Sandoval Manufacturing Co., 1890. R. C. Ingersoll, at age six, holding his father's hand. Note coulter discs held by workmen.

Ingersoll Cooperage Shop. It stood next to the Sandoval Manufacturing Co. Roy Ingersoll is standing in the large door. A. C. Gaylord is at the extreme right.

S. A. Ingersoll tomato canning factory, Sandoval, Ill., where R. C. Ingersoll worked as a small boy.

Sandoval Manufacturing Co., 1898. R. C. Ingersoll is standing in doorway.

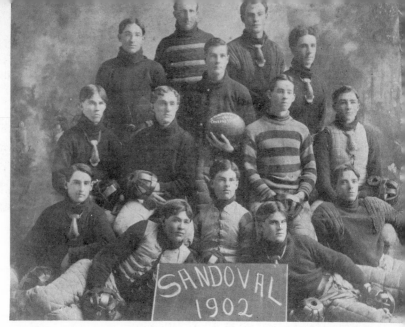

Sandoval central Illinois championship high school football team, 1902.
R. C. Ingersoll, front row center, just under the football.

R. C. Ingersoll, about 1902.

Work force of the Galesburg Coulter Disc Co., 1905. Henry Gaylord is the man with the derby.

After the fire, November 1, 1915, which destroyed the factory started in September, 1904.

After the fire: the re-built plant and new office, showing the landscaping installed by R. C. Ingersoll without his father's knowledge.

Stephen A. Ingersoll home, Galesburg, 1910-1944.

Roy C. Ingersoll home, Galesburg, 1912-1931.

with Lulu Hinchliff on cruise
rd ore boat *Nettleton* from Con-
ht, Ohio, to Duluth.

Another view of Roy and his bride-
to-be aboard ore boat.

Mr. and Mrs. R. C. Ingersoll on
their honeymoon at Niagara
Falls, September, 1911, enroute
to the Adirondacks.

Mr. and Mrs. Stephen A. Ingersoll,
1909.

R. C. I. and night superintendent, Ferd Protzman, in yard of Norwalk Steel
and Iron Co., Norwalk, Ohio, 1910.

Lulu Hinchliff Ingersoll, R. C. I. and Jane in Galesburg, May 1913.

Grandfather Stephen A. Ingersoll with his first grandchild, Jane, 1914.

The sign reads: "Avery 'light-weight' tractor. Doesn't pack the ground. Doesn't waste fuel moving useless dead weight. Travels over soft ground."

The Roy Ingersolls' family Dodge in 1918.

Barbara, Jim, Bob, Jane at grandfather Stephen Ingersoll's farm, Delavan, Wisconsin, 1924.

Roy Ingersoll with his family in 1919. (*Left to right*) Mrs. Stephen A. Ingersoll, Mary Louise Edmondson, Bob, Mrs. Hinchliff, Margaret Sinclair, Lulu Ingersoll, Barbara, Jane, Jim, and Roy.

Mr. and Mrs. Roy C. Ingersoll, on a holiday cruise aboard a U.S. Steel Corporation boat from Gary to Duluth and back.

Present home of Mr. and Mrs. Roy Ingersoll in Winnetka, Illinois.

Holiday at Grand Canyon. Roy at top, Bob fourth from bottom, October, 1925.

Roy aboard C. S. Davis's yacht, Malabar VI, on Lake Michigan.

SEVERE BENDING TEST

1910-14 DISK BLADE
AFTER BENDING TEST

1932 DISK BLADE
AFTER BENDING TEST

Disc testing, showing comparative durability of heat-treated discs.

Comparison of heat-treated disc (left) and non-heat-treated disc tested on same disc harrow.

Discs at work.

C. S. Davis and R. C. Ingersoll testing amphibious tank, Long Lake, near Kalamazoo, Michigan, 1943.

Final assembly line for Beach Busters, 1944.

Amphibious tank, developed and produced for the U. S. Marine Corps by the Ingersoll-Kalamazoo Division of Borg-Warner.

Amphibious tank afloat.

the tall man, bent upon his purpose of talking to his own men.

Watching him, Roy was remembering moments out of the past. The day his father had put him on a bike for the first time and gave him a shove and he was on his way down the street. The bike was just too big for him to reach the pedals, but he rode it standing up. Or the Shetland pony his father had given him. It belonged to all the children but Roy, as the oldest, naturally assumed command.

Or the orchestra another uncle, Edward Gaylord, had started after he moved back to Sandoval from Montana with his family in 1896. Edward was a musician and piano tuner; music was in the blood of the Gaylords, people said. Roy was no musician, but he had bought himself a gleaming trombone and learned to handle it well enough to be in the orchestra, which played at a number of important events in Sandoval, and made trips around the countryside, performing at political rallies.

One close friend of his father's was Philip Shanklin, who was both insurance agent and editor of the local paper. Once he tried to sell Roy's father insurance by pointing out that it would be too bad if Stephen were to die and leave his wife so poor that, to take care of the children, she would have to marry almost the first man who came along. Wouldn't it be better, the insurance man asked, if Mr. Ingersoll left his wife a tidy sum of insurance so that she could take her time and pick a "worthy successor?"

On another occasion this editor published an article to which a local labor organizer took exception and demanded a retraction. This was the editor's opportunity; in the retraction he took occasion to spell out in detail all the complaints he was retracting. After the organizer saw the retraction and the way it was worded, he reportedly told the editor, "Say anything you want about me but please don't print any more of those retractions."

In that moment of crisis, as his father had gone out of the

house, thoughts and memories had jumbled in Roy's mind. Above all the picture of his father in the midst of struggle; all of the years had been a struggle.

This period of the 1890s, and the early part of the next century, were days of mergers and consolidation when some of America's greatest companies were born. One of the attempts in the farm equipment industry sought to merge the reaping and mowing machine industry into a giant $35 million corporation. This was in 1890 and was spearheaded by Colonel A. L. Conger, producer of section knives that were sold to practically all of these companies producing mowers and reapers. His main plant was at Akron, Ohio, and he had another plant in Chicago which was to become the West Pullman Works of the Ingersoll Products Division of Borg-Warner.

Conger had succeeded in obtaining options or tentative agreements for the merging of twenty major companies which included McCormick, Deering, Aultman and Miller, Adriance, Platt and Company, the Plano Manufacturing Company, and others, all of whom were to be brought together into one company.

In a thesis prepared by Norman F. Thomas, a history of the formation and operation of the Minneapolis-Moline Co., an illuminating statement which Conger gave the Associated Press at that time is quoted: "The present demoralization of the business necessitated the formation of a new company. I can recall over eighty companies engaged in the business which have failed, entailing a loss upon farmers, laboring men and manufacturers of between thirty-five and forty million dollars. While some companies have been successful, the general condition of the business was such that it became necessary to give the farmers better machines at lower prices, if possible, without disaster to the manufacturers . . .

"The cost of material has been advancing so that it has become necessary either to raise the price of the machines to the farmers, or, through economy, produce and distribute them more cheaply . . .

"We do not expect to check competition."

This attempt at a major merger in the industry collapsed, however, when a number of the companies involved backed out because they disagreed with the valuation put on some of the other plants.

The next such plan promoted in the farm equipment industry was for two years a source of tremendous concern and worry to Stephen Ingersoll: this was to be a merger of the tillage companies who were customers for his coulter discs. He was fearful, as he told Roy, that if all of these implement companies entered into such a merger their combined requirements for coulter discs would justify the group's putting up a plant of its own to produce the discs. If the Sandoval Manufacturing Company were taken into the merger and became the coulter disc division of such a tremendous combine, it would be a great thing for his company, but if he were left on the outside he would have no place to sell his products. This proposed merger was headed by William A. Vincent, who attempted to form a combine by merging thirty of the plow companies into a $35 million corporation, exactly the same size as had been proposed nine years earlier for the harvesting machine companies. Stephen Ingersoll followed the progress of these negotiations very carefully. On a visit to some of these implement companies he was informed that the merger details had been worked out and that Martin Kingman of the Kingman Plow Company in Peoria was to become president of the combine. Stephen told Roy of his surprise that Kingman was to be chosen as he was president of a comparatively small farm equipment company, measured beside some of the giants of the industry at that time.

One day in 1901 Stephen came home greatly elated. He had important news for the family. The proposed merger of the farm tillage implement manufacturers had collapsed. He had been informed that this happened after James D. Oliver of the Oliver Chilled Plow Company of South Bend refused to enter into the merger. Mr. Oliver was reported to have told this group that he had developed and built up his own business independently over many years, and wished to continue to operate it in that manner.

There was always one more battle his father had to win. And almost always it was not for himself but for someone else. Factories to keep men of the town working. Civic and religious activities. In spite of the great demands of his business he found time to help plan and finance a new Congregational church for Sandoval.

Watching him that fall day, sick and feverish, going to talk to his men, the boy was deeply aware of the heritage of courage he had to uphold.

At eighteen, when he was graduated from Sandoval High School, Roy Ingersoll gave a class oration. He spoke with remarkable maturity, most of the parents who heard the oration agreed. He talked about the potentials of tremendous industrial growth in America because of the nation's abundance of natural resources and means of transportation. He pointed to oil deposits, gas, coal, iron and other ores, the vast lumber resources, the great railroad transportation facilities. He cited also the Great Lakes, which enabled industry to transport ores cheaply from the mines of Michigan and Minnesota.

Patterns of life—like patterns of history—often repeat, even across the chasm of the generations.

Young Stephen had earned and saved ten thousand dollars while teaching school in the winter time and operating a leased farm in the summer; Roy, when he finished high school, had saved the sum of fifteen hundred dollars from his work. It seemed to him like a fortune.

And like his own father he wanted to prove himself, to start out entirely on his own, without the backing of his father's business associations. Having had experience in the factory already, and in his father's cooperage, making apple barrels, he decided to start a barrel factory in Centralia, heart of the Illinois apple district.

Within a few weeks of his graduation, the eighteen-year-old youth had rented himself a building in Centralia, hired ten journeymen coopers, purchased the staves and hoops and other equipment required, and was out every day securing the accounts of the apple growers of the Centralia district.

It was no easy assignment for a boy of eighteen. The coopers who worked for him were a rough breed, many were drifters who moved from place to place, looking for new work and cheap liquor. Nor were the apple growers of this district too inclined to do business with an eighteen-year-old youngster.

But the coopers stayed at their jobs and the orchard people bought his barrels because they were well-made and sold at a fair price. When the rush season came in the fall, the demand was so great that they were working twelve and fourteen hours a day, turning out a daily quota of from 110 to 125 barrels per man. During this rush period, the coopers were getting 7¢ a barrel, and their earnings ran from $45 to $55 a week, a substantial salary at that time.

Over week ends he would come home to Sandoval and his father would go over his carefully-kept records and warn him not to get too large an inventory and to keep up to date on all records of transactions, sales and payments, and especially to watch his accounts receivable.

Like his father also, he ran into difficulties that ultimately took him to Chicago. One of his customers had defaulted on payments for a sizable purchase of barrels. Roy had borrowed money from the Centralia bank to take care of his expanding business and he insisted that past due accounts be settled promptly. This largest past due customer was anxious to settle but, lacking cash, offered to make payment in apples—four carloads of them.

Roy accepted. He shipped the apples to Chicago and put them in cold storage. In December, just before the Christmas holidays, he went to Chicago, called on the top apple brokers on Water Street and began extolling the qualities of the carloads of apples he had in storage. One broker was so impressed at Roy's enthusiasm for apples that he insisted on going over to the warehouse, opening up one of the barrels and seeing for himself.

By the time the youthful barrel-maker was finished, he had sold the entire shipment and made enough to cover the cost of all the barrels and apples, plus the expenses of selling them, plus a modest profit, including computation of time on his trip to Chicago—and he still had an excess of $150 which he paid to the original defaulting customer back in Centralia.

The pattern repeats—almost. As his father a generation back had triumphed in a shifting battle of wheat and oats, Roy won now in a battle of barrels and apples.

For a year he stayed in Centralia and attended the Brown Business College, keeping the cooper plant going in off season, on a limited scale. While there he rented a room in one of the fine old homes of the city with his friends John Preihs and Charles Rogers. Preihs later became a judge in Pana, Illinois.

It was in Sandoval one afternoon at the turn of the century with some of his classmates that he saw a strange and exciting sight parked at the side of the curb—his first automobile. He had no notion then of the role automobiles would play in his life. He and the others crowded around to examine the machine, an Oldsmobile with a curved dashboard and very high wheels. Roy and the other youths stepped aside when the owner came up, and they watched with rapt interest as he cranked the car several times, until it finally started. Then he jumped in behind the wheel and the car started up the street while Roy and his comrades looked on in wordless admiration.

The business school courses were difficult and called for long hours of study. Only one student at the house seemed to find time for the local social whirl. One evening while this man-about-town was out, Roy and the others took the slats out of his bed—all but one slat at each end. They supported the rest of the mattress with hatboxes.

In the morning they heard cries for help. When they opened the door they found their playboy completely bowed in, with his head and feet up and the rest of him sagging to the floor, as the hatboxes had caved in, precisely as Roy had planned it.

In the summer of 1903, Roy went to Chicago to visit a childhood friend, Charles Hurd, and while there he came down with typhoid fever that put him in the old Wesley Hospital on 26th Street and brought his frightened parents from Sandoval to his bedside. According to the charts, his fever was the highest in the whole history of the hospital, ranging up to 107° and once to 107½°, and dropping after ice-baths, which they gave him every four hours, down to 103° or 104°.

For much of this time he was delirious. When he was in his right mind he was hungry; they had him on a diet of virtually nothing but medicated milk. On one occasion he told his mother as she stood at the foot of the hospital bed, "If you come back tomorrow morning and find me dead, it will not be from typhoid fever but from starvation."

At another time he told his nurse, "If I saw a piece of bread across the corridor with a rat gnawing at it, I would crawl out of this bed and get over there and take the bread away from him."

Every time his nurse returned from her lunch, he would make her relate to him a detailed description of everything she had eaten.

In the course of this ordeal, he lost thirty pounds, and drove

his nurses, doctors and family close to nervous breakdowns—
but both he and they survived.

Before coming to Chicago he had planned to enter the University of Illinois; but his illness had made this impossible, it
was too late for registration. In addition, he was told, they
would not accept his credits at Sandoval High as sufficient to
permit his admission, as Sandoval was not then an accredited
school.

A few days later he heard from his friend John Preihs, who
had entered the University of Illinois Law School, of the possibility of a job as assistant to Professor Shattuck, then business
manager of the university. Roy had taken the bookkeeping
course at Brown Business College so he wrote a letter applying
for this position, then went up to the university for the interview and so impressed the professor that he promptly appointed
Roy to the post, at a salary of $40 a month.

Within a few weeks Roy was keeping many of the financial
records of the university, writing the checks for the faculty and
suppliers, paying the bills, and helping to take care of the
routine but vital financial affairs of a university of more than
2500 students and staff. It was quite a responsibility for a
nineteen-year-old youth.

As this experience continued at the university, he found another world unfolding, the university itself, the academic life
around him. It was a far different life from farming and manufacturing, barrel factories and canneries. This world seemed to
encompass all of these and beyond. Talking to students, he
found them exploring new ideas in philosophy and history and
the arts; talking to professors of science, engineering and agriculture, he sensed the fact that a man needed a basic understanding of many fields, that essentially this was higher education, the blending of many worlds and concepts and activities
into a crystalized understanding.

But his work at the university was launched in high excitement. Hardly a week after his arrival, he awoke in his dormitory to the smell of smoke. He and his roommate Preihs raced to the door of their room only to be driven back by smoke and flames in the outer hall.

Hurriedly they began throwing possessions out of the windows of this second-floor room; then as the fire came closer, they jumped to safety. No lives were lost but the entire dormitory burned to the ground. A day or two later Roy came back to dig through the hot ashes to see what might be salvaged. He did uncover his watch among the ruins of the building, but it was black and useless.

Even when he worked at the university he was studying at night at a branch of the Brown Business College, learning shorthand, typewriting and bookkeeping. Living conditions in Champaign were reasonable; on his $45 a month—they had given him a $5 raise after a few months—he was able to pay his board and lodging, his living expenses and save a few dollars besides.

Several times his father stopped off to visit him, while on business trips in the area. The pair would talk about the local gossip of Sandoval and the business and plans for the future. On one of these trips the elder Ingersoll told Roy that he had just entered negotiations to move the plant to Galesburg. As he began to outline his plan, Roy realized its implications.

The people of Galesburg wanted his father and the factory. It would be an expanded operation. Galesburg's Chamber of Commerce and its leading businessmen believed the plant would be of great value and provide employment for many in the town.

The father himself told his son the background of this story. Stephen Ingersoll was trustee of the Southern Collegiate Institute of Albion, located in the southern part of Illinois. Another trustee of this college was C. M. Avery, head of the Avery Company of Peoria, Illinois, one of the large companies producing

steam threshing engines and threshing machines. Stephen Ingersoll had mentioned to Avery that he was planning to move his
plant out of Sandoval, since he wanted to locate it in some place
that would be near his customers and also, if possible, close to
a college so his children could obtain college educations and
still be at home.

Avery suggested Galesburg. It was, he pointed out, within a
radius of only 20 to 90 miles from some of the largest farm
equipment manufacturers in the country. Peoria, Canton, Mon-
mouth, Fort Madison, Moline and Rock Island, Rock Falls and
Rockford and other famous manufacturing centers came within
this area. And Knox College, Avery pointed out—an outstanding Middle West college and one of America's fine co-educa-
tional institutions—was located right there in Galesburg. Avery
persuaded Ingersoll to come to Galesburg, look over the city
and meet the officers and the prominent members of the Galesburg Chamber of Commerce.

Shortly after his return Avery advised him that the businessmen of the Chamber of Commerce wanted to meet with him
further to work out terms for building his plant in Galesburg.
In the meantime, they visited his plant in Sandoval. At the
second meeting to formulate plans they agreed to launch a
$100,000 corporation and to give Stephen $50,000 in stock as
payment for his plant at Sandoval and the expense of moving
the equipment to Galesburg. The purchase did not include any
of the quick assets of the Sandoval Manufacturing Company.
The other $50,000 was to be raised by cash subscriptions from
the citizens of Galesburg.

As his father related all this to his son, Roy had to know every
detail. The new company would be called the Galesburg
Coulter Disc Company, his father said, and the Sandoval firm
would be merged into it. Roy's father with other directors had
purchased a ten-acre tract of land two miles from the center of
Galesburg, where the plant would be built.

Roy had planned on entering the University of Illinois as a special student in the fall of 1903, but the typhoid fever had spoiled that. However, his plan had still been to resign as assistant to the business manager and enter the university in the fall of 1904. The proposed move of family and factory to Galesburg changed these plans.

In the summer of 1904 he resigned his university post in time to return to Sandoval and make preparations for the move to Galesburg—and Knox College. He wanted, more than ever, a college education, and he wanted to be close to this new project as he had been close to all the others, since he posed for a photograph at the age of six, standing beside his father and the workmen outside the Sandoval Manufacturing Company.

Early in September, after stopping en route for two days to see the St. Louis World Fair, he arrived in Galesburg, to become a member of the class of 1908 at Knox College. It was still several days before the college would open for its 1904-05 academic year.

He went on out to see the ten-acre tract, where the new factory was to be built. His father and other directors and people were there discussing the contract and possible building plans. The acreage had been part of a farm and was still covered with uncut cornstalks.

Father and son shook hands and Roy said, "Look at that field, Dad. Somebody has to cut down those cornstalks before you start building."

They glanced at each other and grinned. Roy still had to be part of everything, not remotely but actively, with his whole being and mind, his own two hands.

In a few days before college, Roy Ingersoll took on and finished, alone, the job of clearing off ten acres of cornstalks on this property where his father's new plant would be built, for which strenuous labor the young scion was paid at a rate of twenty cents an hour.

4

Soil and steel

It was a moment of change in America, and particularly, although perhaps not generally understood then or for some time later, in the vital world of the farmer. The mechanization that had come to America with the industrial revolution of the nineteenth century, and that was to bring in the new era of automobiles and planes, and other mechanical wonders, had also reached the farmer and his fields and crops. Few in the cities were aware that a farm revolution, as far reaching as that involved in the new mass-production techniques of industry, was under way or that this change in agricultural methods and techniques would lead to basic changes in our whole civilization.

The mechanized farm was slowly shaping into a reality, and all the other developments of a new century would rest on this mechanization. For it would free man and beast from servitude to ancient tools that took a high tribute in labor and sweat and time, for every kernel of wheat and corn. New machines of the fields freed men to begin new lives, to produce the new things of a new age.

As a supplier of some of the parts that went into this mechanization, the Ingersoll plant in Galesburg was itself to be a part of the change that was beginning to take shape in the midst of the long furrows, in the rich black earth of thousands of midwestern farms.

Whether a family treks with its belongings across a wilderness, or merely from one part of a state to another, moving can assume tremendous proportions. With the Ingersolls, the shift from Sandoval to the metropolis of Galesburg was a project of vast change. Patterns of a lifetime were dislocated and the family itself temporarily scattered.

Stephen Ingersoll was traveling constantly to distant cities on business, or commuting between Sandoval and Galesburg. Winifred and Roy had to come on early to enter Knox College in the fall of 1904. Roy boarded with his uncle, Arthur Gaylord, who had moved to Galesburg to supervise the building of the new plant and become its superintendent. Winifred stayed at Whiting Hall, a dormitory for young ladies at the college.

In January of 1905 the rest of the family moved over en masse, including Roy's brothers, Harold and Stephen Lawrence, four and ten years younger than Roy—and younger sister Jennie, who had brown hair and dark eyes, and who was the pet of the family and got better marks in school than all the others.

The three younger children were at various levels through grade and high school. Harold, frail in early years, was developing into an athlete and football player in high school; young Steve was naturally athletic and good at all sports, especially tennis and basketball. Winifred, the older daughter, was a charming co-ed now, with beautiful hair that had once, back in Sandoval, been the cause of a great family crisis. The preacher's son up the street had thrown lime into her lovely curls as a joke. Winifred had run crying into the house and the brothers had been ready to tear the preacher's boy to shreds. They were restrained only by the admonitions of their father who, although equally outraged, did not believe and would not teach his children to believe in an eye for an eye.

It was, in fact, a quite typical American family with all the small and major calamities, joys, sorrows, quarrels and love that make a family, whatever their strata of society or economics—or their ultimate destinations.

The move to Galesburg took time. In January, before their furniture was shipped from Sandoval, they rented the large furnished home of United States Congressman George W. Prince, who was living in Washington for this session of Congress. The barrel factory and the canning company in Sandoval had been sold, the Sandoval Manufacturing Company was merged into the new Galesburg Coulter Disc Company, which started operations by temporarily renting space in a closed-up plant of the Brown Corn Planter Works, while the new factory began to rise on the tract of land where Roy had cleared away the dead cornstalks.

The Sandoval home and the farm on the edge of town also were sold. Not very long after the sale, oil was discovered on these fields. Stephen Ingersoll always spoke of his joy that this property had proven so rewarding to the purchasers.

He had no time to look back. In Galesburg a new world and life took shape. The factory was almost ready, the children were in school and college, Stephen Ingersoll and his wife Cordelia were searching for a new permanent home. They finally purchased from one of the directors of the new company a two-story brick house on North Academy Street.

New patterns unfolded, in work, in the home, in the family, school, college and church, in the social and academic and cultural world of Galesburg, in what was to the Ingersolls, after the more rural world of Sandoval, a whole new life.

For Roy and Winifred the years at Knox College were the opening of unsuspected vistas. To the practical knowledge Roy had picked up he began to add the rounded education available from Knox's staff of professors, to absorb the wealth of factual information, astronomy, physics, psychology, higher mathematics.

As extra-curricular activities in his spare hours, he went out for sports on a moderate scale, walked four miles a day to and from classes, worked in his father's new plant over week ends and holidays, as he had done in Sandoval, studied voice at the Knox Conservatory of Music for a brief period, and played in the orchestra at the Congregational Church.

He was a little older than most of his classmates because of the year he had worked as drayman when the Sandoval plant was on strike, the year spent in Centralia and the year working at Illinois University. Perhaps this was one reason among many that drew his attention to an auburn-haired young lady who was also a member of the class of 1908. She played the violin in the church orchestra with charm and accomplished technique, having been graduated from Knox College Conservatory the preceding year. Her name, he learned, was Lulu Hinchliff.

She was in several of Roy's classes at the college and got even better grades then he in mathematics. It was not long before they were working out together the problems of physics and exploring the elusive concepts of modern psychology and astronomy.

Fate took a hand in this matter months later, in the form of a mouse which wandered into an economics classroom. All the young ladies of the class leapt upon chairs with cries of terror—all but the auburn-haired young lady who remained calmly in her chair.

Suddenly, however, even Miss Hinchliff emitted a cry, as the injudicious mouse sprang upon her lap. It was then that Roy Ingersoll grabbed the mouse, killed it and threw it from the window.

From that moment on, classmates were sure they knew the ultimate outcome of this romance.

When he was a sophomore he was involved in a class battle with the freshmen. The freshmen had been ordered by the sophomores not to wear their class colors. The freshmen, in defiance, decided after a meeting to wear ties with class colors.

One of them, Clifford Ewart, a grandson of a former President of Knox College and a friend and fraternity brother of Roy's, even went so far as to put a wire through his tie, so that no sophomore could possibly pull it off.

Service was over in the upper story of Beecher Chapel when a melee was started by the sophomores' attempt to tear off the ties of these freshmen. The battle continued down the stairs and on out to the street, until all of the ties were torn off. Thinking the battle was over, Roy went back to the chapel to get his books. As he returned to the campus he saw a pile of some twenty boys, the football coach and a professor trying to pull the youths away to rescue a freshman at the bottom of the heap. Roy pitched in to help.

When they reached the boy, Roy discovered it was his fraternity brother with the wired necktie. Unaware that it was wired, the sophomores were still trying to pull it off. When rescue reached the youth, his face was purple, his eyes bulging and his tongue hanging out. Fortunately, the coach and the others were able to bring him back to consciousness. As a result of their quick action he survived, although for several days his face was a dark violet hue.

The Galesburg Coulter Disc Company, meanwhile, was expanding and spreading its wings. Stephen Ingersoll's factory, while still a small operation in relation to the major steel companies in the East, was beginning to be discussed in the farm belt, in the new mechanized era that was beginning to emerge in farming.

Stephen had purchased new machinery for his Galesburg plant, chiefly from the Williams and White Company of Moline, Illinois. The productivity was increased tremendously over what had been possible in the Sandoval plant. They were increasing their sales of coulter discs to the major farm equipment manufacturers.

The main product was still the coulter discs. The discs they were then producing varied in diameter from 10 to 20 inches; the larger plow discs were not made until later at this plant.

The going was not easy, although they were making fairly good profits. Some of the equipment firms attempted to make their own coulter discs, rather than purchase from outside suppliers, but experience soon proved they could purchase them at less than their manufacturing cost. The big steel companies could still outproduce the comparatively small plant at Galesburg, and could undersell it if necessary.

But the Ingersoll firm was already getting some orders from the equipment people who recognized the standard of quality in the discs this firm manufactured. Stephen Ingersoll was on the road more than ever now, traveling from city to city in the farm equipment manufacturing communities, talking to the leaders of this industry and extoling the merits of the coulters produced at his Galesburg plant. According to the minutes of Directors' Meeting of the Galesburg Coulter Disc Company held September 18, 1905, the salary committee, appointed at a special meeting on August 28th, recommended that the salary of the president, Stephen Ingersoll, be $2,000 a year on a monthly basis, retroactive to April 1, 1905. At that meeting Director Wertman, Chairman of the Salary Committee and President of one of Galesburg's largest banks, made the following salary recommendations: "Your salary committee would respectfully report as follows: President S. A. Ingersoll, salary $2,000 per annum; A. C. Gaylord, Superintendent, $125 per month; H. A. Nelson, Secretary, $55 per month."

At the stockholders' meeting on July 15, 1907, the records show that Roy C. Ingersoll was elected a director without compensation, although it was later voted that all directors not receiving a salary from the company should receive $5 for the attendance at each directors' meeting. At that time Roy was twenty-three years of age and a junior in Knox College. Following meetings of stockholders and directors on July 20, 1908, the record shows: "Director Avery moved that the secretary be instructed to cast a unanimous ballot for R. C. Ingersoll as Vice President and General Manager, motion seconded by Director Churchill and carried." At the meeting of directors on August 1, 1908, the records read in part as follows: "Director Churchill moved that a salary of $65 per month be paid to R. C. Ingersoll for the services for the coming year, motion seconded by Director Wertman and carried."

Farming and its methods, equipment and tools had been the foundation of the Ingersoll business and of much of their lives. It was to continue to be so in the future. The Ingersoll enterprises came in a moment of change; they were a part of the transformation of agriculture from the primitive and medieval occupation it remained until the middle of the nineteenth century, to the modern mechanized industry of the mid-twentieth century.

Yet the world-wide impact and meaning of this industry and the contributions of its modern leaders can be understood only if one understands a little of the lethargy from which it emerged. In few areas of man's work had there been so little change—for so many thousands of years. And in few areas also has so much been accomplished, in just a little more than a century, once the sleeping giant of agriculture awakened.

The world had moved on in the centuries before this awakening, but the farmer had remained where he was, chained to his slow, hand-powered primitive tools. The man with the hoe in eighteenth-century France or England or Ireland or America was still toiling with the same basic tools used in the days of the ancient Egyptian Pharaohs. A farmer of that time, set down on an eighteenth-century farm, could have stepped behind the plow and started to work.

Over these hundreds of years, those who grew the food that

nourished man's progress, stood rooted in seemingly changeless ways.

Roy Ingersoll, discussing this lack of improvement in methods of planting and reaping, stated in a speech in 1949 that with very few exceptions, from Biblical times down to the start of the nineteenth century, "the crooked stick drawn by human beings, oxen or horses, or the wooden hoe, was used to prepare the soil for planting. The hand sickle or the scythe was the only equipment for harvesting . . ."

The plow was one of the earliest inventions of mankind. The Egyptians gave credit for this invention to their sun god, Osiris; the Greeks gave the credit to Zeus; the Romans to Dionysius. America's Farm Equipment Institute, without taking sides on this, states the picture sharply in one of its pamphlets:

"Following this early progress, there was only one significant step forward in the next several thousand years. Eventually man learned to harness animal power to the plow. This was one of the great discoveries of all time, because plowing calls for more power than any other operation in farming. Had man continued through the ages to demonstrate inventive genius, history's pages might not have been littered with the undernourished bones of millions who died from hunger. . . . Except for minor refinements, plows changed but little until the eventful period which began shortly after 1800." *

The awakening had actually begun even a little sooner. The plowshare that cut the furrow and the moldboard that turned over the earth were both formerly made of wood. In the eighteenth century experiments were made with designs of moldboards and plows, to fit different types of soils. Thomas Jefferson made important contributions in this field and became the first Patent Commissioner.

In 1797 a patent was issued on a cast-iron plow. The farmers

---

* *Land of Plenty,* Farm Equipment Institute, Chicago, 1950.

opposed it at first; many insisted that cast iron would poison the soil. The prejudice gradually died away.

Then, suddenly, came the surge in the nineteenth century of new implements and modifications of the old. Cyrus Hall Mc-Cormick in 1831 gave the world the reaper, and in 1837 John Deere "gave to the world the steel plow," which greatly reduced the work load of the farmer. Where four to six oxen were needed to till an acre a day in black gumbo soil, a single pair of horses or mules could do twice as much or more pulling a steel plow instead.

Disc plows were patented in 1847. Coulters, harrow discs and plow discs, on which the Ingersolls built their first enterprise, first assumed sizable commercial proportions after the Civil War.

Other inventions came swiftly in that period. The sulky plow, enabling the farmer for the first time in history to ride behind the plow, came in 1863. The corn planter had appeared in 1839; the self-binding reaper came in 1875. Moldboard and plow-shares made of soft-center steel, which, because of its hard, glass-like surface, would scour in any soil and would not break or crack in the rough going of the prairies, began to appear after the development of this type of steel in 1868.

All of this both improved and lightened the farmer's role; he could do more, he could do it better, cheaper and faster. In Colonial days, before any of these inventions, the job of feeding the colonists had required the full-time efforts of 85 per cent of the working force of the colonies. In 1820, almost three-fourths of America's working force was engaged in agricultural pursuits; by 1940 this was down to 17 per cent.

Once it took a man a day to till half an acre. By 1874 the range lifted to three acres or five. With the advent of the tractor a single man with far less effort could plow ten or twelve acres a day. Where, in 1840, the production of one farm employee fed less than five persons in America, in 1940 one worker fed more than fifteen.

The achievements in the production and mechanization of the farmlands of America form a brilliant, and too often overlooked, chapter in America's development. Behind this achievement was a group of some of the most rugged individualists in our history, leaders and developers of the farm equipment industry, men who shaped the moldboards and plowshares and developed the plow discs and harrows and the modern technology of agriculture out of the tree-branch implements of the past.

One of the most important steps in this advance was the transition from animal to mechanical power. This started with the dawn of the twentieth century and reached its fruition a half-century later.

Mechanical power on farms had been limited chiefly to windmills and treadmills until in the late 1850s came a new device—a steam machine, used to run threshers. Early models were stationary; horses would lug the ponderous steam engine from farm to farm; later, they went under their own power.

Farmers began devising means of using the steam engine for other purposes. This included using these new implements to pull the plow. Earliest attempts at this improvisation were reported in 1860.

After the turn of the century gasoline traction engines began to appear. The first were awkward, ungainly and over-weight—the early models weighed 12½ tons. Gradually they were made lighter and easier to handle and with greater horsepower. By 1906, advertisements began to appear in the farm journals proclaiming the virtues of a wonderful new piece of machinery which at that time was being produced by eleven companies.

This invention was to lift to a peak of intensity the bitter competition that had been building up in the farm equipment industry over the second half of the nineteenth century. It was to develop into a price-cutting war rarely equaled in modern times, as the struggle turned to a nation-wide battle for ascendancy in this field.

And although they did not fully know it then, this invention was also to change the lives and the future of the Ingersolls, for it would help to lead them into widening production and new inventions and developments no one could have foreseen.

Everyone in the farm equipment industry, including Stephen and his son Roy, who was just about to start out on his first trips to the equipment firms, was to be affected by this emerging new mechanical prodigy of the fields.

They called the new prodigy a tractor.

5

Journeys

Roy's education in the rough going that a young salesman of
farm implement parts had to face began even while he was still
finishing his formal education at Knox College. He set out on
his first trip in his senior year, during the mid-winter vacation
period between semesters.

It was a trip that was to give him a good sample of conditions
he would encounter, the people he was to meet, the personal as
well as the business side of each experience and human relationship. For he was a salesman, even then, not only of discs
but also of himself, his ideas, his enthusiasms.

Traveling conditions were far different in those days than
they were to be a half-century later, when jets sped the businessman and salesman to his destination across the continent in
a few hours, and modern communications, transportation facilities and living conditions would be available in even remote
communities. The salesman of that time had to learn to adjust
to whatever conditions he happened to meet. And the more remote the town, usually, the more difficult the conditions.

It was bitter cold, in that mid-winter of 1908, when this college senior set out alone on his first selling trip.

The train jostled through the snowswept darkness, heading
north from Chicago, toward Milwaukee. From there the lone
passenger in the drafty, dimly-lit coach would go on to Horicon,

49

Wisconsin, which depended for its livelihood very largely in that year 1908 on the Van Brunt Manufacturing Company. This firm made grain drills for wheat-growing farmers not only in the United States but in South America as well. Roy had chosen Van Brunt as a starting point because it was a large user of discs for its grain drills.

It was almost midnight. Since he was the sole passenger in the coach and there was still an hour to go before they reached Milwaukee, he tried to turn the seat in front of his around so that he could stretch out and get a few moments of sleep. He found the seat locked in place and called the conductor and explained the situation.

The conductor was not sympathetic. It did not matter, the trainman informed his passenger, that there was no one else in the coach. "It is against the rules to turn the seat. If you want to sleep try it sitting up."

The discourtesy so outraged the young man that it was some years before he forgot it, and even long afterwards, whenever he had to authorize a payment to this railroad for some shipment, he would feel a pang of annoyance.

Shivering, grim-faced and tight-lipped, he sat upright in the seat until they reached Milwaukee and finally, somewhat after 2 A.M., he reached the station stop at Horicon Junction.

It was snowing when he stepped down to the platform. The station was obviously some distance from Horicon; there was no town in sight, no horse-drawn bus, nothing. The only other man on the platform was a passenger who got off the Pullman car in the rear. "The town is quite a distance away," this man told him. "You'll have to walk, you know. If you go along with me, I'll show you the way."

Roy had his luggage to carry, and it was by now 2:30 in the morning and he longed for sleep. But he picked up his baggage and with his new-found companion set off into the night.

When they finally reached the town, he located the village

"night watchman" who carried a kerosene lamp and suggested that Roy would probably want to stay at the best-known hotel in town, the Gessner. The policeman himself unlocked the hotel door, and showed him up to a room that was big enough for a bed but nothing else, not even a washstand.

In the morning around 7:30, Roy went downstairs to get water. The only person around was Mr. Gessner himself, a white-haired German who was known and loved in the town and around whom, Roy was to discover, a whole series of legends had grown.

Mr. Gessner was only too glad to help him. They went out back of the hotel to a barrel that was covered with ice. Gessner broke through the ice, dipped the pitcher in the water and handed it to him. "Now, you can shave all you want," the white-haired hotelkeeper beamed.

Roy decided that he was learning rapidly to be on his own.

At breakfast that morning he found before him on the hotel table a plateful of doughnuts and cakes. These looked very good and he decided to try them while he waited for breakfast to be served. But the doughnuts and cakes apparently had been table decorations for weeks; they were hard and as inedible as the steel discs turned out at the Galesburg factory.

At the Van Brunt plant he asked to see the purchasing agent, Mr. Herman Lange. Like many other purchasing agents on whom he was to call in the years ahead, Lange was to become one of his good friends.

They gave him no orders for coulters or discs and bluntly said that they had no intention of doing so. "Your Galesburg operation is too small. We have to have someone who can guarantee us quantity, real quantity, at the right price."

Roy knew what that meant. The Bethlehem and Crucible steel companies were in the thick of the fight for business and ready to cut prices to the bottom. The Galesburg plant could not stand up against that kind of price cutting.

Lange introduced him to a Mr. Wilcox, who was a brother-in-law of Van Brunt and treasurer of the company. Also to a man who was to be another of Roy's close friends, a young executive lately graduated from the University of Wisconsin, Fred Clausen, later a leading political figure in Wisconsin. Clausen took him out to the experimental laboratory where Van Brunt spent practically all of his time and here Roy had the opportunity of meeting this man who was the inventor of the grain drill.

Roy sold no discs on this visit, or on subsequent calls to the Van Brunt works. It was three years later before he received an order for what they called an "experimental carload" of grain drill discs. The carload order of approximately 10,000 discs was a fraction of the 250,000 to 400,000 discs used annually by this plant. Year after year the percentage of their disc business increased for the Galesburg plant, until finally Galesburg was securing 100 per cent of the requirements of this plant.

Late that afternoon of his first visit, Roy took the train from Horicon to Hartford, Wisconsin, only a few miles away, where he visited the Kissel Manufacturing Company, later called the Kissel Car Company. This company manufactured farm implements, cultivators using grain drill discs, and a line of stationary gasoline engines. From the stationary engines they had developed a gasoline automotive engine and had started production of automobiles.

By today's standards their method of producing these cars was a primitive operation. There were no expensive dies costing hundreds of thousands of dollars that could produce body stampings on giant presses, where items like fenders could be formed two at a time with one stroke of the tremendous press. Here the body parts were made on wooden forms by skilled craftsmen who hammered and shaped fenders and other parts out of a piece of steel. At that time this plant averaged four cars a day.

The Kissel Company produced fine cars but along with some

600 other companies who started to produce automobiles in that era, it was soon involved in all-out competition for popular favor. In a few years the Kissel Car and many other companies were out of business.

Even in the midst of his efforts to sell his discs against growing competition Roy found time to have interest in the human side of all with whom he came in contact. The Van Brunt firm was more than a customer; he looked forward to his visits with Lange and Fred Clausen, to getting out for a visit with Mr. Van Brunt who would show him the new developments and improvements he was making on his grain drill. And there was always some new story Van Brunt had to tell him about his friend Mr. Gessner who ran the hotel.

In one instance he told Roy about the Gessner's golden wedding anniversary and how Gessner rented the Masonic Hall and sent out 400 invitations. Gessner told Mr. Van Brunt that he knew most of the guests would not be able to afford expensive presents, so on the invitations he wrote: "In lieu of a gold wedding present please bring a gold dollar." Van Brunt said that the anniversary was a great success; everybody brought their gold dollar and Papa Gessner wound up with a surplus of $257.

The next year on a visit to Horicon, Mr. Van Brunt told Roy about a revival meeting that one of the churches had during the winter. The Gessners were prominent in Protestant religious circles and Mr. Gessner often attended the revival meetings and mid-weekly prayer meetings held by various churches, and he would testify about the wonderful things that had happened to him in this land of freedom. One of his famous lines came when he became particularly enthusiastic at a meeting, as he talked to the gathering, and, in a burst of his simple, broken-English gratitude, cried out, "It just beats the devil—how much Jesus loves me!"

A year or so later on a visit, Roy went into the hotel to see his old friend Mr. Gessner and could not find him, but he did

see Mrs. Gessner and asked where her husband was. Tears came
to her eyes and she said, "Didn't you know? He passed away last
December." She paused, then said slowly, "You know, before
we moved to Horicon we lived in Milwaukee and Mr. Gessner
founded the Milwaukee Volunteer Fire Department. On the
day of the funeral it was cold and I was not well, and it was
thought best for me not to attend the services. I stayed up in
my room looking out the window to see the funeral procession.
Milwaukee had sent a battalion of the Fire Department all the
way to Horicon for the funeral. The Masons, the Odd Fellows
and Knights of Templars and a number of other groups were in
the funeral procession. It was over a mile long. I looked out of
the window and saw this mile-long procession and realized the
honor that was being paid to my husband." She smiled gently,
and added, "It was the proudest day of my life."

In the early summer of the following year, Roy with his
brother Harold and cousin Henry Gaylord, at that time foreman of the Galesburg Coulter Disc Company, journeyed out
west.

In that year of 1909 the World's Fair was being held in
Seattle and the railroad was giving very low round-trip rates.
Roy had never been west except when his mother had taken him
to visit his Grandfather Gaylord in Nebraska when Roy was
seven years old. He wanted to see it now, places he had read
and studied about, Pike's Peak and all the wonders of Colorado,
the vast acres of farm land that were being opened up in
Montana. He wanted to see Great Falls where his Uncle Edward's family had lived for many years, and Kalispel, the town
in Montana where the Kents, his father's sister and her husband,
lived.

Like most young men of their years they had to do all this
on a limited budget in which a few pennies counted heavily.
On the trains, when they could afford it, they would take a
whole "tourist section"—an upper and lower—and one would

sleep on top and two below. Total cost of the section: $1.50.

They visited Colorado Springs and Denver and Great Falls, Montana. In Billings, Montana, they saw the Billings Brewing Company and Roy was impressed with its slogan painted in large gilt letters: "Brewers of the Beer that Made Milwaukee Jealous." In Great Falls they dined in a restaurant with the sign: "Bill keeps this place—this place keeps Bill. Open forever."

In each city they would drop in also at the most luxurious hotels—the Antlers in Colorado Springs, for example—and stroll through the lobby to get a glimpse of the luxury in which some people traveled. Then they would go over to the YMCA to get rooms for the night, at a cost of fifty-cents apiece. This also entitled them to use the swimming pool.

On the way from Billings to Great Falls they stopped in the Judith Basin in Montana, one of the new farming areas just being opened up and just being planted for the first time. This was dry farming that did not require irrigation.

"Dad would like that land," Harold remarked.

Roy and Henry glanced at him. Didn't Stephen Ingersoll have the plant in Galesburg to handle? Yet Roy knew that his brother Harold was right; their father's love of the soil still ran strong within him. Two years later, in 1911, Stephen Ingersoll had purchased several thousand acres and had begun operation of one of the large wheat farms of Montana.

They rode the train to Spokane, Washington, and on to Portland and Seattle, where they were holding the 1909 World's Fair, which was the object of their junket, and then they went on to Victoria and Vancouver, where they saw the Pacific Ocean and salmon fishermen lowering their nets exactly at sundown on a Sunday evening, because it was illegal to fish commercially before that hour on a Sunday. They had a glimpse of Canadian wilds, and Lake Louise and Glacier. Harold and Henry and Roy drank in this beauty and wonder with the tirelessness of the young.

Homesteading was going on through much of the northwestern part of the States at that time; the trio took the interurban from Spokane. They had invested one dollar for a ticket in a land drawing at Coeur d'Alene, Idaho. If they won they would be entitled to buy 160 acres for a dollar an acre, provided they agreed to work it for two consecutive years at least.

It was fortunate that they did not win the drawing. Roy Ingersoll many years later remarked that it is hard to guess what they would have done had they won.

As it was, on their return they told their father about Montana's Judith Basin and its rich level land. He listened to his two sons and his nephew with a bright gleam of interest as they talked of the good earth in this newly developing area out West.

Roy had kept records of all expenses of the trip, and when he added it all up on his return the entire cost including meals, railroad fare, sleeping quarters, and visits to the Seattle World's Fair, came to exactly $97.80.

Even while Roy was still in college, his father had begun to be aware of changes that had come or were sure to come in this new century. Not all of these changes did he approve of or accept. Even more than his children he stood between two centuries, two ages. One day, he knew, this new era would rush past him, this younger generation taking over.

Harold and Roy had guessed correctly about his longing for the soil. Many times his mind turned from business to thoughts of fields and earth and crops, to the early days in Sandoval when he and Roy had tilled fields on the edge of town.

The family had remained closely knit through the days of school and college and growing up in Galesburg. The house on North Prairie Street with its columns and surrounding trees, its big rooms and high ceilings, its full-size bowling alley in the basement and recreation and dance room on the third floor, was a place of endless activities, comings and goings. Winifred was one of the most popular young ladies of the college.

Roy, with his almost boundless energy, had divided his time between learning everything he could at college, and everything he could learn about the Galesburg factory and its products. He also found time for an evening at the Galesburg Auditorium Theater, or a Knox College concert at Beecher with Lulu Hinchliff.

Harold and younger brother Steve had won reputations for themselves in local sports, basketball, baseball and tennis. And Jennie, the young sister, was still the pet of them all, still getting the best grades and growing from a child into a beautiful young girl.

All of those in his family were close to Roy, and each important to him. Yet there were at that time three women who had a particular influence on his life. One was his mother from whom he inherited much of his will and energy. A second was a Knox College teacher, a Miss Ida McCall, who was quite deaf but who was a wonderful patient lady who had tried to temper her young student's impatience and exuberance with wisdom, even as she taught him classical Latin. "You'll never make much of a Latin student, I'm afraid," she told him once, as he had tried to convince her he deserved a higher mark for the term, "but you'll be a wonderful business man."

The third was Lulu Hinchliff who had become very dear to him. She had a way of seeing life in its most beautiful colors and could make him see the lighter side, the humorous side, even of himself and his own shortcomings.

Often he would walk with Lulu across the Knox College campus and she would listen as his words flowed on about problems at his father's plant, problems of the industry and of finance, of social and economic issues that had to be faced and dealt with before they hurt the country.

Most often he talked of the plant and its immediate goals and she would listen attentively and smile at this young man.

Few young men could be so charming as he, she knew. Yet

there were moments when she wondered which had first claim
—she, or the steel discs being rolled and hammered and pressed
into shape on the machine of the Galesburg Coulter Disc factory.

For more than a year, the Galesburg plant and its products
had become Roy's full-time work. He knew every machine,
every operation, technique, problem and headache; he knew the
job of selling; and the purchasing agents of the main implement
firms were his good friends. The business was progressing slowly
but soundly.

In 1907 there had been a sharp money panic and out at the
plant for a month or two they had been compelled to pay their
workers in script, really little more than I.O.U.s, because there
was no cash to be had; the only cash they received in payment
for their discs was from one company, the LaCrosse Plow Company of LaCrosse, Wisconsin, later to become the tillage division
of Allis-Chalmers. This company paid every bill from its own
cash reserves.

The money panic cleared up and by fall of 1908 business was
increasing. Since graduation in 1908 Roy had taken an active
role in the company and had the title of vice-president and
general manager.

For all his titles, his salary was only $65 a month.

Total sales for the year ending June, 1909, had been $163,-
162—a substantial gain from the $113,000 of the previous
year, when he started work, immediately after being graduated
from Knox. There were new problems ahead as their sales went
up, however; they had to find a sound and reliable source of
supply for the special steel from which their discs were made.
Without an additional supply of steel they could not fill their
increasing orders from the implement companies.

Roy threw himself into these problems after his return from
the western trip. He found relish in work, in the August heat
of that summer in Galesburg.

Most of his family were away, at various summer places. His sister Jennie was up at the Sequonata Club on Pine Lake, later called Charlevoix Lake, five miles outside of Charlevoix, Michigan. Many Galesburg families summered in that district. Lulu Hinchliff was there too that summer with her parents.

It was in the midst of these familiar patterns of their lives that Roy and his family were to learn the meaning of sudden, irrevocable loss.

Jennie was staying with her friends, Helen Trask, and the Trask family, at the lake. The house was close to the swimming beach and the docks where the boat that plied between Charlevoix and Boyne City and Ironton came in with its summer people and its cargo of items for delivery.

Late on the afternoon of August 20, at the Galesburg plant, Roy was summoned to take a long distance call. When he heard the words coming across the wire, it seemed to him the world had smashed at his feet.

Jennie and the others had been in swimming. Although a good swimmer, she had moved in too close to the boat. The suction of the propeller had dragged her under the water. It was sudden and swift. Before anyone could even try to reach her, it was too late.

Her parents were too overcome to go up there, and they asked Roy to make the trip and bring his sister home. This was another kind of journey for him—one that was grim and silent.

At the Sequonata Club special services were held while he was there along with many friends of Jennie's and of the Ingersolls.

To Roy, as to the others in the family, the shock of this loss was deep and lasting, his only relief was to throw himself into the complex details and demands of the plant operations, which more than ever now his father was leaving in his hands.

6

Giants of the fields:
The farm implement makers

IT IS NOT always easy to find glamor, or adventure, in the soil,
yet it is there. It is not always easy to recognize the importance
of what we take for granted—air, water, rain, or the grain in the
fields, the crops that do not fail, the food on the table in a world
where modern methods and machines have in large measure
freed us from drought and the scourge of recurring famines.
Yet without the advent of modern farm implements none of the
rest of our modern world would exist, for it was the coming of
mechanized farming which not only freed millions of human
beings for other kinds of production—in the factories, in science,
in the professions—but also gave the world a food supply greater
than dreamed of in the past centuries, a production that came
directly out of this achievement of mechanized farming. It is an
achievement that equals or exceeds in importance any of the
other great developments and discoveries of the past century
and a half.

The story of this development is peculiarly American, shaped
mainly from 1800 on by men whose parents had come to America seeking freedom from old ways and old ideas, shaped and
molded and brought to reality by men of special courage and
vision. It was, primarily, a story of individuals, men whose

names became symbols of this development—men such as John Deere and J. I. Case, James Oliver, and McCormick.

In Sandoval and later in Galesburg, from early boyhood, Roy had come to know these names, the men and their achievements, and he considered himself even then a part of their world. Stephen Ingersoll, returning from a trip to obtain contracts for his coulter discs from these equipment firms, would relate to him incidents and modern folkloke of the men and their factories.

Roy would listen to his father's stories; he would read the pamphlets and books, that his father brought home, about these firms and their founders; the drama of the men and their lives were a part of his childhood, as the firms they founded and built were to become an important part of his own life and business career.

These companies with which his father, and later Roy himself, were to be intimately concerned in the farm equipment business, represented a very important part of America's industrial and cultural development. He was to be concerned also with the automotive world in later years, but where the story of the automotive industry has in large measure been told many times and in considerable detail, the story of the farm equipment companies and their achievements over many years is not as well known nor has it been widely publicized.

President Eisenhower's Secretary of Agriculture Ezra Benson was quoted as saying of this farm implement story and these companies which made the story come true:

"Almost within my memory we have jumped from oxen to atoms while agriculture in most of the world has stood still. In no other nation today do farmers . . . produce so much food and fiber to feed and clothe so many at such a relatively cheap price."

One of the most illustrious of the men who made this achievement possible was still active in business, and recognized as one of the great names in American agriculture and industry, when Stephen Ingersoll launched the Sandoval Manufacturing Company. This was John Deere, founder of Deere and Company of Moline, Illinois, makers of plows and other farm implements.

Born in 1804, a native of Rutland, Vermont, Deere became a skilled mechanic and blacksmith. He made shovels and hay forks for Vermont's early farmers until difficult economic conditions and tales of opportunities in the West led him to pick up stakes and start out for new land. He traveled by stage coach and canal boat, at length arriving in the community of Grand Detour, Illinois, in 1836. Within forty-eight hours of his arrival, he set up his blacksmith shop and hung out his sign.

The people of the town, the farmers especially, came to the new blacksmith to talk over their problems. Most of them, too, had come only recently from the East and most were in worse trouble now than they had been on the often rocky, difficult eastern farmland. There the wooden plows, sometimes tipped with iron, would at least scour and turn a furrow. But no plow would work, after the first breaking of the soil, in this black sticky earth of the Midwest, the farmers told Deere.

So serious was this situation that many of the settlers were ready to give up and go back East, rather than fight the soil with their plows that could not cut a clean furrow. Could Deere find a way to help them?

So John Deere set to work in his shop to find a way to keep settlers from turning back from the western tide—and found it in a broken saw blade made of high carbon steel, which he shaped into a moldboard and plowshare, the first major step in developing a practical steel plow.

After much experimentation and refinement of his idea, the new steel plow was given a public demonstration in the community, with a borrowed horse to pull the plow through the black earth, while a group of neighboring farmers looked on. They saw a clean-cut furrow, a plow which shed the earth easily and cleanly as it cut through the sticky prairie soil. The steel moldboard was shiny and clean; the pioneer farmers called the plow "John Deere's Selfpolisher," the name by which it was to become known across the nation in decades ahead.

For some time Deere remained in Grand Detour, importing high quality steel from England and later obtaining it in the States, while he and his partner, Major Leonard Andrus, operated as Andrus and Deere. Later he and Deere parted on good terms, Andrus to start the Grand Detour Plow Works, Deere to start Deere and Company in the heart of a new industrial community called Moline, Illinois.

In the mid-nineteenth century, Moline and Rock Island became centers of the farm implement development; this area of the world was a logical center for the new production, because it was close to the newly opening, rich farm lands of the Midwest, close to the Mississippi at a point where the crossing was comparatively easy, and close to the railroad lines then under construction and to well-traveled routes of settlers coming from the East.

In 1847 when Deere moved to Moline, he built a shop where he produced 700 plows a year. Because the railroads had not been extended beyond the Mississippi River at that time, distribution was largely by riverboat and wagon. But by these means of transportation, and later by the railroads as they expanded in the post-bellum era, John Deere's steel plows were shipped and sold in all parts of the country.

In those early days there were not even banks in Moline. The nearest was in Galena, Illinois, or Burlington, Iowa. Most of the farmers paid their bills in produce; in one instance a $200 invoice was paid in postage stamps. Charles Deere, son of the founder, was brought into the company in 1853 and became a vice president after the Civil War. Previous to this, he attended Knox College which was later to be Roy Ingersoll's alma mater. Following the death of John Deere in 1885, Charles was to as-

sume full control as president. Deere and Company by that
time was turning out all kinds of steel plows, cultivators, corn
and cotton planters as well as other farm implements. In 1911,
in a continuation of a program to build a complete implement
line, they brought in six manufacturing firms and twenty-two
sales organizations.

Charles Deere, like his father, was ambitious to see the country grow and expand across the newly-opened fields of the
Midwest and Far West. The company that his father founded
in 1847 was incorporated in 1868 with a net worth of $420,000.
Forty years later that figure would be $14,000,000. By 1959 it
would be $313,985,359.

Deere established the first branch of the company in St.
Louis in 1869, Deere, Mansur and Company in 1870, and ten
other branches in various parts of the nation. Like his father,
too, Charles believed in research and planning. Substantial portions of profits were put back into the business, new designs
and improvements in plows and other implements were developed under his guidance, and a new distribution system was
built to carry the products of this concern throughout the farm
world.

This widening of production horizons continued until the
company which had begun with John Deere's determination to
find help for early settlers in Grand Detour had grown to one
of the largest and most distinguished names and producers in
the farm equipment field.

Succeeding Charles Deere as president in 1907 was William
Butterworth, his son-in-law, who was president during many of
the years when Roy Ingersoll made regular calls at this company, trying to sell it coulter discs and other implement parts
then being made by the Galesburg plant. At first Roy did not
find it easy to convince the executives of this important company that they should purchase discs from Galesburg. Roy
dealt with a number of Deere officials in those years, particu-

larly the purchasing director Herbert Copp and his two assistants, Richard McDannell and Howard Warfield, all of whom became close associates of Roy's. Richard McDannell later was Deere's purchasing director and Howard Warfield afterward was purchasing agent at the Ingersoll Steel plant at New Castle.

Deere's policy of filling out its implement line through important acquisitions continued, particularly in the early years of the century.

Writing in 1947, Deere's former president and board chairman Burton F. Peek, stated that one of the great problems was the seasonal aspect of the farm implement business, in which a sales force employed throughout the year did most of its business in a period of perhaps only a few weeks or months at most.

"The result," he stated, "was that in 1911 in order to sell and service their products more economically and effectively several manufacturers of non-competitive lines . . . pooled their interests and created the present Deere and Company.

"This organization was made up of Deere and Company, Deere and Mansur Company, the Moline Wagon Company, the Van Brunt Manufacturing Company, a pioneer and specialist in the manufacture of grain drills, the Dain Manufacturing Company, a pioneer manufacturer of hay tools, Kemp and Burpee Manufacturing Company, a pioneer manufacturer of manure spreaders, and Syracuse Chilled Plow Company, one of the earliest manufacturers of chilled plows, and Marseilles Manufacturing Company, pioneers in the manufacture and sale of corn shellers and grain elevators.

"Shortly after the re-organization in 1911 a line was completed by the construction of the plant for the manufacturing of harvesting machines. In 1918, visualizing the expansion of farming with mechanical power, Deere and Company, purchased the Waterloo Gasoline Engine Company. It too was a pioneer, being one of the earliest manufacturers of farm tractors. In 1937 a small California company, the Killefer Company, was added to the organization and in 1946 the Lindeman Company at Yakima, Washington was likewise acquired."

Deere and Company was to continue to remain among the top leaders of the field under able leadership. Butterworth became chairman of the board in 1928 and Charles Deere Wiman, a great-grandson of John Deere, succeeded as president. Wiman was a Yale graduate of the class of 1915, a yachtsman who sailed his own boats in the Bermuda races, a captain of artillery in World War I, and a colonel in World War II. He was also devoted to this business which his grandfather had founded and after he left college he came back to Moline and worked as a laborer in factories and branches of the company and in a variety of other difficult jobs, to learn every aspect of this industry.

He later became vice president of Deere in charge of all factory operations, and became president in 1928 succeeding his uncle, William Butterworth. In 1942 Wiman resigned and went into the armed forces as a colonel. He resumed the presidency on his return from the war in 1944, continuing in the business until his death in 1955.

Burton Peek, who was named president in 1942 and became chairman of the board in 1944, originally came into Deere and Company in 1888, when he was sixteen, working as a bookkeeper, and in the shipping department. Peek quit sometime later, went through Harvard Law School, and then came back to the company as general counsel at the urging of Charles Deere.

During all these years the rivalry continued between this company and its next-door neighbor, the Moline Plow, although the executives and the owners, the Deere family and the Stephens family, continued to maintain cordial social relationships.

The rivalry and competition was real enough, however. Top "security" measures were maintained by each firm to keep the other from finding out what new development might be taking place. A new machine would be brought in covered over so that no one at the other company would be able to tell what kind of new equipment had been developed.

Ultimately, despite this protracted industrial "feud," a happy resolution was achieved when Dwight Deere Wiman, a grandson of Charles Deere, married one of the daughters of the Stephens' family.

In 1955 W. A. Hewitt succeeded to the presidency after serving in several posts of importance in the Pacific Tractor and Implement Company in Richmond, California, and in Deere and Company. He had risen to vice president and general manager of the San Francisco branch of the company in 1950 and was elected executive vice president of Deere and Company, in 1954. On the death of Charles Deere Wiman, he was elected president, and under his leadership the company continued to develop its home markets and also to expand into other areas including the purchase of a 75 per cent interest in the Heinrich Lanz Company in Manheim, Germany. By 1959 this company and its subsidiaries operated fourteen plants in the United States as well as plants in Canada, Germany and Mexico.

In the story of the farm world there are family lines and long traditions, which go hand in hand with remarkable technical achievement. Speaking of this extraordinary high technical proficiency, Lloyd Kennedy, Deere's senior vice president, pointed out that the tractor is a far more rugged vehicle than an average car. "If you drove a car over rough rock-strewn fields, you'd soon wreck it completely. But a tractor is built to take that kind of beating all day long."

The general purchasing was directed by Richard Edwards, who was both a director and vice president in charge of the purchasing division. Edwards has been widely recognized for his work in coordinating the purchasing of all the plants, and

Roy, Bob, and Jim Ingersoll always have appreciated the privilege of being his guests at the annual meetings of Deere's
purchasing agents.

There is important meaning in these standards and traditions
still maintained by those who make modern farming possible.
At the sixtieth anniversary celebration of the Ingersoll Steel and
Disc Division of Borg-Warner, in 1944, one of those who attended was Mrs. William Butterworth, granddaughter of John
Deere and widow of the man who was president of the company
for so many years and was beloved by all in his field.

Roy Ingersoll introduced her and told of the honor it was to
have her at this meeting. She was a kind of queen that night, a
symbol of the glory of this industry of which she had been a
part all her life. There was long applause when she stood up
to speak. Her talk was not long, but it was deeply appreciated,
for her presence added a gracious note to the gathering. "Mr.
Ingersoll," she said, "I wish to thank you for the compliment
you have paid me tonight. I appreciate it very much and I
thank you for it. I am glad to be here and do hope to be here
a good many years longer."

Approximately two decades after John Deere arrived, another group in the Moline area launched the Moline Plow
Company in the production of plows of various types, as well as
other farm implements. This was the company whose plant
was to stand side by side with Deere and Company in decades
ahead, two of the great agricultural implement makers, bitter
competitors, even though their executives and officers knew each
other well and enjoyed the byplay of friendship and business
rivalry as part of the daily routine of highly competitive neighbors.

Originally a partnership known as Candee, Swan and Company, implement makers, the Moline Plow Company officially
was formed in 1870, after it took in as a new partner an ambitious young millwright named George Washington Stephens,

who had arrived in Moline in 1843. He ran a flour mill and a sawmill and made furniture, until he decided to try his hand and talents and hard-earned capital in this expanding farm implement industry serving the thousands of farmers and their families now migrating into the rich prairie land.

For more than a half-century, the Stephens family was to direct and in large measure to dominate the fortunes of this company in its production of tillage and harvesting equipment for the farmers not only of Illinois but of all America and the whole world. Many branches were to be established and many smaller farm machinery makers were to be absorbed into the Moline Plow production, until its merger in 1929 with two other companies into the Minneapolis-Moline Company.

As Moline Plow Company's business increased it saw the necessity of having a full line of implements. One of the reaper companies which had not gone into the International merger in 1902 was Adriance, Platt & Company of Poughkeepsie, New York, which had made reapers for Cyrus H. McCormick in 1845. This company was purchased by Moline in 1913. The capital of the Moline Plow Company in 1903 had grown to $3,200,000 and to $9,000,000 by 1910, but with the purchase of Adriance, Platt & Company more capital was required to take care of the expanding business. New capital was brought in and a preferred capital structure of $30,000,000 was established.

In 1915, Moline purchased the Universal Tractor Company of Columbus, Ohio, with its designs, patents and tools. In 1916 it moved the tractor plant to Moline and started production of tractors, producing 2,000 that year. The demand for tractors grew so rapidly, that in 1916 and 1917 a new tractor plant was built in Rock Island; this was later purchased by International Harvester Company and became one of their great tractor producing factories.

In 1918 John N. Willys and his auto company acquired 82 per cent of the common stock of the Moline Plow Company.

Arthur and Charles Stephens resigned from the board of directors since they had sold all of their stock. In 1919 Frank G. Allen was replaced as president by Mr. George M. Peek, a brother of Burton Peek of Deere and Company. The new president was aided by General Hugh S. Johnson who came with Mr. Peek from the War Industries Board.

The farm equipment business continued to expand after the war until the second half of 1920 when depression closed in. The next two years, 1921 and 1922, were probably the most difficult the farm equipment industry has ever had to suffer.[1]

Despite heroic efforts, John N. Willys and his auto company could do little for Moline Plow Company, and in 1923 and early 1924 it was decided to sell properties including the tractor and harvester works. The equipment of the tractor works was sold at auction.

This tractor plant contained some excellent equipment. Roy Ingersoll and his son Robert, out of school on vacation, drove up to Moline, attended the auction and purchased several of the machines needed for the Galesburg plant.

Several years before, the Moline Plow Company had purchased a steel company in Chicago which made carborized steel moldboards, a product somewhat similar to the soft center steel Ingersoll's New Castle plant was furnishing to the plow makers of the country. Moline Plow Company had put on demonstrations for the dealers across the country trying to prove the superiority of this carborized moldboard steel over the soft center steel. To be able to supply plow makers with either type of moldboard steel, the Ingersolls decided to purchase this carborizing plant when they learned it was for sale, and move it to New Castle.

The reorganization of 1923 and 1924 did not cure the many ills and problems of Moline Plow. Factories which formerly belonged to the great company were sold and only a few plants

---

[1] See *Appendix* for chart showing effect of the economic crash of this era.

were left for the next five years after 1924. Then conditions improved. In 1929 the Moline Implement Company was merged into the Minneapolis-Moline Company, along with the Minneapolis Steel Machinery Company, and the Minneapolis Threshing Machine Company. Headquarters were moved to Minneapolis and W. C. McFarland became the first president and chief executive officer of the new company.

Still another great name of the farm implement industry, about which Stephen Ingersoll would talk with his son Roy, was J. I. Case—Jerome Increase Case—who developed the threshing machine. Around his name clustered a kind of folklore of the new farm world in which steam traction engines and threshers were to play such an important part.

Case had been born in 1819 in upper New York State, son of a farmer. At an early age he had become the thresherman of the family, using a primitive threshing implement known as a "Groundhog." As he learned to work this machine, he began to conceive the idea of making one that would do much more of the threshing job automatically. The boy's idea grew in his mind; when he was older he migrated from New York State to Wisconsin, where he launched in 1842 the J. I. Case Company, making threshing machines, first in Rochester, Wisconsin, then in Racine. At the beginning, he took his thresher from farm to farm; later he decided the real business lay in selling the machines rather than working them himself.

Like John Deere and Major Andrus with whom Deere had worked in Grand Detour, Case recognized the plight of America's migrant farmer of that day as resulting from the lack of proper tillage and threshing tools. Crops had been poor as a result of this lack, prices of flour and other commodities had been out of reach in a time of scarcity.

J. I. Case was to become ultimately the "threshing machine king of the world." His machines, like the new plows of John Deere, Oliver Plow, Grand Detour, Moline Plow and others, were freeing the farmer from the backbreaking toil of the hand tools that were available. "We are told," wrote the *Wisconsin Farmer*, with vast respect for these machines of J. I. Case, "that one machine has earned over $1,200 during the season of threshing. Mr. Case has been a practical thresher for some ten years, and knows how to get up a threshing machine just right."

During the earlier years at Sandoval, the J. I. Case Threshing Machine Company was not a customer of the Ingersolls since it did not make tillage tools which use coulter discs until later, when it purchased the Grand Detour Plow Company and the Emerson Brantingham Company, both of which were customers of the Ingersolls for many years. However, the J. I. Case Plow Works, also of Racine, Wisconsin, which was founded by and named after Jerome Increase Case and was headed by his son-in-law, Mr. W. H. Wallis, was one of the earliest customers of Stephen Ingersoll and remained one of the oldest continuous Ingersoll customers until it was sold to Massey-Harris Company in 1928.

Roy later was to become close to officials of this firm; its vice president in charge of purchasing, William La Venture, came all the way from Racine to Norwalk, Ohio in 1910 to see Roy and try to get increased shipments to take care of the Case Plow Companies' expanding needs for soft center moldboard steel.

Mr. Case's "just right" threshing machines were a clattering success with the world's farmers, and the difficult and often truculent Mr. Case kept improving them and working to make them more efficient. In one instance, when a farmer complained that his thresher wouldn't work, and that the J. I. Case experts couldn't seem to repair it, Case himself got on a train and went to see the farmer and worked over this machine, although at that time the firm he headed was one of the world's large producers of farm machinery.

The legend, as reported in a book by historian Stewart Holbrook, states that when Case failed to find the trouble with the thresher, he finally poured kerosene over it, lit it with a match and watched with perverse satisfaction as the machine burned to a charred mass. Then he went back on the train and shipped the farmer a new thresher that operated without any difficulties.

Case concerned himself with the most minute details in the factory to prevent inefficiency and waste. He would even examine the furnaces personally to make sure that the ash burned all the way, and once he became so angry over the wastage of bent nails that he straightened a whole keg of them himself at the anvil. Holbrook also reports that Case once made a bill collector run half a mile to get change totaling fifteen cents. "And get back here," Case is said to have instructed this young man, "prepared to do business in a businesslike manner."

When J. I. Case formed his first threshing machine business in Racine, Wisconsin in 1844 it was known simply as the Racine Threshing Machine Works, J. I. Case, Proprietor. Although called familiarly the Case Company over many years, it officially held this name. In 1876 the proprietor formed another company which he called the J. I. Case Plow Works. In 1880 the original threshing machine works changed from a partnership to a corporation and became the J. I. Case Threshing Machine Company. The two firms which he founded always operated as two separate units—the J. I. Case Threshing Machine Company and the J. I. Case Plow Works.

After Case died in 1891 these two companies were to be run by different groups of his family and associates, and after 1919 when the J. I. Case Threshing Machine Company purchased the Grand Detour Plow Works the two Case firms became rivals and bitter competitors although bearing similar names and both operating in Racine, Wisconsin. The farmers, of course, did not differentiate between the companies and would write simply to "J. I. Case Co., Racine." This created a problem in the Post Office; which letter was meant for which J. I. Case Co.? So vexing was this problem that the post office in Racine had to set up a system for opening all letters addressed to J. I. Case, and in the presence of a representative of each of the two firms had to determine who got which letters. This routine continued until 1928 when the J. I. Case Plow Company was sold to the Massey-Harris Company, who in turn, for a fee, gave up the right to use the name Case.

This problem was not completely solved until 1928, four years after Colonel W. B. Brinton, a Case director, was named head of a committee appointed to find a new president for J. I. Case, to succeed Warren J. Davis. The committee picked Leon Clausen, general works manager at Deere and Company. Before talking to Clausen, however, Brinton personally approached President William Butterworth of Deere, and asked if Deere would object if they made Clausen president of J. I. Case.

Since Clausen was making a fine record at Deere, Butterworth and the Deere directors were reluctant to let him go. However, they agreed not to stand in his way and Clausen became head of the Case Threshing Machine Company and directed the large expansion of this company and development of many new implements until his retirement in 1955.

In 1928, at Clausen's urging, the name of the firm he headed was changed back to simply the J. I. Case Company.

It is somewhat ironic that the man who did so much to put the horse out of business on the farm should have become famous also for the ownership of one of the most famous trotting horses of all time—the record-breaking horse Case himself had named Jay-Eye-See. So well known was this horse that Case himself, trying to pay for some purchases of his wife's at New York Lord and Taylor's, discovered that the horse was better known than the man. The clerk was not ready to accept a $1500 check from Mr. Case of the threshing machine company, but when he identified himself as the owner of Jay-Eye-See, he could have had the store.

One of the great salesmen of J. I. Case threshing machines was a man who became a close friend of Roy's, Merrill C. Meigs, who was later to be a vice president of the Hearst publications. For many years he demonstrated the efficiency of Case machines by putting them through almost incredible stunts. He could balance a tractor on a seesaw. And legend has it that he would move it with such precision that he could nose it gently against an open watch and close it without even scratching the crystal.

Sound in business and production, the Case Company continued to have a certain unique dramatic flare.

In 1957 the American Tractor Company was consolidated with J. I. Case, and Marc B. Rojtman, president of American Tractor, became executive vice president of Case, and in 1958 president. Rojtman proved to be a salesman of distinction and dramatic ability. In the spring of 1958 he staged a precedent-shattering sales meeting in Phoenix, Arizona, setting up three vast tents where he had assembled and displayed fifty-two carloads of Case machinery of all types.

To this unique tented showcase, he brought in by plane, in relays, some 3500 dealers who were flown to Phoenix from all parts of the country. During this Phoenix exposition J. I. Case introduced their Case-O-Matic tractor. Setting up the display and flying the dealers into Phoenix cost the company an estimated $150,000, but the meeting itself was said to have yielded more than $15,000,000 on dealer orders for agricultural tractors and implements. The company stated that this was the largest volume of orders ever received at any previous individual sales meeting, tented or otherwise.

A name equally rich in significance to Roy was the Oliver Chilled Plow Company of South Bend, Indiana, whose chilled cast iron plow was particularly adaptable to the soils of the East and the South. This company was started by James Oliver; he and his plow were to became famous all over the world. Oliver believed in this product with a fervor that was ingrained in his being. "A sewing machine, a Mason and Hamlin organ, and an Oliver plow form a trinity of necessities for a farmer," he would declare.

Known by the slogan, "Plow Makers for the World," the Oliver Company became one of the great firms producing farm equipment of all kinds. It was James Oliver who prevented the great combine of tillage-producing companies, near the end of the nineteenth century, when he told the would-be incorporators that he would continue to operate independently. In 1908, on the death of the founder, his son Joseph succeeded. In 1929, this highly successful company was to form with three other companies into what was ultimately called the Oliver Corporation. The other farm equipment companies in this merger included the Nichols and Shepard Company, the American Seeding Machine Company, and the Hart-Parr Company of Charles City, Iowa, the latter being the first company to begin, in 1901, large scale production of tractors.

It was many years before the Ingersolls, father or son, could sell their discs to the great Oliver Company. The officials of Oliver felt that the Galesburg Coulter Disc Company did not have sufficient volume of production to become a source of supply for them. However, both Stephen and later his son Roy called on this company and a friendly relationship developed. Oliver's purchasing agent, Albert A. Frederick, became a close friend of Roy's. He would take Roy in to meet Joseph Oliver, a distinguished son and successor of the company's founder. A moment of victory came when Frederick finally gave Roy his first real order from Oliver. In later years Oliver became one of Galesburg's most important customers.

The Oliver Company experienced one of its greatest periods of growth and expansion under the leadership of Alva Phelps, former General Motors vice president. During his administration, Phelps launched a $45,000,000 rehabilitation and expansion program. During the same period the company acquired five additional manufacturing plants. In 1950, Phelps relinquished the presidency to A. King McCord, who resigned in 1956 to become president and chief executive officer of Westinghouse Air Brake Company. Phelps again assumed the presidency in 1956 in addition to the chairmanship until 1958 when Carl L. Hecker was elected to the presidency with Phelps continuing as chairman and chief executive officer.

To young Ingersoll, working with these companies and their leaders was a personal adventure in learning how some companies grew strong in a free enterprise system while others faded and passed out of the picture.

Half a century later, at the 60th anniversary of the founding of the Ingersoll Company, he was to state that the story of the Ingersoll Company was, in fact, "the story of countless other industries that have been permitted to grow and prosper and give livelihood and opportunity to many men in this American climate of freedom. The institution was nurtured and grew under the sunshine and gentle rains of our American system of free enterprise. It is truly a product of that system."

Yet as long ago as 1884, when the Stephen Ingersoll factory in Sandoval was launched, most of the major farm equipment companies had been established; hundreds of others had come and gone under the fierce competitive situation. At one time there were approximately 1500 implement companies in the United States, all struggling for a place in the farmer's sun. Many were under-financed; few were large enough and strong enough to stand up against their more rugged competitors. By 1899, the number had dropped to only 715 firms.

Even the larger companies, in both the tillage and harvesting fields, had scarcely enough funds for development and rapid expansion. And the farmer's needs were growing, as mechanization opened new vistas for farm productivity. This was the reason for the seething conditions of this industry, the endless battle for customers, the vigorous price competition, the mergers and attempted mergers of many companies.

The salesmen of those days did not ride as they do today in streamlined cars over sleek modern roads, or fly from one farm customer to the next in planes equipped with radio phones, so that they can call in orders on the spot and get almost immediate delivery. Those earlier sales agents had to walk, or ride in buggies, from one place to the next, and in the spring the roads were often knee-deep in ooze and mud and impassable for weeks. It was a relentless, unglamourous, unknown war.

A story going the rounds in that day in the industry—later recalled by G. E. Lukens in the *Farm Equipment News*—told of a farmer who wished to buy a binder and who went from dealer to dealer, getting each man to cut the price just under that proposed by the previous dealer. In the end, the farmer returned to the first dealer he had called on and this dealer cut the price to $80, ten dollars under what he had paid for the binder wholesale.

This was a difficult era in which Roy's father set out to get orders from the manufacturers who used coulter discs on their implements. Yet he enjoyed it all—the struggles, the people he met, the enduring friendships he made.

In Moline and Rock Island, where many of the firms with which the Ingersolls dealt were located, he would go sometimes, alone or with his father, to the Manufacturers Hotel, a plush, mid-Victorian center that was almost a farm implement manufacturers' club, similar to what the Detroit Athletic and Recess Club became at a later date for America's automobile manufacturers. In this hotel one might see John Deere's son, Charles Deere, or his successor and son-in-law, William Butterworth, or Arthur and George Stephens, sons of the founder of Moline Plow, and many other executives of the farm implement companies. There was an atmosphere of excitement and warmth at this hotel in Moline at the start of the century—a gathering place for the industrialists of the new farm land of the Mid-

west, serious, businesslike, energetic, yet with echoes of a frontier era, which at that time was only a few decades past.

But a half-century later, Roy Ingersoll, by that time head of
a corporation called Borg-Warner with assets in excess of $400,-
000,000 and annual sales of more than $600,000,000, was in
Moline on a business trip and looked for this place that had
been such a symbol to him and to his father. He could find no
trace of the glittering mid-Victorian splendor; the hotel had
been torn down and the space was being used as a parking lot.

7

A bridge across time

HIS EARLY YEARS as salesman, manager and over-all operating director of his father's company in Galesburg were to serve Roy as a kind of bridge between two worlds—the world of farm and plow and tractor and the new emerging automotive world of wheels and clutches and gears. The farm equipment industry was to learn much, especially in tractor production, from the fast-growing automobile industry and its assembly-line, mass-production techniques. Yet in other ways the automobile world drew upon the older farm equipment industry.

An example of this was the story of James A. Craig, operating head of the Janesville Machine Company, of Janesville, Wisconsin. This was the firm where Stephen Ingersoll once had to turn down the dinner invitation of the purchasing director, Mr. Cobb, before he finally obtained an order for his coulter discs. Craig had played an important part in the development of a highly efficient plow which won many national competitions.

One of Craig's close friends was William Durant, later the founder of General Motors. Durant, after he had become a leader in the automotive industry, held a conference with Craig and asked him: "Will you give up that business there and come to Detroit and work for me as one of the managers of General Motors?"

Craig thanked him but declined. "I warn you," Durant persisted, "I'm going to have you working for me, one way or the other."

Craig laughed and said, "Okay, Bill."

Durant made good his promise, not long after that call, by purchasing a controlling interest in the Janesville Machine Company. He advised Craig that General Motors was going to get into the farm equipment field and be competitive with Ford, who had started to produce the Fordson tractor in 1917. Ford was buying implements from different implement producing companies: plows from Oliver, disc harrows from Roderick-Lane of Mansfield, Ohio, and others. Durant told Craig that General Motors had already started on the design of a tractor and that a new plant was to be built at Janesville which, with the Janesville Machine Company, would become the implement division of General Motors.

In addition to tractors the Janesville Machine Company would continue to build other implements particularly those that would be attached and integrated with the tractor.

However, Durant's plan to move General Motors into the farm equipment field did not work out as he had planned, despite the fact that he was so confident about his tractors that he began to advertise the Samson tractor in 1918, nearly two years before they were ready to go into production. Unfortunately, by the time the plant was finished and production ready to start the depression of 1921 also had begun. Because of the depression in the farm implement industry the management of General Motors decided to discontinue production of tractors and to convert this beautiful new plant built for tractor production into an assembly plant for the Chevrolet Division of General Motors. It has continued to be one of General Motors' largest assembly plants.

The role of the tractor had been mounting and continued to mount in importance, however, ever since the days of the steam traction when the farmers discovered that they could hook up "gang plows," combinations of a number of plows, sometimes as many as ten, pulled behind the traction engine at the same time. Later the combustion engine tractors proved far less clumsy and cumbersome for this kind of plowing. In many areas, notably on the large farms of the Midwest, gang disc plows have superseded the moldboard type—it is not unusual to see a tractor plowing with ten or more large plow discs attached.

Case was the leading producer of steam tractor engines. In the 1890s, with the opening up of large tracts of land in the West for agricultural purposes, more power was required for breaking the soil, and this was when farmers started hitching plows to Case's "steam-traction" engines, even though they were not really designed for such use in the fields.

The Ingersolls had personal associations with the tractors as early as 1911, when Stephen Ingersoll bought his ranch in Stanford, Montana, and purchased two tractors from Harry Merritt, at that time Lewistown, Montana, district manager of the Hart-Parr Company of Charles City, Iowa, pioneers in commercial tractor production.

Merritt later became a top official at Allis-Chalmers and from 1926 until his retirement in 1941 was in charge of their tractor division, first as manager and then as vice president. A creative and at the same time an experienced executive, he played a leading role in building the Allis-Chalmers tractor division into a strong position in the highly competitive tractor world of the 1920s.

In 1937 he and his associates developed the Model B tractor, a small tractor that proved particularly useful and popular on small farms. It weighed less than a ton, could do the work of a team of horses, and could do it a great deal better and faster. This "baby tractor" was one of the most successful and profitable items in the Allis-Chalmers production list.

Although Hart-Parr was the first to go into the major tractor production on a large scale, beginning in 1902 the first combustion engine used in modern mechanized tractor farming was produced by a firm with an all-embracing name—the Waterloo Gas and Gasoline Engine Company of Waterloo, Iowa. This company manufactured the "Waterloo Boy" Internal Combustion Tractor. The corporation, name and all, was purchased in 1918 by Deere and Company and became the principal plant for the production of the Deere tractor.

The whole tractor story was the story of a complete new development in the agricultural world. Some writers describe it as "the tractor revolution." From a handful of tractors in the early years of the century it is estimated that there were some 21,000 in use by 1915. Virtually all of the major companies in the equipment field were involved, including International Harvester, which became the leading producer of farm tractors in 1911, taking over that position from the Hart-Parr Company.

In 1915 Henry Ford issued a startling announcement. He and his company were going to produce a "Fordson" tractor. His plan was to carry out in the agricultural field what he had already accomplished in the automotive world: the production of a light, mass-produced tractor without unnecessary ornamental features to be sold at the lowest possible price.

The first of Mr. Ford's tractors came off the line in 1917. Within a year the Fordson was the top selling tractor in the nation. In 1919 more than 50,000 Fordsons were sold and this mass production enabled the price to be cut to $750. By 1920 more than 300 tractors a day were being turned out by Ford.

Despite the popularity of the Ford tractor, however, there were basic underlying difficulties facing the Fordson. These lay primarily in the fact that Ford did not have a complete line of farm equipment to go with his tractor. The farmer was faced with the necessity of dealing with other companies.

Ford continued to lower his price for many years in the battle to hold leadership in this field. From an original price of $885 in 1919, he brought it down to a low of $395 in 1922 in an effort to help the farmer who was suffering from severely depressed prices for farm products.

International Harvester, however, with its Titan tractor, was strongly challenging Ford's leadership, cutting its prices substantially, and at the same time devoting all its knowledge and efforts to improving the Titan and increasing its efficiency.

Other farm implement companies also were fighting for their share of the tractor market. In 1927 Harvester again took the lead in tractors and Ford discontinued American production of tractors, although he continued to produce some in Cork, Ireland. In 1933 this production was terminated at Cork and moved to Ford's plant at Dagenham, England, where it continued production.

It was ten years after Ford discontinued the production of the Fordson tractor that he again started tractor production in the United States. In 1938 he entered into a contract with Harry Ferguson to produce tractors and some of their implements for Mr. Ferguson's company known as Ferguson-Sherman, Inc., and later as Harry Ferguson, Inc.

In 1939 production of the tractors, and later some implements to be used in conjunction with the tractors, was started at Ford's River Rouge plant. This was a new type of tractor called the Ferguson System Tractor which had, attached directly to the tractor, several implements such as plows, discs, and harrows with a hydraulic lift for raising and lowering these implements. This system, developed by Ferguson, had, when plowing, the advantage that the harder the pull the greater the traction on the rear wheels, which permitted the construction of a tractor much lighter in weight than those previously manufactured with the same plowing capacity.

In the alliance with Ferguson the Ford Company became a contracting manufacturer of the tractor itself and some of the implements that were sold to Ferguson, which was a merchandising organization. The merchandising was handled first by the Sherman brothers, Eber and his brother George. Later Roger Kyes, sales manager for Empire Plow Company of Cleveland, was persuaded to work with Ferguson a couple of days a week as a consultant on merchandising plans. After 1940 he devoted all of his time to this company. He was made Executive Vice President and, knowing practically every dealer across the country, he immediately started to build an organization and to expand the implement lines. He hired Horace D'Angelo as Treasurer. Soon after this Kyes was made President and General Manager of Harry Ferguson, Inc. During the war they secured material allocations for production of tractors and some implements which enabled them to keep their operation going during the war period. At the end of the war two important men were added to the organization who were to play a most important part in the future of Harry Ferguson, Inc., both before and after the consolidation with Massey-Harris. These were Al Thornbrough, a graduate of Kansas State College and Harvard Business School, and Herman G. Klemm who had been an outstanding design engineer for the Glenn L. Martin Aircraft Co. during World War II.

The relationship between Ford and Ferguson was not a harmonious one and in 1946 the contract was terminated. When the break between the two came, Ford began to manufacture a tractor of his own but Ferguson was left without a plant in which to produce his tractor or any of his implements.

As head of Ferguson, Inc., Kyes purchased a plant in Cleveland, but when the financing and stock issue which Cyrus Eaton of Cleveland had undertaken was withdrawn, Ferguson was left in a serious predicament, for Ford had given termination of deliveries on July 1, 1948. Kyes suggested liquidation of the company, but Ferguson decided to continue. Finally Kyes resigned to become a vice president of General Motors. Ferguson approached Borg-Warner. A five year contract was negotiated by Albert Thornbrough, then Ferguson's able Director of Purchases, whereby Detroit Gear would produce everything from the engine and the wheels to the transmission, clutch, differential, axle, and other parts.

Another man who played a role in this exciting industrial drama was Horace D'Angelo, then executive-vice president of Ferguson. Of his role the magazine *Business Week* reported: "D'Angelo took his operating group to Borg-Warner Corporation to convince the company it wouldn't lose money by tooling up to make axles and pumps for the struggling Ferguson crew. They met Roy C. Ingersoll, President, who agreed to help them out."

By November, 1948, Borg-Warner's Detroit Gear and Warner Automotive Divisions were making shipments under the contract with Ferguson. This contract lasted for nearly ten years. The company continued to expand the production of its tractors and the many implements designed by Mr. Klemm. He later was to become a director and Vice President of Engineering after Ferguson was merged with Massey-Harris Co.

The Massey-Ferguson Company also had a lengthy history dating back to 1847 when the Massey Company, of Ontario, Canada, produced various types of mowers and reapers. The Harris Company, established in Ontario in 1857, also made reapers and mowers. These two companies merged in 1891. Seven months later, Massey-Harris brought in another company, Patterson-Wisner, which had also been a combine of two large implement companies in Canada. Other acquisitions followed.

Throughout the years, Massey-Harris was known as one of the big three in Canada, the other two being International Harvester of Canada and the Cockshutt Plow Company. It was in 1928 that they purchased the J. I. Case Plow Works of Racine, Wisconsin.

Massey-Harris continued to be a dominant factor in the Canadian fields as well as in England, Australia, America and elsewhere.

The Ferguson Company continued to grow, and in 1954 James S. Duncan, president of Massey-Harris, purchased the company owned and controlled by Harry Ferguson for a sum reported to be approximately $17,000,000, which was the value of the 1,805,055 shares of Massey-Harris common stock that was delivered to Ferguson in the exchange. Duncan became President of the Massey-Harris-Ferguson Company and Ferguson, Chairman. At the time of the consolidation in 1954, Thornbrough was moved to the Racine, Wisconsin operations of Massey-Harris where he became Director of Procurement for all United States plants. In 1957 he was named President and Chief Operating Officer of the Company which by then had changed its name to Massey-Ferguson, Inc.

Under the direction of Thornbrough the company made tremendous strides. He liquidated obsolete inventory, closed some inefficient plants, brought out new implements designed by Herman Klemm and his staff, and greatly increased sales and distribution.

Borg-Warner continued to furnish transmissions, differentials, axles, and hydraulic pumps until December 31, 1957. At that time Massey-Harris-Ferguson, Inc. decided to have these components made in England where the wage rate was approximately 70¢ an hour as compared with $2.60 to $2.80 in the Detroit plant. Agricultural implement parts could be brought into the country without duty. Because of this tremendous wage differential, Borg-Warner was unable to compete.

Although Ford terminated shipments to Ferguson as of July 1, 1948, the Ford-Ferguson differences were not finally resolved until several years later.

Ferguson brought a civil suit against Ford for $341,600,000 in which he charged that Ford was infringing on his patents and was really building the Ferguson System tractor. The suit was finally concluded in 1952 by an agreement between the two companies under which Ford paid Ferguson $9,500,000 and made some minor changes in the design of the Ford tractor to avoid patent infringement.

The profound effect that Henry Ford had in the development of the farm tractor can scarcely be over-estimated. Although Mr. Ford tended to minimize his role in the tractor field through the observation that he was only "trying to find out how low the price might be at which farmers would buy tractors in quantities equivalent to automobiles," he nonetheless must be credited with several real contributions to progress in the tractor field.

Foremost among these was his recognition of the fact that there was a vast untapped market demand for a smaller, lighter, and less expensive tractor for use on the smaller farms. Prior to the introduction of the Fordson, the farm implement manufacturers believed they were serving their customers satisfactorily by supplying them with huge, heavy tractors with all the horsepower that could be built into them.

But Ford quickly changed all this. The overwhelming and speedy response to his Fordson demonstrated beyond all doubt that thousands of farmers wanted small tractors to ease the workload on the smaller farms and that these farmers were ready to part with some of their hard-earned dollars to purchase such machines. Once these facts were established, the tractor producers quickly evaluated the broad dimensions of this new market and accepted the challenge by redesigning existing models to specifications which called for less weight, less power, and smaller size.

Another advancement that expedited the progress rate of the tractor industry was Ford's concept of specially-built implements that integrated the operation of the tractor with that of the implement.

Up to that time the tractor was generally considered as merely a new form of pulling power which replaced the horse. Furthermore, there was a widely accepted view that tractors could be used economically only for pulling plows.

But Mr. Ford envisioned a much broader role than this for his tractor. He was well aware of the fact that virtually all implements except the plow, the cultivator, and some tillage implements had moving parts which had to be propelled by some force when they were used. By equipping his light, low-cost tractor with specially-designed implements, Mr. Ford is said to have set the stage for the development of the power take-off— a small unit which provides for the direct transmission of power from the tractor to the implement. The power take-off is considered one of the great advancements in tractor-implement history.

Equally important was Ford's contribution to the manufacturing technique of the tractor itself. Before the Fordsons went on the market the manufacturing methods, standards, and designs of the tractor producers were largely akin to those of the implement makers and, in the opinion of agricultural historians, were not as advanced as those in the new but fast-growing automobile industry.

Ford demonstrated that the basic manufacturing technology of the automobile shops could be applied successfully to the tractor factories and thus paved the way for greater development in the tractor field. The ensuing years were to bring forth a whole new breed of tractors that were to perform better, cost and weigh less, last longer, handle easier, and attract many more buyers than the heavy and cumbersome models.

Following the termination of the contract with Ferguson, the Ford Motor Co. decided to remain in the tractor and implement business. In keeping with this decision, certain directors and officers of the Company organized the Dearborn Motors Corporation in November, 1946, for the purpose of marketing Ford tractors and a line of implements to go with them.

The first president of Dearborn Motors was Frank R. Pierce who was elected Nov. 29, 1946. Under his management the new corporation grew rapidly. In 1947 Dearborn purchased Wood Bros., Inc., Des Moines, Ia., which produced corn pickers, combines, corn-harvesters, grain drills, and corn planters. Through this purchase and by arrangement with independent outside suppliers, Dearborn was able to effect a sizable expansion in its implement line. Shortly after its organization in 1946 it had 18 implements in the line. As of December, 1949, it had 249 implements and attachments. By June, 1952, the number had grown to 400.

Mr. Pierce was killed in an airplane accident and was succeeded by Thomas A. Farrell who had been a vice president under Mr. Pierce. Mr. Farrell was elected to the office in December, 1953.

Meanwhile Dearborn Motors had been reorganized and had become the Tractor Division of Ford Motor Company, effective Aug. 1, 1953. Farrell resigned January 15, 1954 and Irving A. Duffy succeeded him as General Manager of the Tractor Division. Duffy had come to the Ford Motor Co. in 1949 as Director of Purchases.

Roy had many negotiating sessions with Col. Duffy while he was Director of Purchases, including those in 1952 when Roy was helping Swain Russey, President and General Manager of Warner Gear Division, negotiate a five-year Ford automatic transmission contract which was an expansion of the original transmission contract. In spite of the very considerable difference between the ideas of Duffy and Ingersoll as to what constituted a reasonable price, each respected the other's views in regard to achieving a fair contract. The two men eventually became very close friends.

As under his predecessors, the tractor and implement business continued to grow under Duffy's management. Early in 1955, after nearly 40 years of single model production, Ford announced five new farm tractors in two power classes, one with 134 cubic inch engine and another with 172 cubic inches. During the spring of the same year, the first tri-cycle type row crop tractors in Ford history were introduced. This meant that for the first time Ford tractors could be used with front mounted equipment.

In 1955, the Tractor and Implement Division, the name by which it is known today, produced 66,656 tractors, a 29% increase over 1954 production. The Company's tractor production in 1955 represented 20.2% of industry production of wheel type farm tractors.

Duffy continued as general manager of the Tractor and Implement Division until January, 1957, when he was promoted to group vice president in charge of several manufacturing divisions. Duffy is also a director of Ford.

At that time Merritt D. Hill became General Manager of the Division. He had joined Dearborn Motors shortly after it was founded. Beginning in February, 1947, he was a director of Dearborn and Vice President in Charge of Sales. He remained in this capacity until he became Assistant General Manager of the Division, the position he held prior to his current post.

Among the key men in this operation is Irving R. Kappler, General Purchasing Agent for the Tractor and Implement Division. He came to Dearborn Motors in August, 1947, and became Vice President in Charge of Purchasing in June, 1950. When Dearborn became the Tractor Division in August, 1953, he was named the Division's General Purchasing Agent.

The men who ran the farm equipment companies and the sales managers, development engineers, and purchasing agents with whom Roy Ingersoll dealt were numbered among his closest friends. Many of these friendships lasted over decades. Roy enjoyed talking with these men, drawing out their stories, and gaining their confidence. Mr. Brantingham of Emerson Brantingham in Rockford, Illinois, would tell him of problems in raising funds for expansion. "Littleness is a crime, I guess," he told Roy. "Back in New York in 1911, when I went to talk about a refinancing plan, and told them how much I needed, I was turned down because they said it was too small. However, they did advise me that if I would increase the amount of required financing several times over and take some other company into the plan, why they would have financing for me."

Brantingham agreed to this, the financing was arranged, and Emerson was able to build one of the finest farm equipment plants in Rockford.

One of the companies Roy "called on" was the Grand Detour Plow Company in Dixon, Illinois, a firm which was to become a part of J. I. Case Company. Here he met his life-long friend, Alfred Leland, who later would be head of an important Emerson-Brantingham division of Case. Through Leland he met a colorful and engaging personality, the president of the company, Colonel W. B. Brinton, his son Bradford, and his daughter Helen.

On many occasions he dined at their home, built by the firm's founder, the former partner of John Deere, Major Leonard Andrus. This was a large house on the banks of the Rock River and Roy considered it one of the most beautiful homes he had ever been in.

Half a century later, when Roy Ingersoll and his wife were on vacation in Phoenix, Arizona, they and the Lelands who had been Roy's friends since the days back in 1907 in Dixon, spent an afternoon with the daughter of Colonel Brinton, Miss Helen Brinton, and they talked of old times and this beautiful house by the river. Roy told her: "In the powder room, on the dresser, I saw a matched set of toilet articles, mirror and brushes and combs, all of solid silver, gleaming and beautiful, and I told myself that if one day I were ever to become rich enough to afford it, I would buy such a set for my own home."

Helen Brinton smiled and commented, "Roy, you're chairman of the board now of one of America's great corporations. Did you get the set you promised yourself?"

Ingersoll could only shake his head.

The companies and men with whom he dealt in those first two decades of the century represented an era of change, leaders in the new dawn of modern living and improvements. Some were or would become world famous, some known only within their own fields; yet all were part of a tremendous contribution to our age. One day he would call on a firm named Allis-Chalmers of Milwaukee, famous for years as producers of power plant equipment including turbines, generators, heavy machinery and later to enter the farm equipment industry as builders of tractors, plows, disc harrows and other farm implements, in addition to its other widely diversified products. Another day it would be the LaCrosse Plow Company which later became a part of Allis-Chalmers.

Allis-Chalmers' story went back deep into America's history and development. It was started in 1847 when two young men hung up their sign on a rough-hewn building in Milwaukee: "Decker and Seville—Manufacturers of French Burr Millstones, Grist and Saw Mill Supplies." Ten years later they had the largest iron business in Milwaukee, employing seventy-five men. In 1861 the company was taken over by Edward P. Allis. By 1867 they were doing $150,000 worth of business a year and began manufacturing steam engines. By the turn of the century they were producing some of the largest steam engines ever produced. In 1901 they merged with the Frazer and Chalmers Company of Chicago and became the Allis-Chalmers Company.

This enterprise continued in the development of specialized equipment, including turbines and generators, and became one of the largest producers of power station equipment in the country. It went into the tractor business in 1914, during the

presidency of General Otto H. Falk. It was in 1926 that Harry
C. Merritt was brought in to head up the tractor division. Merritt launched a major expansion program which included the
purchase of the Monarch Tractor Company of Springfield,
Illinois in 1928, and the LaCrosse Plow Company in 1929.

Young Ingersoll became closely associated with Fred Haker
who was the purchasing agent of this company and one of the
most beloved figures in the farm equipment world. He also
knew well this firm's president, Walter Geist, who died in 1951
and was succeeded by his good friend and former farm equipment sales manager, William A. Roberts. In 1955 Robert S.
Stevenson succeeded to the post upon the death of Mr. Roberts.

Stevenson had been with Allis-Chalmers Manufacturing
Company since 1932. A graduate of Washington State College,
he started with the company as a tractor salesman in the Kansas
City sales office in 1933 and spent the next three years there and
in Omaha, Nebraska. He returned to the home office in Milwaukee in 1936 and for the next fourteen years filled various
sales and managerial positions. Stevenson was named vice president of the tractor group in 1951 and executive vice president
of the company in 1952. In April, 1955 he was elected president. In 1957-1958 he was president of the Farm Equipment
Institute.

One of the earliest of the Ingersoll customers in the 1880s
and 1890s while they were still at Sandoval, was B. F. Avery
and Sons Company of Louisville, Kentucky. The head of this
company was Captain C. F. Huhlein, an important early leader
in this field. This company, which produced chilled plows,
cotton-planters and other equipment particularly adapted to
southern states, was ultimately purchased in 1944 by the Minneapolis-Moline Company.

In Kentucky he would visit with Charles Birnsteil, purchasing agent at B. F. Avery; Birnsteil and his wife would always
give him a home-cooked sample of southern hospitality. Or in

Racine it would be his friend Harry Barr, who began at J. I. Case in 1910 as an apprentice and rose to be vice president in charge of purchasing. One of the most distinguished and respected leaders of the industry, he rose step by step in this company over long years of service. He was elected a director of Case in 1952, almost a half century after he began to work there.

Or Theo Brown, research and design engineer at Deere and Company, who would often show Roy his diaries in which, with engineering care for details, he had noted down the day-to-day events and progress he was making on new developments. These diaries ran into volumes and were like a personal history of the age.

In 1959 eighty-year-old Theo Brown recalled these days and his long association with Roy Ingersoll. "When we wanted something done," Mr. Brown said, "Roy got it done for us in a hurry and he did not stop until the job was finished."

On farm implements of all kinds Brown had a total of 158 patents issued to him, many of them in connection with the development of the modern tractor.

Many of the men knew Roy's father and had dealt with him over past years, but despite Roy's youth and the roughness of competition few tried to take advantage. There was one man who did try to get a better price than Roy was ready to sell his discs for. This was U. G. Orendorff of Parlin and Orendorff, a Canton, Ohio company which later became part of International Harvester. In that instance, Orendorff found himself outmaneuvered by a resourceful younger man.

This was in 1912, at the time of year when Roy was negotiating to sell discs to Orendorff's firm. Several competitors were trying to get this business, including Reuben Michener, sales manager for the Crucible Steel Company, and Clifford J. Ellis, western sales manager of Bethlehem Steel. After each one had negotiated with Orendorff's purchasing director, Carl Proebsting, they would then be sent in to talk to Orendorff himself. In this instance, Orendorff was trying to shave the price of discs down to $2.75 per hundred pounds from Roy's quotation of $2.85. He told Roy that his competitors had already agreed. Roy told him he could not meet the price and would have to let the business go. Mr. Orendorff countered: "Your father would never let this business go that way. Why don't you call him?" Roy explained that there was no phone at his father's ranch in Montana. Mr. Orendorff suggested that Roy wire him.

The following morning Roy returned to this firm's office with a typed message on a telegraph blank, "$2.85 IS OUR LOWEST PRICE STOP WE CANNOT AFFORD TO SELL BELOW COST EVEN IF WE LOSE ORDER AS RESULT." Orendorff had apparently not signed with any other competitors and they had already left town. Faced with this telegram he finally agreed to Roy's price, and gave him the contract.

But since the telegraph office in Galesburg was closed by the time Roy got home the night before, and had not yet opened when he left for Canton to see Orendorff the next morning, Roy's associates were not quite clear as to how he obtained that telegram. Roy never revealed what had happened.

Just before and at the end of the century the often ruthless practices in the farm equipment industry had become disastrous, both to dealers as well as to manufacturers. Out of this devastating situation, particularly for the harvesting producers of reapers and binders, came a logical realization. If these companies were to live, to grow and develop, to perform the research essential for continued progress, so that the industry could better serve the farmer and his needs, a merger of some of the major companies was inevitable.

The world-famed corporation, International Harvester, whose products sell in every nation on earth, was formed in 1902 by the merging of five companies—two large manufacturers of harvesting equipment, the McCormick Company and the Deering Company, both of Chicago, and three smaller manufacturers, the Milwaukee Harvester Company, the Warder, Bushnell and Glessner Company, and the Plano Manufacturing Company. All of these were on the harvesting end; later in 1904, the company acquired the Keystone Company and thereby began to move also into tillage equipment and haying tools.

Immediately following the original consolidation, Harvester had brought in D. M. Osborne and Company of Auburn, New York, maker of haying machines, the Weber Wagon Company of Chicago, in 1904, and the Kemp Manure Spreader Company in 1906.

In a brochure entitled "Roots in Chicago" published by International Harvester in 1947, it was stated:

"Additional companies and factories were purchased outright by the new corporation as a rapid means of acquiring proved machines in demand in the farming areas. D. M. Osborne & Company, Auburn, New York, brought haying machines into the line. With the machines came a well-earned reputation among eastern farmers. The Keystone Company, Rock Falls, Illinois, brought the company a popular line of haying machines, corn shellers and disc harrows. Purchase of the Weber Wagon Company in Chicago brought farm wagons into the rapidly growing line. The Kemp manure spreader was also purchased. An empty factory in Akron, Ohio, provided extra manufacturing space which later served as the birthplace of the company's high-wheeled trucks for farmers, the forerunner of today's line of International trucks. A later purchase, in 1919, of the Parlin & Orendorff Company, Canton, Illinois, provided a well-established line of plows, tillage implements, planters, beet machines, and potato diggers. In 1920 the factory and grain drill lines of the American Seeding Machine Company of Richmond, Indiana were purchased.

"Thus, in less than one hundred years the little McCormick factory on the north bank of the sluggish Chicago River grew into a group of major farm machinery factories in Chicago and many other cities, with management centered in general offices in Chicago." *

International Harvester began its experiments with farm tractors very shortly after the formation of the company. This production placed them in a leading position during the 'teens, and this was strengthened by accelerated production for the World War I needs. After the war came the period of far more intense tractor research and development. Most of the work was carried on at their tractor works in Chicago.

Additional plants were added to the company including the purchase of the huge tractor plant of the Moline Plow Company in Rock Island, Illinois, to be known as the Farmall Works, which was used primarily for the production of Farmall tractors. Truck production, also an important aspect of International, began in Akron, Ohio, in 1907. This was to become one of the new important facets of the Harvester Company production. In large measure it was co-ordinated, however, with their other farm equipment production. As one of their brochures states this, there were "trucks to haul the farm produce its machines had helped to grow, as well as the loads of industry and commerce which had sprung into being around the nation's rapidly expanding agriculture."

About the time World War II erupted, Harvester had five plants in Chicago with a total employment of approximately 30,000 and 15 additional plants in other parts of America and Canada with an additional employment of 60,000 plus a number of affiliated companies and plants abroad.

In the postwar period, also, this company conducted a wide expanding program which reached out not only to virtually every area in America, but of the world.

---

* For dates and other statistical data on these purchases, see appendix 2.

Two very important companies Roy Ingersoll had difficulty trying to sell in the early days were International Harvester and Deere and Company. Of the two, Harvester was perhaps the more difficult. Ingersoll's persistence and enthusiasm had won him the friendship of Harvester's purchasing agent, Arthur Aranson, whom Roy always saw when in Chicago.

International was a company of extraordinarily high standards, and extraordinary men, from its first president, Cyrus H. McCormick, son of the inventor of the reaper, on down the years. The achievements of this company make it one of the outstanding corporate structures of the world. Yet its officials had time for concern with customers and suppliers, however great or small. Aranson was still assistant purchasing agent when Roy began to try to "sell" International, although International's real interest in coulter discs did not come until their purchase of Parlin-Orendorff in 1919, which put them into the tillage field on a full-scale basis, and of the American Seeding Machine Company of Richmond, Indiana, both of which had been customers of the Ingersolls for many years.

Aranson's boss, then vice president and purchasing director, was a Mr. Edgar, a kindly, meticulous man who invariably arrived at the stroke of 8:00 in the morning; Roy knew that he could set his watch by Mr. Edgar's arrival. Although Mr. Edgar made no purchases of discs from Roy's company, he was always friendly and genial and enjoyed showing his caller a book he had kept for many years, containing the golf scores of every game he had ever played.

Arthur Aranson was not quite as meticulous as Mr. Edgar. Although Harvester still clung to its 8 o'clock starting time after Aranson became purchasing director, he was sometimes not as punctual as his predecessor. Roy had been trying to make a sale for some years to Aranson, without success. One morning he was waiting outside Aranson's office, precisely at 8. All of the other top executives of the firm came in, but no Aranson.

Finally, long after opening time, the purchasing agent did show up, apologized for keeping Roy waiting and explained that he had had to stop in at the Deering works on some business.

Roy was sure his friend had been out late the night before and overslept but the purchasing agent grinned and insisted, "No, Roy, I really did have something important to do."

Roy said, "Art, the only important thing you really have to do is to buy some of my company's coulter discs."

To his surprise, Aranson said, "All right, if your price is right we will give you part of our business."

The order he gave, when the contract was finally drawn up, amounted to over $300,000—the largest single order the Galesburg plant had ever received up until that point.

"When I got on the coach and headed back to Galesburg that evening," Roy remembered later, "I was the happiest man who ever boarded a Chicago, Burlington and Quincy train."

He was to come to know many of the International Harvester Company officials well over the years ahead and a warm relationship was to develop. One of these was Fowler McCormick, who was president of International from 1941 to 1946 and chairman of the board from 1946 to 1951. This period in office included the years of World War II, during which Harvester produced more than a billion dollars worth of materials to support the Allied cause.

Roy Ingersoll saw in International Harvester a company which virtually typifies the American free enterprise system at its best—an organization in which men of outstanding ability can rise to the very top.

A prime example is John L. McCaffrey. He began his business life in 1909 as a clerk in the Cincinnati sales branch of International Harvester and rose to become chief executive officer of the corporation.

Mr. McCaffrey gained a depth of experience and an intimate knowledge of his industry by selling the products of his company in many parts of the country for many years. In 1940 he became vice president. Other promotions followed quickly. He was appointed First Vice President in 1945, then succeeded Fowler McCormick as President in 1946 and served in this post for ten years. He was Chairman from 1956 until his retirement in 1958. During these years of his chief stewardship—from 1946 to 1958—Harvester's annual sales grew from $482,327,755 to $1,098,389,000 and earnings rose from $22,326,257 to $42,987,000. McCaffrey's development of a broad expansion program, involving expenditures of close to $150,000,000 and reorganization of the company's structure on a full divisional basis, materially aided the large growth of this company.

Frank W. Jenks became President of International Harvester in 1957 and took on the additional responsibility of Chief Executive Officer in 1958. Roy Ingersoll, who for many years had recognized the executive ability of Frank Jenks, nominated him for a directorship on the Board of The United States Chamber of Commerce and worked closely with him on this Board for several years.

Frank Jenks, like his predecessor John McCaffrey, had started his business career as a junior clerk in 1914, at International Harvester's sales office in Richmond, Virginia. Jenks, having acquired extensive sales experience in travels throughout the country, was made Vice President in 1944 and Executive Vice President in 1956. A year later he became President. For the quarter ending April 30, 1959, Jenks was able to report the largest sales and profits for any like period in the history of his company. The management of International Harvester long has stressed research and development, and from the laboratories and engineering departments of this great company there have emerged and still come many new or improved machines to further mechanize the farm and increase the farmers' productivity.

A company is no stronger than the men who help to establish

and to direct its policies, and International fortunately has such men at the helm. Another of its leaders is Harry O. Bercher, who became an Executive Vice President and a Director of the company. Bercher's aggressive planning and forceful personality have been responsible for the development of many of Harvester's important policies and procedures.

The story of Bercher's business career is also one of continuing success built on ability, demonstrated from the first day he started to work in Harvester's iron ore mines at Hibbing, Minnesota, in 1928. He received successive promotions to executive positions in the company's general office in Chicago, in the Benham Coal Mines in Kentucky, and in the Wisconsin Steel Works until, in December 1945, he became General Manager of the Steel Division. In December 1947 he was also appointed Director of the Purchasing and Traffic Departments of the company, and in 1953 he was elected a Vice President, continuing to have supervision of both the Steel Division and Purchasing and Traffic.

The only serious dispute Roy Ingersoll ever had with Harry was on a salmon fishing trip to Canada. Roy was sure he had the largest salmon catch of the day, which Harry strongly disputed. On arriving back at camp the scales showed Harry's weighing 34 pounds—three pounds more than Roy's largest.

Another of Harvester's important young executives is Brooks McCormick, a dynamic and penetrating young man who became associated with International Harvester immediately after his graduation from Yale in 1940 and who rose to become an Executive Vice President in 1957. He held many important manufacturing and sales positions in the United States and in Britain. In 1952 he was elected Managing Director of Harvester's British subsidiary. It was there—in England in 1955—that Roy Ingersoll first met Brooks.

Another International Harvester executive who became a friend of Roy's was William C. Schumacher, who was named an

Executive Vice President in 1957. Starting with Harvester in 1917 as a warehouseman in Jacksonville, Florida, Schumacher rose through various sales and office positions to become, in 1946, General Manager of the company's Motor Truck Division and, in 1953, Vice President of the parent corporation.

All of these friends and many others in the two companies helped to form the close relationship which has existed over many years between International Harvester and Borg-Warner.

There was always brittle humor, warm friendship, high standards and sharp interplay of minds and purposes among these men. On one occasion Herbert Copp of Deere and Company was talking to Roy at a Farm Equipment Institute meeting at the Congress Hotel in Chicago when Leon Clausen joined them. This was about a year after Clausen had resigned from Deere to become president of Case. During the conversation, Leon said with a grin, "Herb, have you noticed how J. I. Case's stock has gone up since I took over the management?"

Copp said, "Yes, Leon, and I want to congratulate you. But I also wanted to ask you—have you noticed how Deere and Company stock has gone up since you left?"

There were a number of major mergers in this industry, particularly during the late 'teens and 'twenties. One of the several companies merged into the Massey-Harris Company was a Verity Plow Company of Bradford, Ontario, owned by the Verity family and headed by C. M. Verity and his brother. Verity Plow Company was one of the early customers of the Ingersolls' coulters and later of their plow discs. Mr. Verity was a very close friend of Stephen Ingersoll's and also of Roy's; Verity's son, Morley F. Verity, became general manager of the company, and when it merged into Massey, was placed in charge of several Massey-Harris plants.

When Roy began calling at this company, the senior Verity often suggested to him that the Ingersolls ought to set up a plant in Canada for the production of coulters and discs. However, the next day Roy visited Harry H. Biggert, then general manager of the Canadian works of International Harvester Company at Hamilton, Ontario, and later executive vice president of J. I. Case, and Roy talked to him about it. This was in the days before World War I. Biggert told him, "Roy, sure we'd like you to have a plant up here. But I'm a friend of yours and I'd suggest before you establish a plant in this country with only about 8 million people, make sure that you have fully exploited your potential in the United States with its 90 million population."

Roy W. Gifford, who later became assistant general maneger at the Detroit Gear Division of Borg-Warner, had charge of building new plants for Massey-Harris in France and Australia. Massey at that time had only one plant in the United States where they made mowing machines, in Batavia, New York. However, after Massey-Harris acquired the J. I. Case Plow Company in 1928, this plant with additions they made, for years became their principal tractor manufacturing plant.

Mergers in the industry had special significance to Roy Ingersoll. The day came, many years after Roy's first visit to Horicon, Wisconsin, as a salesman, when the Van Brunt Company was to be sold. But Mr. Van Brunt set up certain stipulations about the sale. Determined that no harm should come through this sale to the community of Horicon where he had lived and worked and prospered with his company—on which all the town now depended—he insisted that the purchaser agree in the contract not to move the plant from the community.

To stand by this pledge he had to turn down one offer for $4,500,000.

Eventually he sold the company for a smaller price to Deere and Company who accepted the stipulation. Half the price was paid in cash and the other half in Deere and Company 7 per cent non-callable preferred stock.

The preferred stock eventually sold for as high as $200 a

share and brought the Van Brunt family a tidy profit in addition.

The Ingersoll companies at Galesburg, Illinois, and New Castle, Indiana, had come to play an increasingly important role in this farm equipment industry. The first ten years after Roy joined the Galesburg Coulter Disc Company sales had increased over 1000 per cent, and by 1920, the last year before the severe recession of 1921 and 1922, they had increased nearly 1300 per cent.

The New Castle plant, from the time of acquisition in July 1, 1917, had increased over 100 per cent; in the depression of 1921-1922, by effecting great economies, both of these plants were able to operate in the black even though sales were very much curtailed.

In October of 1920 came the most precipitous decline in farm industry's sales that the manufacturers had ever experienced. Overnight, order cancellations began to flood the Galesburg plant, reflecting what was happening throughout the industry. At the start of the month the books had been loaded with orders; by the end of the month there were hardly enough to keep the factory going for another week.

With the farmers in bad shape and farm prices on a toboggan, virtually all the farm equipment manufacturers began to close down or, at best, run only part time. Galesburg was down to 20 per cent of normal output. To make matters worse, it had contracted for large quantities of steel slabs for the New Castle mill that could not be canceled. They had to be paid for and held in inventory until business began coming back to what President Harding called "Normalcy."

Yet it was here, in the midst of postwar recession, widespread unemployment and industrial inactivity, that Roy Ingersoll achieved a significant contribution that enabled the implement producers to furnish their disc harrows and plows with blades that would stand up and hold their cutting edge under the increasingly severe requirements of the tractor-drawn implements.

In 1920, as the economic recession spread, a challenge came to him. It came in the form of a harrow disc, like thousands furnished from the Galesburg plant. But this one no longer had the sharp keen edge it had when first shipped out. It was cracked and chipped from its use and abuse in the fields. Its edges were twisted and bent and contorted. Obviously it had encountered rocks, limestone, hidden stumps and roots that had pulled and torn it, twisted and broken its fine edge.

The disc lay on Roy's desk in the Galesburg plant, where he stayed late one evening, alone, catching up with work that had had to wait while he was away. Often, while he worked, his eyes strayed to the battered disc—and his mind to the problem it presented.

It was returned by one of his implement customers to show him the problem they were up against. This disc was an Ingersoll product, equal in quality and durability to any being produced anywhere in the world. It was the best to be had, Roy knew, and it wasn't good enough.

These discs had to work in every kind of soil, under every kind of condition. When the going was rough, as it was on many farms, it was only natural that eventually the discs cracked and twisted, their edges became bent and uneven, until finally they were as useless as the one on his desk.

Natural? Yes, his mind admitted, but not necessarily inevitable. The idea hovered in the evening quiet. Could some method be found to produce discs which would last longer, even under the worst soil conditions?

Alone that night, his mind played with possibilities—with techniques in steel, methods of hardening and toughening the discs. His other work forgotten, he walked slowly through the plant, past the shadowy lines of presses where the discs were being produced.

What was the answer? Two days later, on a selling trip, he asked himself this question as, while changing trains in Indianapolis, he stood outside the Atkins Saw Company. He had no idea then, of course, that one day, as head of Borg-Warner, he would be directing the destinies of this company, one of the world's leading producers of saws of all types.

As he gazed into this plant he noted the furnaces which brought the circular saw blades up to quenching temperature, after which they were quenched in oil. It was a process which warped the saw blades; the shape could be restored only by putting the saws between platens sixty inches in diameter and keeping them there for a lengthy period. Roy was aware that the steel used for his coulter discs was the same quality as that used by Atkins.

The technique of restoring the saws to shape after the heat treating was far too expensive to employ with the coulter discs, turned out not individually but by the thousands daily. When the saws came out of the oil quenching tank they were not only distorted but also hard and brittle. Platens held the saws inside a furnace, at a uniform temperature required for this "drawing operation," which not only restored the shape but also put into the steel strength and ductility, eliminating the brittleness.

To develop any kind of heat-treating technique that could be used in the mass production of discs with their sharp keen-edged blades, and still maintain the exact contour and dimensions of the discs, would, he knew, involve hundreds of tests and experiments, for they would have to achieve a delicate balance in which the blade would have maximum hardness and still retain the strength to withstand the treatment it met behind high speed tractors working in rocky and other difficult types of soils.

All the way back to Galesburg he considered the possibilities. It was a time of depression—but prosperity would come back to the farms and the farmers as it always had and always would, stronger than before.

The time to experiment was now.

Back in Galesburg he went to his father, with whom he had talked over business problems for a quarter of a century, ever since, as a boy, he had been the older man's "first assistant" at Sandoval.

It was a big dream, Stephen Ingersoll told his son, and one with far-reaching implications. Perhaps he would fail, as had the big steel companies, with all the facilities at their disposal. But perhaps now an Ingersoll would find a way.

It was no vast laboratory staffed with technicians that Roy Ingersoll, with his father's backing, set up in the Galesburg plant. It was a small section where he could work with whatever equipment and material were available, in whatever time he could find. Though he was running the Galesburg plant and traveling to the farm equipment and automobile companies, trying to secure orders which would keep the company going, he made time for his experiments.

Painstakingly, step by step, he began his tests to develop a controlled heat-treatment for the steel discs. Half a dozen full-sized notebooks were filled with rows of figures in which he compiled information gained from these tests. And out of these fat notebooks came a technique unique in the steel industry.

The process that he developed wasn't a simple one. It was a complex procedure involving many technical intricacies, each the result of long and patient experimentation.

As it evolved, the discs were rolled and formed and then subjected to the proper controlled heat; then they were cooled quickly by quenching in oil baths. Each step had to be perfectly designed and perfectly carried out; each brought its own special problems. An oil had to be found, for instance, that would not flash into flame when the red-hot disc was plunged into it. A way had to be found to keep the tanks of oil cool, but not so cool that the discs would harden too quickly and become brittle and breakable as glass.

Once through the heat treatment, the discs had to go on to "drawing presses" where, by means of special electrically heated clamps they were held in place and shaped to the exacting measurements and contours required. All of this had to be precisely controlled to give the proper hardness and toughness as well as exact contour.

These intricate, technical problems Roy Ingersoll worked on and solved, one by one, until in his unpretentious "laboratory" at Galesburg, he was able to produce discs which satisfied the incredibly exacting demands of this quest: they were perfect in contour, curvature and measurement, uniform in hardness and had proved, in tests in the plant, that they would far outlast any other steel discs being made.

Then came final tests in the fields. Gangs of harrow discs, alternately heat-treated and untreated, were attached to tractors and hauled by them through rocks and every other rugged soil condition a farmer might possibly encounter.

The results were staggering. The untreated discs, under the tremendous punishment, were bent at the edges, bashed in, and practically as usless as the harrow discs which had been returned by Roy's implement customers with a plea for him to do something to correct and overcome this situation.

The heat-treated discs, though rolled and ground to fine edge, held their edge and shape even under this intense battering. There was no question that Roy Ingersoll had developed a process that would more than double the life of a disc, no matter under what conditions it was used.

In the farm equipment world, the word of the new wonder discs spread like a spring wind across the fields.

International Harvester was first in line, asking for samples for test purposes. Only a few days later Art Aranson called with a unique request. International's president, Mr. Alexander Legge, after seeing these tests, insisted that their large inventory of 200,000 discs be sent to Galesburg to be heat treated. International would pay for the entire expense, including freight charges each way. Roy agreed to do this, although a considerable proportion of these discs were products of his competitors' plants.

Farmers began hearing of the new, longer-lasting discs and asking questions of their equipment suppliers. Equipment salesmen wanted the new discs on their plows. Manufacturers turned to their own suppliers with demands for Galesburg heat-treated discs.

The patent process that Roy Ingersoll had so painstakingly evolved over the months made no headlines or sensational stories in the daily press. Yet it was a development that had a big impact on this industry that was trying desperately to meet the problems produced by the tractor age. The Galesburg Coulter Disc Company was certainly not one of the giants of the industry, but the giants were now aware of its existence.

In the past, the Ingersolls had had to struggle for every small gain in their share of the market for coulters and discs; for several years they had secured less than 10 per cent of the total volume of business done.

Now, suddenly, equipment companies were calling, wiring and sending representatives to Galesburg, all wanting the new heat-treated discs. There was no longer any question of finding customers for the plant's product. The question now was how soon equipment could be installed to meet the greatly increased demand for their discs.

The sales of discs annually ran into many millions. Galesburg was fast making strides toward becoming the largest disc producer in the world. There was still, however, plenty of competition, as other firms tried feverishly to develop a process that would produce a disc of equal quality. But one of the giants, Bethlehem Steel Company's Cambria plant, paid Galesburg the supreme compliment: in 1925 it gave up entirely its attempts to develop and manufacture a heat-treated disc that would compete with Roy's, and bowed out of the disc business entirely.

But this triumph was part of the future.

It was a long way ahead of the early days at Galesburg, Roy's first selling trip to Horicon, Dixon, Moline, Rockford and other cities where farm equipment firms were located.

Before the heat-treating experiments could even have been dreamed of, there were hurdles that had had to be conquered. One of the most important was to obtain a reliable source of steel for Galesburg's soaring needs.

8

Wanted: One steel mill

ONLY A FEW companies in America produced the grade of steel required to make the coulters and discs manufactured at Galesburg and used by farmers in plowing and harrowing the earth. Crucible Steel Company was one. Cambria at Johnstown, Pennsylvania, which later became a part of Bethlehem, was a second. The Norwalk Steel and Iron Company, a comparatively small operation, was a third.

For many months the Galesburg factory had depended almost entirely on this Norwalk, Ohio, plant for its steel requirements. But early in 1909 the shipments had begun to slow down and then almost to disappear.

With the threat of idle machines and men confronting them, and unfilled orders piling up, the Ingersolls couldn't delay longer. At his father's suggestion, Roy hopped the first train to Norwalk to find out why they were not receiving the quota of steel promised by this company.

He found a roaring chaos. Although the Ohio plant had a full backlog of orders, and was producing at capacity, its finances were in such confusion that it had no funds either to meet payrolls or buy the pig iron needed for the open hearths to keep production going. It was a situation that would have disheartened many an older, more experienced man. But Roy Ingersoll simply could not afford defeat.

Galesburg needed steel of the fine grade produced at Norwalk. The plant must be kept going. Wiring back to Galesburg for money, Roy began to meet the payroll and buy the pig iron himself. Within a period of weeks, he had spent $50,000 of Galesburg's cash to keep the shaky plant in operation.

But his troubles, he soon discovered, were not over. The steel shipments from Norwalk were still arriving in dribbles, far below the percentage of Norwalk's production promised for Galesburg. Then the story came out. The plant's operators, on the lookout for cash, were shipping their product to other customers.

Furious at the way he was being treated, Roy telephoned his father that he would not advance another cent to the company; that he would stay there and see that he got sufficient steel to take care of the amount of money already advanced to the company. His father said, "You know how badly we need this steel, but I agree with you that it would be a mistake for us to go on advancing money to keep them operating under these conditions."

"Right," Roy told him. "And we'll see who gets steel this time."

The answer was nobody. With no more money forthcoming from the Ingersolls, the operators of the Norwalk plant were forced to close down only days later, but Roy had secured several carloads of steel, sufficient to take care of the funds he had advanced. Roy called Galesburg and stated that he had a plan for getting the plant into operation. The Galesburg directors agreed to come to Norwalk to explore this proposal.

The day on which they arrived was bitter, the wind icy and penetrating; snow swirled wet and stinging against the faces of the men who stood silent and disconsolate in the hush of this closed-down steel mill. The spectacle around them held a ghost-like aura: smokestacks and vents and cranes loomed like twisted gargoyles; the open hearths, whose roofs had already fallen in, were chill and forlorn; the buildings silhouetted for a moment against lead-gray sky, then half obscured in the sleet and mist.

To some of the men in the group, this January 3, 1910 meeting at the steel mill in Norwalk, Ohio, seemed hardly a propitious start for a new year or a new decade.

The Norwalk Steel and Iron Company had been their chief supplier of steel. It was, until it shut down three days before, one of the few companies producing the special grade of steel needed for the sharp-edged coulter discs. All the directors were aware that major steel suppliers in the Pittsburgh area would shed no tears if the relatively small but growing Galesburg company—the only firm producing those discs in the very heart of the farm area—had to go out of business for lack of raw steel.

Such was the free-swinging philosophy of rugged competition that still prevailed at the dawn of 1910.

The directors had come to Norwalk in a moment of crisis, at the urgent telephoned insistence of this young man who stood before them now in the swirling snow—twenty-five-year-old Roy C. Ingersoll, broad shouldered, with an oval face and a slightly misshapen nose, broken while playing tackle for Knox College against an emerging young university called Notre Dame. The stripling youth was the only one of the group with an air of confidence in the midst of the caved-in hearths, the already-rusting rolls, the snow drifting like a rumpled white shroud across the mill.

"This Norwalk mill is bankrupt but it's not in bad shape. We could lease it from the receivers and have it back in operation in ten days," he had assured them over the phone. "Then we can make our own steel and we won't have to depend on our competitors—Crucible or Cambria—to stay in business."

The courts still had to appoint the receivers of the bankrupt mill before the leases could even be drawn, but Roy Ingersoll explained on the phone—and repeated here, in the midst of the snow—that all of this was mere detail.

It had sounded plausible and possible as young Roy outlined his findings and proposals to his father and some of the directors individually over the long distance telephone.

But here on the scene, as the directors stood in the bleak immobility of the plant itself, the suggestion began to take on the contours of a nightmare.

The young man carefully surveyed each member of this group before him. They were much older than he, all except Charlie Stoup, the young plant superintendent of the closed mill, who had driven Roy out this morning from the Norwalk Hotel in his one-cylinder Brush automobile.

The other men were close friends of his family's, of his father in particular. Some of them, he was sure, would support him in this project to try to get the mill back into production. Others appeared unsure.

"Charlie Stoup tells me," Ingersoll persisted in persuasive tones, "that we can get the lease and can get the men back to their jobs and can put this place back in operation for practically nothing more than meeting the unpaid back payroll."

They appeared impressed by his enthusiasm, but far from certain about his proposed strategy in this crisis. One of the directors, however, had made up his mind.

"Gentlemen, this is all hair-brained nonsense," he announced. "This Norwalk mill is finished. Nobody's going to get it back into production now or ten months from now. Look at this morgue!"

The tall white-haired speaker was Willis E. Terry, Sr., one of the most influential members of Coulter Disc's board of directors, and one of Galesburg's most respected and leading businessmen.

Roy Ingersoll answered with supreme deference: "But, sir, without the production of this mill, where will my father turn for the kind of steel that has to go into our discs? Without this special, high carbon steel——"

"I want to tell you, Roy," Terry reiterated, "first, last and all the time: you can't make it work. Nobody could make it work."

Against the snow and the elusive forms of the mill itself, the two men seemed to stand apart, but each respected the other's viewpoint.

Clearly, the logic of the younger man was strong, almost irrefutable, but full of peril; the conservative approach of the older man was less risky in one sense but invited disaster in another.

Looking around him at the others, the older man knew by their expressions that Roy had won.

"All right," Terry said with a smile, "if this thing fails, which I'm sure it will, I'm going to say 'I told you so.' And if by some streak of chance it should come out all right, well—I'll call you a fool for luck."

In the midst of the snow and sleet, the board took a formal vote. With the exception of one dissenter, it was unanimous for Roy Ingersoll's plan.

Within a week after that vote, the open hearths and heating furnaces had been repaired, the roofs restored, the rolls cleaned and made ready. A payroll had been put together by young Ingersoll from funds sent from Galesburg to meet sums due the workers; the men were back and operations were underway.

Within one month the mill was producing more steel than ever before in its history. In addition to turning out steel for discs, it was again turning out "soft-center" steel for mold-boards, plow shares and other specialized sections of a plow. Soft-center steel has three layers—hard, soft and hard—a particularly durable "sandwich" for work in gumbo and sticky soils. When tempered this steel has a hard glassy surface which prevents the soil from sticking to the moldboard. The mill was supplying not only the steel requirements of Galesburg, but also those of several other farm implement concerns.

But to the young man who had won a vote of confidence there in the snow, this victory focused in his thoughts a truth that was to shape his life—the almost mystical interdependence of men and machines and plants and the glittering array of products they produce in a free society.

He had had his first rough-and-tumble fight in the arena of big business, and had come out the winner. But there was to be no rest or opportunity to relax and take bows. He had to get the Norwalk plant back into production and back on its financial feet.

The manufacture of steel in a mill like this one was a new challenge. He plunged into it with all the enthusiasm of a teen-ager investigating the intricacies of his first jalopy. He learned how to make soft-center steel for plows and the special two- and five-ply varieties used in penitentiaries—jail bar steel for prison windows and doors, sawproof because it was made of alternate soft and hard layers.

He was lonely in Norwalk, away from his family and, most especially, for the girl back in Galesburg. He spent every waking moment at the plant, poring over the books, studying reports, worrying about taking proper care of his customers' orders and seeing to it that delivery promises were kept.

Roy's hard work soon began to pay off. As America took to its wheels, and steel production started to zoom in an effort to keep up with the demand for cars, the Norwalk plant became a greater and greater asset. It gave the Ingersolls a dependable source of supply for their own and their customers' needs. It also enhanced their growing reputation as manufacturers of steel products at a time when steel was becoming increasingly hard to get.

But these blue skies over Norwalk could not continue forever. And they didn't.

The Ingersolls did not own the now booming steel plant in

Norwalk; they had only leased it. And in the middle of 1910, the receivers who had been leasing the mill to the Galesburg company decided to put it up for sale.

The Ingersolls faced another crisis. Roy wanted the mill because he saw the great potentials for expansion in this basic industry. He had breathed new life into it, put it on its feet, and in a short time had greatly increased its capacity. As far as he was concerned, it was his child. Unfortunately, several other companies had their eyes on it, among them the giant known as Crucible Steel.

Roy was willing to tangle with anything twice his size—but Crucible!

During the months in Norwalk, he had been too occupied with work to make many friends, but in the course of business he had come to know wise, ninety-four-year-old John Gardiner, who was still the active president of the Norwalk National Bank; his bearded seventy-year-old son, Edmund, the bank's treasurer; and his grandson, Charles Gardiner, then cashier but later vice president and director. As regularly as Roy made his weekly trip to the bank, the old man would call him into his office for a chat and to find out how things were going at the mill.

The old man and the young would sit together in that curious, old-fashioned room, with the bank president's hunting dog sprawled before the wood-burning stove, on the yellow pineboard floor. And from the old man's keen mind, sharpened by years of experience, Roy learned much that was to serve him well in the years ahead.

Old John lived by standards out of another age. He had built many things in his life—blast furnaces and portions of a railroad that eventually became part of the New York Central. He had been president of a railroad and he told Roy that he had made several fortunes, and lost some of them. But he had no regrets.

"You know what my rule is, Roy, my philosophy of life?" he would say, shaking a finger at his young companion. "It's this: I learned early in my life never to cry over spilt milk, but to go out and get myself another cow. That's what I've always done."

Now, faced with the possibility of losing his mill, Roy went to the old man for advice.

"Get control of it," old John advised immediately. "Buy it."

"But how?" Roy persisted.

The old man considered for a moment. "If you could buy up several big blocks of the company's bonds, with a face value of say, $1,500,000, you could control the plant. And you could probably locate them and buy them in for a good deal less than their real value so that it should not cost now more than four or five hundred thousand."

"But that would still take more cash than we could raise."

"I know," said the older man, "and we don't have it either. But the big banks in Toledo and Cleveland do. Show them your figures, what you've been doing with the mill. Get them to loan you the money to buy these bonds at these depreciated prices."

Roy Ingersoll took the train to Cleveland. He had almost convinced the big-city bankers that they should put up the necessary cash when the word got back to big Crucible, and before Roy could get the deal settled, the company had bought up the outstanding bonds. Roy's mill was gone.

"You can't beat that kind of cash on the barrelhead," the old banker tried to console his young friend. "You better start looking for that other cow."

"Well, we've got several months' supply of steel," Roy answered, bouncing back from his disappointment. "That gives me a little time to go cow-hunting."

As it turned out, he didn't have to look long or far. Now that it had gobbled up the Norwalk plant, Crucible needed customers for its output—and who was more logical than the Galesburg Company they had just dispossessed?

Crucible had the steel, Galesburg had the money to buy it. But the price was high. "Impossible, Mr. Wharton," Roy bluntly told the company's sales manager, who was later to become Crucible's president. Galesburg's directors agreed with Roy and began to make plans and secure financing for their own steel mill. When word of this maneuver leaked back to Crucible, the price came down fast.

Roy was able to negotiate a five-year contract which guaranteed the Galesburg plant a steady supply of high carbon steel to meet its growing needs at a price pegged to the cost of the pig iron. He believed that pig iron was and would remain a stable-priced product on which to base the price of his disc steel. His foresight paid off. His insistence on this clause in the contract made late in 1911 saved his company hundreds of thousands of dollars in the next few years, especially after World War I started in 1914 and steel prices skyrocketed.

The negotiations with Crucible were important to him, but not as important as those he was conducting evenings and week ends on the front porch of a pleasant house in Galesburg. Talented Lulu Hinchliff had not been content to sit quietly at home while her college sweetheart made his first forays into the world of big business. She was not only teaching violin but also performing; she had made two successful cross-country concert tours. Before she became too engrossed in her career, Roy knew he must take action.

Spring was beautiful that year when Roy asked the all-important question and was accepted. Never in his life had he made a sale that meant to him a fraction of this one, he told his friends.

Crucible executives, wooing Roy as he was courting Lulu, didn't let the young couple's betrothal pass unnoticed. How about a holiday trip on one of its ore boats, they suggested. It was an ore boat ride *de luxe*. For on this trip were Crucible's president, C. C. Ramsey, and his wife, and the company's treas-

urer, George A. Turville, and his wife. With these as chaperones, Roy and Lulu, his sister Winifred, and her Knox College
fiance, Arvid Zetterberg, set out in gala mood.

Try though they might to conceal it, their happiness was
quite apparent to all. Convinced finally that they were not
honeymooners, the conductor on the train which took them
and their chaperones from Cleveland to Conneaut, Ohio, insisted, "Well, when people have the kind of look you two have,
I say you're going to be married soon."

At Conneaut they boarded the ore boat. There followed sun-
filled days and moonlit nights on the Great Lakes, with the
waves lapping against the heavily-loaded vessel, as Roy and
Lulu talked and planned for their future. A home in Galesburg,
where they could be near their families and their friends . . .
and children. Business was fascinating to him, Roy told her, but
she would always come first. He was a family man by instinct
and upbringing. Soon, he promised, he would not have to work
so hard; he could be with her more of the time.

Wise far beyond her years, tall and lovely Lulu pressed his
hand and made no answer.

A young man so curious about everything connected with his
world, and so charged with energy, could not, however, relax
completely even under such romantic conditions. Roy watched,
fascinated, as ore and coal were loaded and unloaded. He paced
the deck, investigating every nook and hatchway. At Sault St.
Marie he was up at dawn to see the vessel pass through the
canal locks into Lake Superior.

And, before the voyage was over, he was summoned by telegram back to Galesburg to settle a contract problem.

"It won't always be like this. Soon I won't have to work so
hard." Lulu smiled as he said good-by and hurried down the
ladder to the small boat that would take him ashore at Detroit.
The words already had a familiar ring.

They were married that autumn, and honeymooned in the

Adirondacks, where there were no steel mills, no contracts, no ore boats. They went on to that mecca of honeymooners, Niagara Falls, and en route, by odd chance, they met again the conductor who had prophesied their marriage earlier. "I said you'd be married in a month," he recalled, as he took their tickets. "Somehow, I always know."

Back in Galesburg, they began housekeeping with high hopes and a big mortgage. A shrewd young businessman he might be, but Roy had been able to make a down payment of only $2,500 on the $8,500 house he had bought for his bride. The remainder he had contracted to pay off at the rate of $60 a month.

But the directors of the Galesburg plant were for the most part family men. They knew from experience that two could not live as cheaply as one. They gave Roy a raise from $125 to $175 a month.

With Roy able to take over much of the management of the Galesburg plant, and his younger brother Harold helping on many of the company's problems although still in college, Father Ingersoll began to cast longing eyes and thoughts more and more to the world he had not forgotten—the soil and what it could grow. His sons had told him two years before about the fertile land of Montana, rich for growing wheat. In his mind's eye, he could picture outflung fields, grain waving in the western breeze; he could smell the sweet aroma of earth.

In the summer of 1911, while Roy was negotiating his successful contracts with Crucible, and with Lulu, his father bought his first land since coming to Galesburg: a wheat farm of 3,000 acres at Stanford, Montana. Once embarked on this new career, he steadily added to his holdings, and spent much of his time in Montana with Roy's brother Harold, who became manager of the ranch on his graduation from Knox College in 1912.

Stephen also bought a farm on the Illinois River, and became a hero to his neighbors when he successfully fought a flood, and won, by building the dike higher with sandbags. He acquired land in Colorado, where he grew alfalfa and sugar beets by the thousands of tons. He purchased a sheep ranch and added to it until it was one of the largest in Montana.

For Father Ingersoll, lover of good soil, fine horses and his fellow man, it was the fulfillment of the dreams of decades earlier, when he had operated a farm and taught school, and saved the money to start a grain elevator in Sandoval. It was a time of smooth seas, a moment of curious calm, in the turbulent lives of these people.

Assisted by his younger brother Harold, during the winters when Harold was not needed to operate the Montana farm holdings, Roy was handling most of the day-to-day operations at the plant, bringing in new business, increasing products and profits. Roy, Harold and their father held many conferences on future plans. As war broke out in Europe and Allied food needs became vital in the struggle against the Central Powers, the farm equipment industry boomed. And Roy's shrewdness in negotiating the contract with Crucible, with its pegged-on pig-iron price clause, became evident. The Galesburg plant, with this advantage, could meet its competition and still turn out discs of the highest quality at a satisfactory profit.

Roy's home life was running as smoothly as the plant. In July, 1912, Lulu had presented him with their first child, a daughter whom they named Jane. Two years later, their first son, Robert Stephen Ingersoll, was born. A daughter, Barbara, born in 1916, and a son, James, in 1918, made their family complete.

And, as another added fragment of this serene family portrait, in 1914 he had paid off in full the mortgage on their Galesburg home!

This serenity of their world was broken abruptly a year later, on the night of November 1, 1915, when Roy answered the telephone to hear the words: "The plant is on fire!"

All night, shivering in the late autumn cold, he stood and watched as the flames licked hungry tongues against his father's life work. There was no way of halting the conflagration once it had been whipped up by the winds. It seemed as if the whole building was on fire at once. Firemen could only stand by, helpless.

As dawn came, Roy Ingersoll stared at the mass of still half-burning, half-smoldering ruins. It was two days before the fire-swept plant had cooled enough so that the wreckage could be investigated and the loss estimated. The verdict then was unequivocal: the plant was a ruined hulk; every inch had been burned or damaged beyond use. Even the records and papers in the office vault had been scorched by the heat.

But fire or no fire, customers were expecting deliveries. With his father's full backing, Roy took over. Rolling up his sleeves, he and Henry Gaylord, the plant superintendent, organized factory crews to clean up the wreckage of the plant, and to sort out the salvagable stock.

As he took these first necessary steps, his thoughts were racing ahead with plans to get the plant back into operation. He ordered a temporary wooden structure built over what was left of the factory, prevailed on companies to turn out needed equipment in record-breaking time, bought more from the Kingman Plow Company of Peoria, which had closed down. Within four weeks, the makeshift wooden structure was completed, the new equipment had been installed, the factory wheels were once more turning.

By this time, working with architects and builders far into the night, Roy had carried out his next step. While the plant operated under its umbrella of wood and tarpaper, which kept out the rain and some of the bitter Illinois winter, around and above it the new permanent building was going up. By spring, without interruption or delay to the plant's production, the new building was practically complete, and by the following autumn, when his father returned from his summer in Montana, it was finished, down to a fine new driveway and landscaping.

Roy had suggested the roadway for a very practical reason. The fire, he felt, might have been brought under control if there had been a good road leading into the plant. He wanted to take every possible precaution against a second such catastrophe. So a new road was built from the factory gates to the building, and a handsome landscaping job completed at the same time.

James Ingersoll, Roy's youngest son, likes to relate the family legend about this occasion when his grandfather, Stephen A., first saw the landscaping and roadbuildings at the completely restored Galesburg plant.

"Grandfather was out at the ranch at that time and Dad contracted with the local landscape people to put in trees and shrubbery and the lawn, and flowers around the office, and when Grandfather came back, he was met at the station and went right out to the plant.

"Going in the newly-built long driveway to the plant, past all the new shrubbery and trees, grandfather didn't say one word, so the story goes. But when he got inside he saw an old friend who had been selling the company equipment parts for many years and he said to this man, 'Say, do we owe you any money as of right now?'

" 'Why no, Mr. Ingersoll,' the man said, flustered. 'Nothing past due. Just the regular current account.'

" 'Well, I suggest you go see Mr. Reinhardt and get whatever we owe now before we go bankrupt. My son seems to have spent all the company's money on the shrubbery.' "

Remembering this moment, Roy was to tell a friend, "I

knew he was angry. But I also knew he would be back later to find out just how much all that work did cost and I had a detailed statement ready to hand him.

"The job was very reasonably done. The whole thing, including the road, cost only a few thousand dollars. Later father admitted he was proud of it."

The pride was justified; for several years the company took the prize for having the best landscaped plant in Illinois.

A few years afterward, when the company built a new office building at New Castle, the older Ingersoll hired a landscape architect himself, and paid considerably more for the job than Roy had paid in Galesburg.

Late in 1916 Crucible Steel decided not to renew its five-year contract with Galesburg.

For months the Ingersolls had been aware that the larger company was unhappy with a contract that was quite advantageous to the Galesburg plant, providing it with steel at an attractive basis in the midst of a wartime price rise. Roy had been seeking new sources of supply against the day when Crucible would discontinue furnishing them steel, at least at the terms provided in the expiring contract.

In 1917, Galesburg was buying some steel of lighter grade from the Indiana Rolling Mill Company in New Castle, Indiana, as well as from other companies who had learned how to produce the quality steel required for coulter discs. The Indiana firm did not make its steel, but rolled the steel billets and slabs into the thickness or gauge required. It served Galesburg's needs, however, and, as Roy told his father, he had a hunch the mill itself could be bought.

"I'm going to Pittsburgh, Roy," his father replied. "I've got to talk to Crucible. I think they'll change their minds."

"Maybe," Roy said. "But, if not, don't forget New Castle."

Several days later he received a telephone call from his father in New Castle, Indiana. He had not been able to work out a satisfactory contract with Crucible. His father informed Roy laconically that he had just bought the New Castle steel mill, as Roy had suggested.

"You'd better get over here, son," said the older man, "and start taking the inventory."

9

Let in the clutch

The coming of the new century with its greater mechanism and production lines brought many changes in the industrial life of the nation. The additional requirements of steel products were bringing new miracles of alloys and improved techniques of steel-making. Electric melting furnaces were taking the place of the slow and expensive crucible pot methods of making tool and alloy steels.

The Ingersolls, who had acquired a taste for steel-making in the open hearths at Norwalk, and now had acquired outright the New Castle mill, had put themselves and their company into the steel production world in a wholly new way. For New Castle was a plant with vast potentials in steel production of all kinds and varieties, especially after the Ingersolls with Roy and later his brother Harold directing, added new rolling mills and a battery of the latest electric steel-making furnaces. Then the mill not only rolled but also melted steel of the highest quality, for uses far beyond the world of farming in which Stephen Ingersoll had begun.

Aware of all these possibilities, Roy Ingersoll surveyed the rapidly changing world about him.

A whole new mode of living was coming into being during this decade of the 'teens. On highways that were still mostly dirt roads, the growing colossus of the automobile was beginning to cast its fender-shaped shadows. Overhead, planes were rare but people talked of the day when they might cruise in comfort across the skies at 150 miles an hour. The radio and television and talking movies were still subjects for the Sunday supplements.

But in workshops and laboratories and improvised garages men were experimenting in an effort to make the dreams come true. Above all this was so in the automotive world, and the auto parts companies which, in these early days particularly, researched, invented, and produced the thousand and one parts that went into the American car.

They were all types of men—laborers, artisans, craftsmen, who loved their tools and benches as an artist loves brush and easel. They were men of pioneer stock and immigrants so newly arrived in America that they had difficulty making themselves understood in a strange new tongue. But they had one thing in common—vision. With their own hands they took the raw material and shaped it and, if they failed at first, picked up the pieces and started again.

It was a curious time, that era before the automotive world became only a handful of major companies, capable of producing most of their own needs. In the decades from 1900 to 1920, there were several hundred American car makers, many turning out experimental models. Some were doomed to vanish after they had put out only a few cars, others destined to become the great names of the future: Cadillac, Dodge, Nash, Ford, Studebaker, Buick, Chevrolet, Oldsmobile, among many others.

At the same time there were the pioneers in the manufacture of automotive parts, experimenting ceaselessly to find new ideas for improving on the original sputtering horseless carriage.

Some of the improvements were obviously significant. Others, to the layman, seemed obscure. There was a queer-looking disc plate which cushioned the clutch as it engaged the whirling flywheel and kept the car from jerking like a lively colt. There was a new design for the radiator and a new method of welding on a running board. There were experiments and development of self-starters, spark plugs, electric lights, carburetors, universal joints, transmissions and ignition systems. The evolution of the car came step by step; the men who were part of it helped to mold the pattern of our age.

In 1911 Stephen Ingersoll purchased a seven passenger Premier car made in Indianapolis. Not long afterward, Louis Hill, railroad pioneer and president of the Great Northern, staged an endurance test for automobiles all the way out to Montana. The roads in those days were mostly unpaved, muddy and difficult, and often little more than cowpaths. Stephen Ingersoll and his wife, Cordelia, participated in this endurance test in his car, driving by day and stopping by night at rendevous points where they slept in Pullman cars provided by Mr. Hill.

Many of the cars ran into trouble over this arduous route, some with blowouts or mechanical breakdowns. Others slid off at some muddy point into a ditch from which they had to be pulled out. It was difficult going, yet, as the Ingersolls realized, it was luxury compared to what the pioneers with their covered wagons had endured only a few decades earlier. The Premier came through with all six cylinders performing smoothly.

But even in that pre-super highways era, many people wanted their own car, including the Roy Ingersolls. They purchased their first automobile in 1918, a secondhand Dodge sedan, for which they had been saving for several years. Roy went to Chicago to pick it up and phoned Lulu in Galesburg to take the train to Aurora, which was forty miles out of Chicago. He would meet her there at the Burlington station at 1:30 that day and they would drive home together.

However, the dealer did not have the car ready and it was 1 o'clock in the blazing hot afternoon before Roy started out for Aurora. On the outskirts of Chicago, the paved road turned into an unpaved single lane.

When he reached Naperville he failed to observe a 10-mile-an-hour speed sign. A policeman stepped from behind a tree and blew his whistle. He charged that Roy was doing 15 miles an hour. Roy countered that he had not seen any sign. He used his best selling efforts—to no avail. The officer insisted that Roy had to go to the police court.

On the way over Roy asked the policeman: "Do you happen to be a married man?"

The officer said, "I sure am."

"I just wonder," Roy persisted, "if you happen to be married to a red-headed wife?"

The officer shook his head, puzzled.

Roy went on, "Well, I am, and she's been waiting for me in the Aurora Railroad Station since 1:30 in all this heat, and it's 2:30 already and I'm still 15 miles away."

The officer finally relented, on condition that Roy drive him back to his station behind the tree, which Roy was glad to do, as he wanted to see that 10-mile speed limit sign for himself.

He finally reached Aurora—two hours late. Lulu was extremely sympathetic when she heard all he had been through, and they drove back to Galesburg proudly in their secondhand Dodge.

Dramatically symbolizing the era of experiment and invention in which so many men of that day were involved, is the story of the development of the single-plate clutch, which was one day to be standard equipment on virtually all American cars.

The clutch was the brain child of two men who were to become intimately involved in the life and fortunes of Roy Ingersoll. Neither had a degree in engineering. At that time neither even knew how to drive a car. One was a mechanical genius named Gus Nelson, who had learned all he knew at work benches in Moline factories. The other was a young bookkeeper named George Borg, son of the founder of Borg & Beck, makers of machines for automatically producing wagon poles. George was a youth who combined courage and willingness to try the new with an almost extrasensory ability to know what would pay.

It was inevitable that the destinies of two such unfettered middle westerners—Roy Ingersoll and George Borg—should become linked.

Old Charles W. Borg, who had emigrated to America from Sweden in the mid-nineteenth century, was a man of force, with solid, old-fashioned ideas of business, but with imagination, too, and the ability to go along with progress even when it developed through the headstrong and unpredictable practices of his son George. There was a streak of stubbornness in his nature; once started on a new project, Charles refused to let go and admit defeat.

Many stories are told about colorful Charles Borg and his equally colorful son. One of the most famous concerns the time, at the close of World War I, when the two stopped at a Chicago bank seeking to raise $200,000 with which they planned to buy a new plant in Chicago. The banker was cordial but cautious. Two hundred thousand dollars was a lot of money. "Do you happen to have any collateral?" he asked politely.

Charles shook his head. "Collateral?" he echoed in his heavy Swedish accent. "No, what is that?" Then, seeing refusal in the banker's face, he added, "But I do got half a million dollars in Liberty bonds. Maybe that do all right instead of collateral?"

The speechless banker could only nod his acceptance—and the story went the rounds of America's financial marts until it has become part of the folklore of the world of stocks and bonds, and of clutches and gears.

But this was much later, after Charles Borg and Marshall Beck had formed their partnership, and George, with only a business-college training, had streamlined the company, shortened up Mr. Beck's lengthy letters about which customers complained constantly, and tried to get the firm on a sound business basis. Charles W. didn't mind his son's taking over— to an extent. But he still held the majority control of stock. "Always remember, George," he would tell his son, "I still got control."

To keep their plant going, they took on job work, and some of the jobs included the making of small parts for the growing automobile companies. One day they were asked by the Velie Motor Company to try their hands at an admittedly difficult item—a clutch.

In those experimental days in the automobile industry, clutches were mostly of the cone type which made engagement extremely rough when starting the car. There was no uniformity either in clutches or in gear shifts. The Velie Company had developed a clutch, but it would not work satisfactorily.

George Borg called in his chief mechanical assistant, Gus Nelson, and told him he was sure that working together they could develop one that would perform better. The two men set to work on the problem and eventually invented a single-plate clutch.

Tried on the machinery in the shop, it worked. But would it work in a car? Neither of the men whose invention was later to be used on one-third of all the automobiles in America knew anything about the new horseless carriage. Neither of them, nor anyone else in the shop, owned a car, or could drive one. They had a clutch, but no car on which they could even test it.

Charles W., who had little faith in automobiles in any case, balked at putting up the cash to buy one for a lot of foolish experimentation. But George and Gus together finally prevailed upon him not to force abandonment of the clutch project for lack of testing equipment. Reluctantly, he authorized purchase of a secondhand car. Cost: $475.

The clutch was installed and the great moment came for

the demonstration. Nelson, who had been chosen for the try-out, settled himself behind the wheel, the motor was started, and Gus let in the clutch. With an ear-shattering roar and a cloud of smoke that enveloped them all, the car bolted forward and crashed head-on, with a sickening crunch, into a brick wall.

Gus climbed out of the wreck unhurt, except for his pride. "It's no good," he said disconsolately, shaking his head, and everyone agreed with him. But it was at this moment that Charles W., the man who didn't believe in automobiles, showed his stubbornness. "Don't quit on it, George. Keep on, you'll get it. You don't get a baby without you suffer pain."

And Gus went back to work.

Soon they had developed a single-plate clutch that overcame the troubles of their first one, and this time it worked, not only on the lathe but also in the somewhat banged-up secondhand test car. This was the basic design which was to be used in millions of American automobiles.

But unfortunately, at that time, after they had designed this workable prototype for the automotive future, they found it extremely difficult to convince any of the automobile companies to buy it, or even to give it a trial run.

With unflagging persistence, George Borg took the clutch to firms in Detroit and Toledo and Cleveland; he talked with the executives of firms that were just beginning to make their names known in American life. Some listened politely; some gave him only a few seconds. All said no.

George kept on doggedly, searching for a company with enough progressiveness to try the new clutch. In Indianapolis, where he had just been turned down by the Marmon people, he bought a cup of coffee and a plate of beans, and took the train for Kenosha, Wisconsin, and the Jeffrey factory.

He was at the plant early, explained to the receptionist what he was trying to sell, and sat down to wait. The noon hour came and went, and George sat. He had just enough money in his pocket for his train fare home to Moline, with nothing left over for food. Through the long afternoon he waited until, shortly before 5 P.M., a harassed looking man appeared.

"Mr. Bill," the receptionist said to him, "this man wishes to talk to you. It's something about a clutch."

Mr. Bill whirled. "Clutch? What about a clutch?"

"I've got a clutch that will revolutionize the automobile industry," George Borg began, launching into his talk before he could be cut off. "I've got a clutch that will not only work smoothly but in addition will stand up under all kinds——"

"Listen," the other man managed to break in finally, "do you have any blueprints with you?"

Young Borg looked at him in astonishment.

This Mr. Bill was serious.

"Of course I have blueprints," George half shouted in his excitement. "Here, sir. Right here."

He drew them out of his brief case. Mr. Bill looked at him. "We'll show them to our engineers at once. They'll know."

For half an hour, while George waited, the engineers examined the designs. Then George was on the phone to Gus Nelson in Moline, arranging for a sample to be shipped that night.

"If your clutch holds up under full-fledged test conditions, and if it works, you'll have our contract," George was promised. He started home to Moline like a man in a trance.

Only later did George Borg learn the difficult situation in which this Jeffrey firm—later to become Nash Motors, maker of the Rambler car—found itself at that critical moment. It had accepted a large government order for trucks to be used by the Army in defensive maneuvers along the Mexican border. But complaints came in constantly that the clutches were breaking down. Unless remedial steps were taken, the company had been notified, the order would be canceled.

Soon Borg was to receive a phone call from Mr. Bill.

"The contract is yours," the words came over the phone. "We want you to get into production immediately. We'll need forty clutches a day to start, and you'll have to increase the number steadily."

Within hours, wheels began to turn in the plant of Borg & Beck, turning out the first clutches. Soon Jeffrey was using them in its passenger cars, as well as in its trucks. Business grew; the plant expanded and the number of workers increased.

In 1910, there were exactly six of these clutches in all the world. By 1918, at the end of the war, there were 200,000. By the 1950s, there would be 16,000,000—and the number continued to grow.

As the automobile age dawned, parts manufacturers worked day and night to discover and invent and engineer new ways to make cars run faster and more smoothly; to make them function under all kinds of conditions and on all kinds of roads. Drivers complained and swore as they tried to get their stalled engines started or to change a tire on the side of the dirt road on a Sunday afternoon. A man loved and hated his car, and studied the advertisements of next year's models, whether he drove a Cadillac or a Packard, or one of Mr. Ford's "Tin Lizzies" about which so many ballads were written. The car was the rolling symbol of the future, and parts makers and car manufacturers and drivers and owners all wanted to be part of it.

Roy Ingersoll was no exception.

Since his father had summoned him, only a year or two earlier, to come to New Castle and take over the steel mill the older man had bought, Roy had made many changes and improvements. Now, far from its origin as a shovel factory in 1904, it was producing many types of steel for many different customers.

There had been no open hearth or electric steel melting

furnaces in the mill when the Ingersolls acquired it. They purchased steel slabs from which they rolled disc and coulter, saw
and section knife steel, as well as the steel required for their
shovel factory which was under the management of Arvid P.
Zetterberg, who had married Stephen Ingersoll's daughter. The
mill was named the Indiana Rolling Mill Company.

Roy added a new rolling mill and a number of furnaces and,
after his brother Harold joined as plant manager in 1920, together they greatly increased the capacity and range of the New
Castle works.

Always known for the high quality of its products, even its
shovels had been of high grade metal, it evolved gradually into
a plant that produced specialty steels for many different purposes. For the Atkins Saw Company in Indianapolis, it made
saw steel. It turned out also, each year, thousands of tons of
section knife steel to be used on mowing machines in the grain
and hayfields of the nation and sold them to all the great companies—International Harvester, Canada's Massey-Harris, and
Deere and Company, who had just started to make mowing and
reaping implements, and many others. It supplied the steel, too,
for the discs and coulters which continued to roll steadily from
the Galesburg factory.

Roy also was thinking of the automotive world. Clutches
needed disc plates, too—different in size and shape and purpose
from those used on harrows and plows, but still discs. And a
well-equipped factory could turn them out. Why shouldn't
their Galesburg plant?

Learning that the leading producers of clutches were Borg
& Beck in Moline, Ingersoll carefully made a note to call on
them. George Borg was the man to see, he had been told, but
George was out of the plant when Roy showed up and he spoke
instead to Gus Nelson.

Together, with Roy leading the way, the two men talked new

machines and tolerances and gears and the steel products that were changing the face of the world—talked about everything except actual business.

It was a language Gus understood and enjoyed. And at last, there in the plant, amid the roar of the factory, they arrived at the real purpose of Ingersoll's visit: Borg & Beck were having trouble keeping up with their orders, they commented. Perhaps his Galesburg factory could make some of the clutch plates they required.

Gus Nelson stared into the hazy light which marked late afternoon in the plant. Here was a man who understood his problems, a man after his own heart. But his answer, when it came, was noncommittal. "George Borg ought to be in tomorrow. You'd better talk to him about it."

When Borg and Ingersoll met, several days later, each instantly recognized the drive and the power of the other. Each had something to offer the other. An agreement was soon reached and within a few months the Galesburg plant was beginning to turn out friction discs for the Borg & Beck clutches.

And when Borg began to realize, later on, that because of the higher level of employment in Moline, there was nowhere to grow and no manpower to make growth possible, Roy Ingersoll was one of the first men to learn about it.

"What would you think of leasing or building an additional plant in Galesburg? We've got lots of good workers there," he suggested.

Borg asked questions. Ingersoll waxed enthusiastic about Galesburg and its virtues—economically, socially, educationally, geographically.

Roy talked and Borg listened and, like many others, before Roy's persuasive words he saw the light! The place to lease or build a plant, of course, was in Galesburg, not far from the Galesburg Coulter Disc Company.

For bookkeeper and timekeeper at Borg & Beck's Galesburg branch, Roy suggested one of his friends, Lawrence Seen, whose father had been with the older Ingersoll in Sandoval. The family had moved to Galesburg with the factory, and Seen has been with the company ever since. In 1959, he was still actively serving the Borg & Beck division of Borg-Warner as director of purchases.

Borg & Beck was Ingersoll's first customer in the clutch business, but it wasn't long before he had others. Some of the automotive companies of that time, just before the war, were using multiple disc clutches requiring four, six, or seven clutch discs, many of which could be made by the Ingersoll's Galesburg plant. The New Castle plant, with its improved mills, was turning out a fine grade of high carbon steel for these clutch plates and discs.

By 1917, when America got into the war, the volume was very large. It was even necessary for Roy to go to Washington to see James A. Carr, president of the American Seeding Machine Company who was serving the War Administration Board on steel allocations. Roy was able, because so many of these clutches were going into trucks and other vehicles for the Army, as well as for agricultural discs, to get a sufficient allocation of steel to fill the war orders.

Immediately after the war, following a brief slackening in orders, came a post-war boom that lifted production at the Galesburg and New Castle plants to the highest in the company's history. Until October, 1920, they were working at capacity level and had a larger backlog of orders to fill than ever before. The growing automotive industry as well as the veteran farm equipment industry, was riding the crest of prosperity.

But the prosperity was as fickle and almost as elusive, for some months at least, as the stable peace the nation sought but failed to build. In 1920, the depression had struck suddenly and violently.

In early spring the automotive industry had shown some signs of slowing up; orders had fallen sharply, unemployment was widespread here as in the farm industry. Some car manufacturers had been forced to close down.

At this period, during long months of his experimenting with heat-treated discs, Roy had been thinking mainly of discs that would give longer service on the farms. It soon became evident, however, that heat-treated discs would be of value in other fields as well.

Borg & Beck continued to use thousands of untreated discs from the Galesburg factory for their clutches, but the Long Manufacturing Company of Detroit, which in 1922 began to produce a new type of clutch, tried out the Galesburg electric heat-treated discs, and found that they gave improved performance, durability and wear.

The Long Company, organized in 1903 with $100 cash and a machine which fabricated copper and brass into spiral tubing, had made its name as a manufacturer of radiators for the ever-growing automobile industry. By 1920, J. Lester Dryden, who had taken over the company's direction in 1911, after the death of its founder, J. B. Long, was looking for diversification. He found it in the new clutch design.

As he worked constantly to improve it, the new clutch grew in popularity until within a few years Long and the firm of Borg & Beck were producing, between them, the clutches for many of America's leading cars. Both came to use Galesburg-made discs, and both were eventually to become a part of Borg-Warner. The third great producer in this field, the Rockford Drilling Machine Company of Rockford, Illinois, also was to be a part of Borg-Warner; it was never in competition with the others, however, for its main production was concentrated on manufacture of a large percentage of the clutches used by the farm implement and tractor companies.

Meanwhile, the Galesburg and New Castle plants were expanding and broadening their operations. Discs and clutches were only a part of their business. From the new furnaces in New Castle came tool and saw steels, soft center and high carbon, high-manganese steel and steel alloys that were finding a hundred uses in American industry—for the automotive world, for plowshares and moldboards, for the needs of the Galesburg plant and the special requirements of other companies as well.

Soft-center steel slabs were first purchased in 1922, after Charles W. Stoup became superintendent of the new department for the manufacture of soft-center and other kinds of plow steel. Electric furnaces were first installed at this plant in 1927, when they began the manufacture of soft-center steel themselves, from ingots produced in their own electric furnaces. Solid stainless steel was first made in 1930.

Much of the development of this plant had been carried on by Roy and his brother Harold; they worked closely together in meeting and solving the problems of this factory. Harold was placed in charge of the steel production at the mill and many of the important improvements and additions were conceived and carried out under his direction. He was to become plant manager in 1939, and general manager of these works in 1945. In 1950, he was to become president of the Ingersoll Steel Division, one of five Ingersoll divisions in Borg-Warner.

In Galesburg they were making stampings and parts for some of the auto companies, as well as all the clutch covers and other stampings for Long. For Buick they were making a difficult engine stamping.

And at the Ingersoll's New Castle plant a little later, Stephen Lawrence Ingersoll, "baby brother" of the family, developed

a new kind of stainless steel that ultimately, under the trade-
name of Inga-clad, was to be a major, highly successful break-
through in laminated steel.

Young Stephen had come into the firm fresh out of the University of Pittsburgh's courses in engineering and metallurgy.
He set to work on a big idea—a method of making steel that
would be stainless on one side, welded to soft low carbon steel
on the other. With the same painstaking effort that had made
Roy's heat-treated disc a success, Stephen experimented until
he found the answer.

Two slabs of stainless steel, the facing sides polished and
coated with a chrome compound to keep them from fusing
under heat and rolling, were welded together at the edges. This
stainless steel sandwich was put into a mold and entirely en-
cased with the soft, low-carbon steel, in its red-hot molten state.

As this red-hot sandwich began to cool, it was reduced to
proper thickness in the rolling mills until, from a slab several
inches thick and only a few feet long, it was rolled and elon-
gated into a sheet perhaps ¼ of an inch thick and 12 to 14 feet
in length.

The edges and ends of the sheet were then sheared off, the
two sheets were separated—each a thin 20 per cent portion of
stainless with a thicker layer of low-carbon, soft steel fused to
its back.

This product was used for many purposes: for the linings of
dairy tanks and milk containers, for lunch counter coverings,
for laundries and supermarkets and drug stores where the rust-
proof qualities of stainless were required on one side only.
These sheets sold at a much lower price than solid sheets of
stainless steel.

There were those who said that molten steel ran in the veins
of the Ingersoll family. Father Stephen, and son, Stephen,
Harold and Roy—all of them loved steel. They lived it and

breathed it, and dreamed of additional products which they could make from it in coming years.

Borg & Beck moved their operations to Chicago in 1918, and it was ten years later, in February 1928, over a luncheon table in the Windy City, that George Borg broached a subject that had been whispered, but not openly discussed, in the financial district of Chicago: Some of the auto parts makers, the strong independent ones, the leaders in the field, he told his old friend Roy Ingersoll, wanted to merge.

"We'd keep our identities as firms, Roy," George said. "But by joining together we could help each other. Nobody could push us around, either. Not if they knew we're not one company but four or eight or twelve."

Roy listened. There were advantages and disadvantages.

"We're not settled on anything yet; we're still holding meetings over in the Chicago Club. Just informal get-togethers. Talking the plans over. Charles Davis and Ray Johnson of Warner Gear, Eric Eckstrom and Levin Faust of Mechanics Universal Joint Company, J. R. Francis of Marvel-Schebler Carburetor. And Borg & Beck. And——"

He looked at Roy Ingersoll across the table and grinned.

Ingersoll did not answer.

He understood their reasoning. The automotive-parts manufacturers were specialists. The alert parts manufacturers would always have a role in the auto industry; the car makers needed them and welcomed their contributions. At the same time, it was obvious that in unity there was strength.

In unity perhaps there would be strength. Certainly their bargaining position would be strengthened if they were not just one company but four or six or even more. "It will be the way of tomorrow," Borg prophesied.

Ingersoll did not answer Borg's implied invitation to join in with this new group immediately. Outside the window were the lights of Michigan Avenue and, beyond it, the darkness of the lake. As he gazed out, he did not try to guess where all this would lead, although intuitively he knew that in this new organization lay the future for these firms and perhaps eventually for the Ingersoll interests as well.

Each of them was a proud and strong company, each was successful in its own right. This would be a combine of strength, not weakness.

10

"...or hang separately"

ANNOUNCEMENT OF THIS new company, composed of automotive parts makers, was electrifying news in financial and industrial centers across the nation. The coming together of four outstanding firms—Marvel Carburetor, Mechanics Universal Joint, Warner Gear and Borg & Beck, was a development of tremendous importance. Each of these companies was successful and each an important factor in the over-all picture of America's vast automotive production.

In a speech delivered before the Motor and Accessory Manufacturers Association in New York in 1929, C. S. Davis was reported to have stated in part regarding the philosophy of this new company, "In the ideal merger a management organization should provide a central control strong enough to harmonize the activities and add to the financial stability of the units. On the other hand, the local management of the units should have authority and responsibility broad enough to preserve and foster their initiative to the fullest degree . . .

"Above all, the men in control of a merger should recognize that they can build and maintain their institution only on the solid foundation of contribution to the public good. They translate this to mean, very simply, that while making a reasonable profit for themselves they must offer a better product at a lower price than the consumer can continuously buy elsewhere."

Fortune Magazine quoted him further as saying that the only acceptable motives for a merger were the desire to diversify, to pool management talent and financial resources, and to eliminate waste.

Another early policy statement declared, "We can give better engineering, better production, and better service to the automotive manufacturers at a fair price. In short we can better serve the auto makers, and in so doing serve Borg-Warner, its subsidiaries, its employees, and its stockholders."

The men of this merger were strong individuals, men who had built their parts companies from the smallest beginnings and were now banding together to protect them. Like George Borg, Charles Davis and the others, they were realistic, tough-skinned, self-made leaders who constantly had to meet and excel the competition on its own terms. You produced, you met the competition, or you failed.

From the dawn of the automobile era, it had been this way. The number of car manufacturers had dwindled from more than 500 that sprang up during the first two decades of the century to 50 or 60 firms by the 1920s. Among the auto parts producers, casualties were even higher. Thousands of companies had been born, struggled their few moments, and died. The suppliers had to battle not only their own competition but also the major car manufacturers themselves, who could, and did, cut off one or more of their parts suppliers and "roll their own," right in their own plant.

Survivors in such warfare had to be men of ability and foresight, and above all, men of courage and daring, with their careers, fortunes and futures always at stake.

Yet, in spite of this trend, car manufacturers depended to a tremendous extent on the particular parts maker who was alert and farsighted and could come up with a new and better design. This dependence was to continue in many cases, and was to develop sound and lasting relationships in many instances.

The auto companies must make the decision any manufacturer faces whether to "make or buy" and, although on many occasions the car maker has resolved the equation by establishing production within his own plants, in countless other instances he has looked to the parts maker for the new development—the answer to some difficult problem.

Roy Ingersoll, concerned as he often was over a seeming trend toward integration, was the first to point out that the automobile manufacturers had been extremely good to the growing units of Borg-Warner and continued to urge that Borg-Warner maintain its important place in the auto parts field by meeting competitive prices and developing new products in areas where its divisions were outstanding specialists.

The standardized transmission, the single disc clutch, non-slip differentials, the self-starter, are only a few of the new developments that came from the independent parts makers of America. One might think wheels were the most important and integral parts of a car. Yet most of the wheels on American vehicles were still by the end of the 1950s being purchased by car makers from independent parts makers.

From the beginning, however, every customer was a potential competitor. The car manufacturer, having made his own units, was always in an exceptional position to know what they should cost, and even if he was not currently making a unit, he was usually equipped, if need be, to tool up if he thought he could make one better. It was only in the face of this tremendous challenge that the parts maker could survive, by bettering the car maker at his own game and his own price.

Among the most important of these men were the founders and builders of Warner Gear which was to become the world's largest independent producer of automobile transmissions. Originally, around 1900, two brothers—Tom and Harry Warner —had become interested in the production of an automotive differential.

To get financing for their company in Muncie, Indiana, the brothers became associated with Abbot L. Johnson and J. G. Johnson, important Muncie industrialists, interested in lumber and banking particularly. The actual founders of the enterprise as finally evolved in 1901 were the two Johnsons and two associates, Col. William E. Hitchcock and Thomas Morgan. The Warners left the firm later and turned to other fields.

Yet equally significant in the development of Warner Gear, and of Borg-Warner, was a man who hardly seemed to fit the mold of the rugged individualist of the early automotive era. He was a Harvard graduate, a yachtsman and for a brief period at least, a reporter for the *New York Times*.

The story of Charles Strout Davis, born in Terre Haute, Indiana, in 1877, really begins with an automobile show—the first ever held in America, in the year 1900, in New York City. Young Davis, just out of Harvard and working as reporter and yachting editor on the *New York Times,* covered the show and wrote a report about it that startled some of his editors: he appeared to believe that the horseless carriage was about to put the horse and buggy out of business.

Three years later, a man with whom Davis was to be associated in business for most of his life, Ray Johnson, general manager and son of the founder of the firm that was one day to be known throughout the world as the Warner Gear Company, arrived in New York City to attend the 1903 show. No one paid much attention to his arrival or to the exhibit he staged in an obscure corner of the old Madison Square Garden.

Young Johnson had brought along an odd-looking set of gears, and to anyone who would stop to ask about it, he would explain that this was what was called a differential. "It goes on the rear axle, right in the center," he would continue, "and conveys the power from the drive shaft to the two rear wheels. You see, the rear axle has to be separated in the center, because when you're going around a curve one wheel has to go faster than the other. The differential is designed to convey the driving power to . . ."

But by this time most of his listeners were on their way to the next exhibit.

The public did not understand, and the experts and larger car manufacturers—the people who knew what the young man was talking about—were more interested in the products of concerns of which they had heard.

Finally, however, an elderly gentleman approached, examining the differential Johnson was exhibiting, asked a number of seemingly aimless questions, and finally said, "What quantity could you let me have?"

Quantity did not worry Johnson. He had dozens of differentials with him, and several hundred more on the shelves back in Muncie. Swinging easily in the chair in which he sat opposite his customer, he said confidently, "Any quantity you can use."

"Good," the man stated brusquely. "We'll need 4,000 to start."

Johnson gasped and, before he could recover his equilibrium, toppled over backward in his chair. His customer helped him up, dusted him off, and inquired with calm persistence. "How soon can you deliver?"

The man then introduced himself. His name, he said, was Ransom E. Olds. He was head of a Michigan automobile company, later to be a part of General Motors, that was making a car he had named the Oldsmobile.

Once Johnson had recovered from his shock, the order blank was filled out and he hurried home to get production started. More orders were to follow in a steady flow, not only from Oldsmobile but from other manufacturers who had begun to hear of the quality of the products of Warner Gear. Within a year the plant had to expand.

Warner Gear became one of the great names in the auto

parts industry and the Warner transmission was used in literally millions of cars of almost every leading make. The products of this company came to include transmissions, clutches, steering gears, rear axles and differentials.

Charley Davis meantime had left the *New York Times* and returned to Terre Haute where he served his apprenticeship in industrial enterprise by working in his stepfather's coal business. In 1904 he married Florence Grace Johnson, attractive daughter of Warner Gear's founder, Abbot Johnson.

Growing lonesome for his daughter, Abbot Johnson induced Davis to give up the coal business, come to Muncie and become an officer of the Glascock Brothers Manufacturing Company, which Johnson also controlled, and which made toys, baby walkers and strollers, children's handcars and toy automobiles. Davis and his wife moved back to Muncie, two years after their marriage.

Davis helped to lift Glascock Brothers to a high level of production and sales. Ray Johnson, who succeeded his father as head of Warner Gear, recognized his brother-in-law's executive abilities demonstrated in this success, and induced Davis in 1919 to come into Warner Gear as secretary-treasurer.

In 1920 with the sharp downturn of business, the automotive world, like the farm-equipment business, was heavily hit with canceled orders, closed-up factories and unemployment.

The number of major car manufacturers at that time was less than fifty. Many of these companies were manufacturing their own parts and buying less from outside firms. With the curtailing of business and industrial production as depression set in, the integration tendency increased. Warner Gear suddenly found itself at a standstill.

It was Charles Davis who came up with an idea that seemed to make sense: a standardized transmission that could be used in all makes of cars and did not have to be custom made for each manufacturer.

At a gathering of directors and other officers of the firm, Davis put forth his suggestion in his gentle, unruffled tones: "We've got to gamble to do it. We can make and sell these transmissions at a more reasonable price than any individual company, if we can get real mass production. We can only achieve that by making the same transmission for several companies at once, not tailor making it to meet each engineer's idea of the transmission he thinks he requires."

The others were startled. How could you plan your cost ratio on mass production figures, when you had no mass production, no product to sell, and no customers?

"That is our gamble," Davis told them, his voice calm as before, but with a new hardness that underscored his meaning. "We must invest enough to get this standard transmission into production. We must price it low enough to sell. And we must find buyers."

The engineers went to work on this "impossible" assignment and came up with a standardized all-purpose transmission of the gear-shift type—this was, of course, long before the development of automatic transmissions. They estimated that the new model, the T-64, could be sold for about $35, on an estimated run of 80,000. This price was less than half the price charged for the tailor-made jobs. If production went higher, the cost would be less.

The next problem was to find buyers. Engineers of the great companies reacted coolly to the whole idea. The T-64 was all right as transmissions went but—well, there were other matters that seemed to them more urgent. Bargain or not, the engineers preferred their own designs.

Davis, however, was not prepared to sit back and let them sluff off his new design or this new idea of standardized transmission for America's cars. When the engineers proved aloof and indifferent, he went directly to the top, to the heads of the major companies. One of the first on whom he called was Harry

Jewett, president of Paige Motor Company and one of the outstanding car manufacturers of that day.

Jewett was interested. The design was a real engineering
achievement, the quality of Warner Gear products was established and unquestioned, and the price, Davis and his associates
informed Jewett—though they didn't quote a figure—would be
less than half of what it cost him to make his own transmissions.

Jewett, intrigued, told them he would like to place an order
for a few thousand. Davis replied quickly that this wouldn't be
possible; the low price was contingent on Mr. Jewett's giving
them virtually all his business for the coming year. He did not
add that, even with all of Paige's requirements, Warner Gear
would still be selling the transmission below cost, if it did not
get other customers as well.

The urbane Mr. Davis was a man of steel below the surface.
He could handle a racing yacht or a sloop in a rough storm on
the Great Lakes with a coolness and skill that astounded friends
who did not recognize the qualities of reserve and strength and
utter calm that guided this man's life.

Nor did Davis hesitate now. They had to sell at below cost
to Paige if they wanted to win. Mr. Jewett, perhaps only partially aware of the tension of the moment, asked for time. He
wanted his engineers to have a chance to study the new transmission thoroughly, to go over every detail of the blueprints
and test the product itself in operation.

Davis and his group went home to wait.

They waited several weeks before word came from Jewett:
the transmission was fine, he said, but since all the company's
needs for a year were involved, he felt he had to get bids from
other manufacturers before committing himself. Now Warner
Gear, and eleven other companies, were being asked to submit
their bids.

The chips were down. Warner Gear's development of the

T-64 had, apparently, stirred up its competitors in the parts manufacturing world. Now how low did Warner Gear dare go in its price?

Davis kept his own counsel as he pondered this problem, and a story had developed around his ultimate bid which has become well known in the automobile world. On the day their bid was to be submitted, the story goes, Davis and Ray Johnson and a group of their associates left Muncie for Detroit, still with no idea what price they should ask for their new transmission. "I'm waiting for a hunch," Davis said.

The time for their meetings drew near, but no hunch. On the spur of the moment, Davis picked up the Detroit telephone directory, opened it, and put his finger on a number. It was, according to the story, 2985, and an hour later the figure Warner Gear submitted to Paige for its transmission was $29.85.

This was several dollars under that of its nearest competitor, and Warner Gear was awarded the contract for all Paige's transmissions for the year upcoming.

Almost immediately afterward, Warner Gear added the Chalmers car to its list of customers, and soon other manufacturers began to come in. The T-64 was a triumph; the production figures at Warner Gear once more began to climb.

Some years after the formation of Borg-Warner, Roy Ingersoll and Charles Davis were reminiscing about the old days, and Ingersoll brought up the question of the telephone number that set the price of the T-64. "Frankly, I've never believed that story," Roy said. "You're just too good a businessman to do anything like that by chance."

Davis regarded his associate with a smile. After a silence, Ingersoll added, "Charlie, my bet is you let your finger slide down the page till you came to the number that was just about what you wanted."

Davis laughed at Roy's shrewd observation but still made no

answer. Later Ingersoll was to state that he was certain, from the half-humorous, half-serious expression on Davis' face, that his own suggestion had struck very close to the truth.

The company's output of transmissions continued to soar, year after year, as did parking brake assemblies, which it put into production in 1921, the year after the revolutionary T-64 had been introduced. One of the firm's most successful specialties in use, Warner Gear's parking assemblies, are numbered in the millions.

To fill all its orders, the Warner Gear plant was expanded time after time, until it covered half a dozen city blocks. After Warner Gear had merged into Borg-Warner, Ford turned to the company for a portion of its transmissions in 1930, in its changeover from the foot-pedal to the standard lever gear-shift type, and a new plant unit had to be built to take care of this large customer. This new plant, two miles west of the city, had to be enlarged many times, so that eventually the building was a half-mile long and contained some 1,550,000 square feet of floor space.

It was this aggressive and constantly growing concern which was to become one—and the largest—of the four companies joined together in the new firm of Borg-Warner. At the time the combination was effected, Warner Gear was furnishing transmissions to the following automotive concerns: Auburn, Reo, Chrysler, Paige, Jordan, Locomobile, Velie, Gardner, Marmon, Graham Brothers, Moon, Rickenbacker, Stewart Motor Truck and half a dozen others.

Who first conceived the idea of bringing these small but powerful companies together into one family? No one is quite sure. There were a number of people involved, certainly, in the earliest negotiations, but in the opinion of at least one of them, Gustavus Shallberg, who was George Borg's lawyer in Moline, attorney for Borg & Beck and later executive vice president of Borg-Warner, the germ of the plan originated with

General view, Ingersoll Steel Division, New Castle, Ind., 1959.

Office, Ingersoll Steel Division, 1959.

Chicago works, Ingersoll Products Division, 1959.

Making bathtubs in Chicago plant of Ingersoll Products Division.

Making washtubs.

How discs are made at Chicago plant, Ingersoll Products Division.

Grinding room.

Heat treat lines.

Atkins Saw 100th Anniversary: *(left to right)* W. A. Atkins, R. S. Ingersoll, R. C. Ingersoll, S. J. Roush, and Carl Meister. In rear: a portrait of E. C. Atkins, founder of the company.

R. C. Ingersoll and staff of Chicago plant of Ingersoll division at final assembly station of Bendix Washing Machine lines, 1947.

Borg-Warner plant in Letchworth, England.

Warner Gear plant No. 3, Muncie, Ind. (Largest B-W plant: 1,408,505 sq. ft.)

York Division, Decatur, Ill. works, 1959.

York Development Laboratory, York, Pa., 1959.

R. C. Ingersoll with Carl Sandburg and R. S. Ingersoll during a tour of B-W Building while under construction, August, 1957.

Navy E awarded Ingersoll Steel and Disc Division, Kalamazoo Works, 194.

Borg-Warner Building (and headquarters), 200 South Michigan Avenue, opposite Art Institute, Chicago.

Products displayed in Borg-Warner Exhibition Hall in Borg-Warner Building.

Exhibit in B-W headquarters.

RESEARCH CENTER

TREMENDOUS AS ARE THE ACCOM-
PLISHMENTS OF OUR RESEARCH
LABORATORIES TODAY IN SPEAR-
HEADING INDUSTRIAL GROWTH AND
BETTERING THE LIVING STANDARDS
OF OUR PEOPLE, WE CAN BE CERTAIN
THAT THESE WILL BE DWARFED BY
TECHNOLOGICAL ACHIEVEMENTS OF
TOMORROW ··· MAY BORG-WARNER,
THROUGH THE EFFORTS OF THE
DEDICATED MEN AND WOMEN OF THIS
RESEARCH CENTER, MAKE ITS FULL
CONTRIBUTION TO THE BUILDING OF
AN EVEN STRONGER AND INCREAS-
INGLY DYNAMIC AMERICA.

FROM AN ADDRESS BY ROY C. INGERSOLL, THEN PRESIDENT AND
CHAIRMAN OF THE BOARD OF BORG-WARNER CORPORATION, JANUARY 16, 1956

BORG-WARNER CORPORATION

Plaque at entrance of Roy C. Ingersoll Research Center.

Roy C. Ingersoll Research Center of B-W, Des Plaines, Ill.

Testing instruments, Ingersoll Research Center.

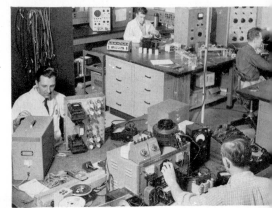

Chemical analysis.

Roy Ingersoll, center, and Robert Ingersoll on his right, on official tour of Research Center.

Operating committee, Borg-Warner Corp.: (*Left to right*) Harry P. Troendl
Group Vice-President; Albert Steg, Vice-President and Treasurer; L. G. Porte
Executive Vice-President; Robert S. Ingersoll, President and Chief Executiv
Officer; Roy C. Ingersoll, Chairman of the Board; Robert W. Murphy, Vic
President, General Counsel and Chairman of Executive Committee; Stanley
Roush, Group Vice-President; Joseph M. Gartner, Committee Secretary an
Executive Assistant to the Chairman.

Board of Directors, Borg-Warner Corp.: (*Left to right*) Roy C. Ingersoll, Chair-
man (*lower right at head of table*); Robert S. Ingersoll, President and Chief
Executive Officer; Robert W. Murphy, Vice-President, General Counsel and
Chairman of Executive Committee; H. G. Ingersoll; George S. Moore; John E.
Johnson; E. F. Ball; G. A. Freeman, Jr.; C. S. Davis, Jr.; H. H. Gehlbach, Sec-
retary; E. S. Russey, Vice-President; W. G. Karnes; John Madden; Ray P.
Johnson; A. W. Duncan; J. Russell Forgan; Paul H. Davis, Chairman of Finance
and Compensation Committee; Albert Steg, Vice-President and Treasurer;
Lester G. Porter, Executive Vice-President.

R. C. Ingersoll receiving honorary degree, Doctor
of Commercial Science, Millikin University, 1957.

Roy Ingersoll (extreme left) and Mrs. Roy Ingersoll (extreme right)
with their two sons, two daughters, a son-in-law, two daughters-in-law,
and fourteen grandchildren (seven grandsons and seven granddaugh-
ters; another granddaughter has since been born). Easter, 1953,
Winnetka, Illinois.

Stephen A. Ingersoll with his sons, 1935. Stephen, left, Roy, center, Harold, right.

Roy C. Ingersoll (right), with his sons Robert S. Ingersoll, President, Borg-Warner Corp., and James H. Ingersoll, President, Ingersoll Products Division, beside portrait of Stephen A. Ingersoll, on the 75th anniversary of the Ingersoll Division of Borg-Warner, 1959.

Mr. and Mrs. Roy Ingersoll, 1959.

Top to bottom: Mrs. Jane Hardy (daughter), Mrs. Barbara McClintock (daughter), Robert S. Ingersoll (son), James H. Ingersoll (son), 1959.

John Fletcher and Paul H. Davis, no relation to C. S. Davis, a prominent Chicago broker, head of Paul H. Davis brokerage house. Fletcher was the banker who had helped the Borgs finance their first Chicago plant; he had since become a partner in the brokerage house of John Burnham & Company and had handled the details, ten years earlier, when Charles Borg retired and his son George had become president of Borg & Beck.

It was these two men primarily who set the wheels and gears of this meshing of many companies into operation. Paul Davis, in fact, became closely associated with Borg-Warner's history and was to become and to remain a Borg-Warner director over the years, providing wise and practical advice at many critical points in the company's development and playing an important role on many of the company's committees, particularly those concerned with planning, research and organization.

Fletcher represented the Marvel-Schebler Carburetor Corporation and was anxious to see this company merge into some larger group to give it a stronger position. From this, and chats with Paul Davis, the idea of a number of auto parts makers coming together began to take hold, and he discussed it with Borg. The Mechanics Universal Joint Company was the third plant to be involved. And Warner Gear, represented by Paul Davis & Company, was the fourth. It was Paul Davis, no relative of Charles but later a friend and associate, and John Fletcher who handled the technical details of the negotiations, with Gus Shallberg doing much of the legal work, and the buying up of shares of outsiders so that the four companies would become wholly-owned subsidiaries of the Borg-Warner Corporation.

The problems to be solved before the proposed merger could be effected were almost endless. For long hours financiers, company heads and their lawyers and advisers met and negotiated. A number of these negotiations were held in private in room 503 of the Chicago Club.

At last they were finished and the merger details ironed out.

The announcement echoed joltingly across the automobile and industrial worlds.

The basic details of the merger which evolved from these protracted sessions were as follows:

One June 5, 1928, the newly-formed Borg-Warner Corporation, with offices at 310 South Michigan Avenue, Chicago, acquired 150,000 shares at $10 per share par value of Borg & Beck stock in exchange for 150,000 shares at $10 per share par value of Borg-Warner stock.

On the same date it acquired 90,000 shares of the Marvel Carburetor Company stock at $10 per share par value, in exchange for 90,000 shares of Borg-Warner at the same value.

On the same date Borg-Warner acquired 140,000 shares of Warner Gear Common, and 70,00 shares of Warner Gear preferred stock, in exchange for 150,000 shares of Borg-Warner common.

On June 15, Borg-Warner acquired 75,000 shares of the Mechanics Universal Joint Company stock on payment of $2,950,000 in cash.

The whole transaction, which had taken months to arrange, was completed on December 12, 1928, when Borg-Warner acquired 12,000 outstanding shares of Warner Gear common stock for $1,200,000 cash.

George Borg was elected first president of Borg-Warner on June 5, 1928, and Charles Davis was named chairman of the board. Within six months, however, the irrepressible Borg decided that he needed more time to devote to his other interests. He suggested to Davis that they switch jobs. This was duly carried out by the board. On March 22, 1929, Davis became president and Borg chairman of the board.

It cannot be said that the new company at the start was anything like the well coordinated firm of diversified yet correlated and interrelated companies into which it was to evolve under the successive presidencies of C. S. Davis and Roy and his son Bob Ingersoll. At first it was simply a holding company, a central office functioning as headquarters for a handful of subsidiaries, all of whom were directed by men of stubborn individualism, with ideas of their own about how their business should be run. But there were nevertheless certain clear premises on which it was built. One was that by hanging together they stood less chance of being choked out of business separately. As a "department store of the auto industry" they had new strength to ride out the storms of depression or the sudden obsolescence of a product· through a new invention. To these firms no longer would the grim catch-phrase of the auto parts suppliers apply: "If you lose a major customer today, you can find yourself out of business tomorrow."

In the development of mass production concepts and techniques, the formation of Borg-Warner represented a bold and at that time still little understood pattern, an exciting but still nebulous new *motif* in the tapestry of American enterprise.

When the new company emerged from the "inner circle" of the Chicago Club, the Ingersolls were not a part of it. They were going their own way, alone, as they had for so many years.

Stephen, Sr., though president until December 11, 1927, was devoting most of his time to his farms and more concerned about his wool and beet production than the output of the New Castle and Galesburg plants. Roy was directing both, in close association with his brothers Harold and Steve and Arvid Zetterberg, his brother-in-law.

With the New Castle mill supplying all the steel the Galesburg plant needed and turning out many other things besides, Roy Ingersoll was forever testing new products and new ideas. Whatever could be pressed or stamped or rolled or formed from steel was "grist" to his mills. The diversification program he was later to bring to Borg-Warner had its inception in Galesburg and New Castle in the 1920s, when he experimented with scores of products—some successful, some total failures.

But life had never been all business to Roy Ingersoll. As he had told Lulu Hinchliff, back in the days before they were married, he was primarily a home-and-family man. Business fascinated him, but not to the exclusion of everything else.

In the Ingersoll's comfortable home on the outskirts of Galesburg, Roy was the typical American husband and father, a blend of disciplinarian, companion and head of the household.

Although constantly traveling on business for his company, he would rush home, making every effort to be there on Saturday nights to join his two sons, Jim and Bob, and a half dozen of their friends, for an evening of swimming and games at the YMCA and afterward take them all home for a supper of waffles and sausages Mrs. Ingersoll had prepared.

He loved to walk fast and the boys had long since learned to let him stride ahead, figuring that they could catch up with him later. They were still letting him exceed their speed thirty years later when, in his seventy-fifth year, he was still outwalking his sons and his guests.

On Sunday mornings he was equally occupied, for he was superintendent of Sunday school at the Galesburg Congregational Church, a post he considered of prime importance.

Success in the Sunday school program he considered as vital as success in anything else in his life. One of his accomplishments, and one in which he took enormous pleasure, was to raise the attendance at Sunday school by a considerable percentage.

To do it, he had to keep constantly on the job, working with teachers and students, checking up on absentees, and keeping long lists of figures and data with comparative records from the previous week and the previous year. Just as production in the Ingersoll's plants had gone up year after year, so had the attendance of youngsters in their religious classes.

Whatever he did had to be done with every ounce of his

energy. At company picnics he would enter into the games and potato-sack races with as much gusto as he tackled a new production problem at the plant. He played to win, just as he worked to win. The compulsion to do his best, to excel, to win the victory—this was and has remained the motivating force of his life.

By 1927, this compulsion to succeed had brought the Ingersoll's enterprises to a point where major investment bankers were urging the family, which now held all of the stock of the companies, to put it on the market. A re-organization was effected by which the New Castle and the Galesburg plants, which before had been two corporate entities, were merged into one. New stock was issued and for the first time the public was able to buy shares. Two million dollars of the family's holdings were sold.

At the same time, Stephen A. Ingersoll gave up the presidency to his son Roy and became chairman of the board; young Stephen became vice president; Harold Ingersoll, treasurer; and A. P. Zetterberg, who had married Winifred Ingersoll, secretary. Helen Nelson, who had been a part of the firm since its first days in Galesburg, in 1904, and had been close to the family throughout all these years, became assistant secretary.

The company was in top financial condition, with a cash reserve of approximately $2,000,000. Father Ingersoll always insisted on keeping his companies in a good cash position and this concept of keeping liquid cash reserves was carried on by his son in his management of the Ingersoll interests and, later, of Borg-Warner.

Early in 1929, Roy's brother Steve resigned as vice president and acquired a plant in Chicago that had been operated as a forging division of the Whitman and Barnes Company, whose main plant was in Akron, Ohio. Steve installed rolling mills and began developing coated alloy steels and aluminum sheets.

Cousin Henry Gaylord left at the same time to work with Steve in this new rolling mill, situated on the south side of Chicago, in West Pullman.

On another industrial front, at almost the same time, new action was developing: Paul Davis, John Fletcher and George Borg were holding lengthy sessions with the new president of the Ingersoll Steel Disc Company in Galesburg—Roy Ingersoll—trying to convince him to bring Ingersoll's plants into the new combine called Borg-Warner. Roy saw the advantages and the dangers.

George Borg presented strong arguments. Borg-Warner needed Ingersoll, and the Ingersoll interests could go right on supplying steel stampings for automotive parts, clutch covers and plates, and harrow and plow discs for the farm equipment firms. "Roy, you won't be losing any business, and you'll be opening the door to new markets. You'll be part of this whole new idea."

Roy smiled at his friend and commented quietly, "And also, of course, you'll have a guaranteed source of steel to fill the needs of all these companies of yours, George."

George Borg grinned. "Well, sure, I don't say *we* don't gain out of it, too. It's a good deal—for you and us."

Roy took the proposal home and presented it to the family. Lengthy family debates and discussions followed. Roy and his brothers favored the move; Stephen Ingersoll, Sr., had serious doubts.

However, basically, the decision was up to Roy and his brothers and sister, and his father did not try to influence them.

For his part, Roy was not primarily concerned with losing the Ingersoll identity by moving into the Chicago firm—he was sure that this would not happen—but was fearful of losing certain customers. He was particularly apprehensive about the Long Manufacturing Company of Detroit, which had become a large customer of the Ingersolls.

"We'll come in," he told John Fletcher and Paul Davis finally, "but only if Long does, too, as we would not want to lose them as a customer."

By bringing in Long, he reminded Fletcher and Davis, the new firm would get additional clutch business as well as Long's big slice of the automobile radiator production, which included the radiator "core" for many American cars, among them Ford.

"Why don't you talk to Lester Dryden?" he asked Fletcher. The two men—Roy Ingersoll and Dryden, had for many years been close friends and Dryden had taken over as president of Long after the death of the firm's founder, J. S. Long, in 1912.

There were more discussions and negotiations. Dryden agreed at last to bring his company into Borg-Warner if Ingersoll joined up, too. On December 16, 1928, the board of directors of the Galesburg Coulter Disc Company agreed to this plan and to an exchange of their 100,000 outstanding shares of stock with Borg-Warner on a share-for-share basis.

Fifty per cent of the Galesburg Company's stock was held by the public but all stockholders except one—the owner of 1000 shares—agreed to make the transfer. The one holdout, a New Yorker, insisted on a price which Borg-Warner considered excessive but changed his mind finally and sold his block of stock at a price the company considered moderate and fair.

The actual date of the closing of the purchase, apart from the 1000 shares, was January 24, 1929. The Long Manufacturing Company came in a short time later, after agreement had been reached on terms with Dryden, the officers and stockholders.

Following the merger, Roy Ingersoll found that the *whole* pattern of living had changed. He was not only still president of the new Borg-Warner subsidiary, he also became a member of the Borg-Warner board of directors and was chosen for its executive committee as well.

In the line of these duties, he found himself commuting back

and forth several times a month between Galesburg and Chicago, where he had established offices in the Borg-Warner headquarters.

Stephen Ingersoll, Sr., watched all of this going on and wished
it well. But privately, to some of his old friends and associates,
he admitted that he still nursed grave doubts about what was
going to happen. "Here in Galesburg, we were big frogs in a
little puddle. But now we're in that big pond called Borg-
Warner, you will probably never hear of the Ingersolls again."

But for once, and for all his wisdom, Stephen Ingersoll was
wrong.

11

"Steel can be a hard master..."

ALTHOUGH FEW were aware of it at the time, storm lay just ahead. Within a few months of the formation of Borg-Warner and the bringing in of the Ingersoll plants, the onset of economic crash and depression was to sweep across the nation and the world. There had been some indications, although few, of this impending crisis which was to test the metal of the fledgling corporation of auto parts makers.

A hint of this came to Roy Ingersoll one day through his friend, Jack Bohmker, general manager of David Bradley Manufacturing Works of Kankakee, Illinois, a Sears-Roebuck subsidiary, as the two men stood in front of the Sears Building in Chicago one bright spring day in 1929. A student of economics, Bohmker had long been worried about the fact that the farm industry had not advanced with the rest of the economy.

"Farming is basic in our economic structure," he told Roy, "and unless this lag is corrected we will not continue this apparent prosperity. I believe that the stocks which are soaring to such heights now will be selling for half of today's prices in less than a year."

Roy was startled at this prediction from a man whose judgment he respected so completely. But the prediction was to be fulfilled in the months immediately ahead. The challenge to Borg-Warner in that period was serious, but the developing

163

strength and stamina of the firm showed itself. Roy Ingersoll was to say later that in his opinion one of the important factors that enabled Borg-Warner to weather the storm so well was the strong cash position of all the companies that came in to the corporation at that time. "We learned," Ingersoll was to say, "the tremendous value of having money to meet the bills."

It was in the fall of 1929 that the bright coin of post-World War I prosperity ran out. Suddenly and catastrophically the stock market plunged to depths few had believed possible; overnight people who had been living in luxury found themselves destitute and without work. As the months of depression dragged on, and the ranks of unemployment grew, certain areas and businesses were hard put to survive.

The American farmers were the worst hit. Farm prices had dropped to all-time lows; the farmers were losing their homes and their fields; in many areas they were rioting to prevent foreclosures on their land. The farm equipment industry, as a result, was in an almost unbelievable situation; orders had shrunk to 15 per cent of the pre-depression level. And as those orders shrank, the call for Ingersoll plow and harrow discs and other farm equipment components shrank along with them.

The ship called Borg-Warner was scarcely out of the harbor when the storm broke and the test came. The strength and wisdom in its concept of unity and diversification was revealed almost from the start; yet it would not have been possible without the men behind it—individualistic, refusing to admit defeat, caught in a serious dilemma but willing to fight their way out of it with their minds and talents and machines, as they had before.

Faced with a loss of nearly 85 per cent of the farm disc business because of curtailed orders, Roy at once set himself a new assignment: Into what new shape could he turn his disc blanks, his slabs of steel piled up at New Castle? At the plant in Galesburg, at the mill in New Castle, he turned his energies to a new idea: If they could not be sold to the farm equipment industry, why not make them into discs for the wheels of trucks—the center, structural section of the wheel to which the hub and rim would be attached?

The truck wheel has a thick center of about ⅜ of an inch, from which extends a flange, tapering down to about ⅛ of an inch in thickness. Evolving a method of producing this tapered metal form out of a single piece of flat steel presented a challenging problem.

At the time Roy Ingersoll began considering the idea of turning some of his manufacturing equipment into the production of truck wheels, one manufacturer was producing most of the steel wheels that kept America's trucks moving. It was the Budd Wheel Company of Detroit.

The method employed by Budd, a patented process licensed for use from a French firm, involved a spinning technique that tapered the truck wheel from the thick center to the thin edge. After some months of experiment in the first period of the 1930s, Ingersoll developed a process known as "skip-rolling" in which the mills were so constructed that they skipped the center part of the wheel, while they tapered the steel blank from its octagonal shape into a circular pattern.

The Kelsey-Hayes Wheel Company, manufacturer of wheels for American automobiles, was anxious to expand into the truck-wheel business, but had no patents in this field. When George Kennedy, the company's president, learned of Ingersoll's new skipmill truck-wheel method, he got in touch with Roy. Chevrolet was brought into the negotiations and eventually a three-way contract was drawn up: Borg-Warner was to produce the steel wheel and ship it to Kelsey-Hayes, who, after adding the outer section or rim, would send it on to Chevrolet.

The new wheel discs had scarcely begun to roll out of the Galesburg plant when Ingersoll received a message from Budd.

Ingersoll was infringing on his patents, he was told, and must cease and desist at once.

Roy's reply to this was that the skip-roll method was entirely his own development, based on patents he had obtained, and it in no way used any of the spinning processes employed by Budd.

The issue exploded into a grim all-out court action as Ingersoll fought for the right to make truck wheels by a method he had spent months of time and thousands of dollars developing. The battle was for stakes that ran into tens of millions of dollars of sales. Edward Budd, Sr., president and founder of the firm, was, in Ingersoll's own words, "a very fine gentleman whom I respected very much." But he added, "At the same time, I knew very definitely that we were not infringing in any way on his patents and it was very important to us and to our rights that we win this case."

When Budd himself was on the witness stand, at the height of the trial, Carleton Hill, attorney for the Ingersoll firm, began to question him regarding his claim that he had a process similar to that developed by Ingersoll, on which the patents Ingersoll had secured were based. Hill asked the Budd company president if his firm had produced any wheels by this process upon which he claimed the Ingersoll Company was infringing.

Mr. Budd answered that his firm had not.

The attorney wanted to know why.

Budd hesitated. Then he replied that it was a thing to be desired but the method of making them was not commercially practical.

The lawyer turned to the court to point out that Mr. Budd claimed they were infringing upon a process that was not commercially practical, while the process they were actually using was so practical that they were turning out tens of thousands of these wheels for the commercial market every month.

It was, without question, an extremely complicated matter, involving dozens of charts, models, diagrams and blueprints. These, coupled with the contradictory testimony, most of it couched in highly technical terms, produced a maze completely bewildering to a layman.

Out of the confusion came a decision against the Ingersolls and in favor of Budd. However, Ingersoll immediately appealed and the three judges of the Court of Appeals unanimously reversed the original findings. The Supreme Court of the United States refused to review their decision. Borg-Warner and Ingersoll Steel were free to make as many millions of wheels for America's trucks as their "skip-roll" machines could produce.

Over these years warm friendship was built between Roy and George Kennedy, president of Kelsey-Hayes.

During this same period, under the leadership of Kennedy and later President Perry Williams, who assumed office after Kennedy became chairman of the board, this company grew from a relatively small, financially weak company to one of the strongest of the auto parts makers.

The battle—and the victory—was a symbol of a way and a creed. It was by way of announcement that neither this new corporation called Borg-Warner nor its subsidiaries would placidly give up its rights even though defending them involved long and costly court battles.

In 1951 a new process of making notched agricultural discs was developed at the Ingersoll Products Division by James Ingersoll, Roy's younger son. Valuable patents were subsequently granted to this youthful inventor and were contributed to Borg-Warner. Both the method and the apparatus for producing these superior notched agricultural discs have become widely recognized in the industry.

Within a year after the Ingersolls joined Borg-Warner, another difficult problem developed. It became excessively costly, with the depression deepening, to ship and process steel slabs from companies in Chicago, Gary, and other steel centers. The slabs had to go first to New Castle, where they were rolled into sheets and cut into disc blanks before being shipped to Galesburg for fabrication into finished discs. A more centralized plant was essential. The Borg-Warner board authorized the purchase of the Chicago Rolling Mill Company in West Pullman.

The price of $800,000 was approximately the market value of the land, buildings and the extensive rolling mill equipment that young Steve Ingersoll had installed.

It was at this time that S. A. Ingersoll resigned as chairman of the Galesburg company board of directors. In March of this same year, he was named permanent honorary chairman of the board "in recognition of his services in founding and building the business to its present substantial position."

Confronted with the sizable West Pullman plant, large areas of which were still unused, Roy Ingersoll began to search out new products. In Galesburg and later, in 1931, when he and his family moved to Chicago and took up residence in suburban Oak Park, Ingersoll was working on several products to augment sales and profits. Some of them worked out successfully; others did not. But even on the failures, the practical Ingersoll almost always managed to salvage some profit, if only a little.

Heading the list of the smaller new products Ingersoll tried out were axes, to add to the line of shovels manufactured at their New Castle plant. His theory was that they could be sold to hardware jobbers along with the shovels, spades and scoops which had always been primary products of the New Castle operation. Aiding him in this axe development was a young engineer named Stuart Battles whom he had brought with him to Chicago from Galesburg to help develop new equipment and new products.

In August, 1936, Stuart Battles bought the original plant of the Galesburg Coulter Disc Company in Galesburg, selling it later to Admiral Corporation, a competitor of Borg-Warner's Norge, as production plant for Admiral's refrigerators. Visiting Galesburg years afterward, to attend a Knox College trustee meeting, Roy drove out to see the old plant and found that the landscaping he had developed after the fire had been eliminated to make room for factory additions. It was a double blow to realize that the beautiful grounds had been done away with to provide for the expansion of a competitor of Borg-Warner's Norge Division.

Like everything else he attempted, the Ingersoll axe-making method had to be new, different and—hopefully—better. Instead of using the standard method—two pieces of steel folded together around the form where the axe handle was to go and welded together at the edges with a strip of high-carbon cutting steel—Ingersoll devised a method of punching a hole into the axe head while, in the process of shaping and forging, it was still white-hot. This gave him a single piece of high-carbon steel which when finished and properly tempered could be used as a hammer or wedge, and would hold an edge much better than the earlier type.

However, as Ingersoll readily admitted later, "We were newcomers in the axe business and it was, we found, a world all its own; the woodsmen and others who used axes regularly had their favorites and changing to something new and untried was almost unheard of."

Even so, the axes were moderately successful. But when the American Fork and Hoe Company offered to buy all the axe-making equipment and stock at a price which would net his company considerable profit, Ingersoll decided to get out of axe-making and pursue the policy of his old banking friend in Norwalk: "Never cry over spilt milk, just find another cow."

Among many other products with which he became involved were the washing machine tubs. In the early 1930s, virtually all the major companies, with the notable exception of Maytag, used porcelain steel tubs, which were formed on deep drawing toggle * presses, sprayed with porcelain enamel, and baked.

The process was simple, compared to the "skip-rolling" method of manufacturing truck wheels, but it would involve putting in new tub-making machinery including presses, rolling equipment and enameling furnaces. Before he did this, Ingersoll visited a number of washing machine manufacturers and discussed his project with them. Several urged him to go ahead. Despite the depression, the washing machine business was doing well. People who never before had done their own laundry were buying washers on time as one more "economy measure."

At first, the new equipment for the washing machines was limited to the presses and machines for shaping the tubs; the enameling was farmed out to the Benjamin Electric Company in Des Plaines, about 25 miles northwest of Chicago. This involved an extra shipping charge, as well as payment for the outside processing. Eventually, as the demand for the tubs increased, the West Pullman plant installed its own continuous enameling furnaces, some approximately 150 feet long, so that the entire process could be completed there.

In his search for new products, and wider diversification, Roy Ingersoll had a smash success in the washtubs. Business in this field grew rapidly until his mill was turning out several thousand units a day, and had acquired 40 per cent of the nation's business in washtubs.

In 1935, a friend came to Roy Ingersoll with a suggestion: that he personally buy a steel rolling mill in Chicago Heights, the 17-acre plant known as Calumet Steel. It was what was known as a "re-rolling mill," where old railroad rails and axles from freight cars and billets were re-rolled into new products. In their new forms, they became bars used in reinforcing con-

---

* A toggle press is one which holds the steel to prevent wrinkles during the deep-drawing operations.

crete and many other items of importance in the building and
agricultural implement industries. Much of this was made out
of the rails, which were split into three parts—the head, webb
and flange—and heated in large billet furnaces to proper tem-
peratures, so they could be rolled, "like so much slightly melted
butter," as one Calumet worker expressed it.

The re-rolling mill, with its amazing techniques for turning
locomotive rails and freight car axles into totally new and
different products, had been successful for many years but,
with the death of the founder, the plant had gone steadily down-
hill, a process which was accelerated during the depression.
Early in 1935 it was being offered to Ingersoll for approximately
$250,000, which was a fraction of the value.

Despite the fact that this was an offer to him personally that
he was able to finance, he informed his friend that, much as he
would like to buy it himself, he was employed by Borg-Warner
and felt that he must offer it to them first. But if they turned
it down, then he wanted it. Borg-Warner's directors, however,
advised Roy enthusiastically that this type of acquisition fitted
into Borg-Warner's program. They purchased it—and promptly
elected Roy its president and chief executive officer, to manage
this plant and do everything necessary to put it on a profit-
making basis.

Ingersoll brought in a young Pittsburgh steel man, Bruce
Caldwell, and placed him in charge. Ingersoll installed as comptroller and financial overseer a young financial expert named
Lester Porter whom he had hired a year before for the Ingersoll West Pullman Works. Porter was one day to be executive
vice president of Borg Warner.

When they took over this Calumet plant in June, 1935, its
condition was perilously close to that of the Norwalk plant on
the snowy January day years before when Roy had convinced
the directors of his father's company that it could be salvaged.
And once again, as in that earlier day, an almost unbelievable

resuscitation resulted from the faith, courage and initiative of these men.

It was the first of July and stifling hot the day Caldwell arrived to find a plant that was shut down, out of inventory, but with its credit and finances restored by Borg-Warner.

Caldwell, backed by Ingersoll and Borg-Warner, set to work, with Ingersoll and Porter building new inventories, bringing back old customers and adding new ones as well. Once again the obsolete rails began to roll through the mill, to emerge as fence posts, bars of many shapes and structural tubing.

In order to increase sales, Boyd Jack, an imaginative sales executive with many years of selling experience, was employed. Under his direction the mill's capacity was soon sold to a growing list of customers.

One of the Borg-Warner products most widely seen is the Gold Crown steel fence post, formed out of these rails and sold, by the millions, to farmers throughout this country. Coming off the production line at Calumet at the rate of many thousand per day, these posts are said to be given the greatest care and preparation of any in this country.

It was Roy who gave them their name—Gold Crown. He felt that they needed an identifying mark and name and hit upon the idea of the gold crown because it would stand out against fields and sky. The tops are painted a golden yellow for six inches from the top. The sight of these green and gold fence posts is a familiar one in many parts of America.

In 1959 a $6,500,000 expansion and improvement program at this plant was nearing completion, converting the Calumet Division from a re-rolling mill to a combination of steel-producing and re-rolling units. This expansion program included the installation of electric furnaces for the melting of 120,000 tons of steel annually and the approximate doubling of the rolling mill capacity.

With the Calumet plant rescued from dismantling and oblivion, as was the Norwalk mill, and once more a profitable operation, Ingersoll was ready to tackle something new. In 1937 he found it, in the shape of a run-down plant in Kalamazoo, Michigan. Formerly known as the Pressed Steel Products Company, it was turning out teeth for hay rakes, harrow teeth, and similar products for agricultural machinery, along with some cast-iron hot air furnaces for home-heating.

Having bought it and added it to Borg-Warner's Ingersoll Division, Roy started once more on a resuscitation job. Henry Gaylord was shifted from Chicago to become plant manager. A line of stabilizers for automobiles was added and Ingersoll himself set up a modified version of his Galesburg heat-treating system to use on them. So successful did they become that eventually they were used on most of America's cars.

Next he turned his attention to the furnaces and after some investigation went to Roy Walker, head of the heating and plumbing department at Sears Roebuck, with plans for a furnace that would be all steel except for cast-iron grates and firebox. With Walker's co-operation, he was able to get the new furnace into production in such quantities that the cost of the new dies —an investment of tens of thousands of dollars—was amortized within a comparatively few years and the Kalamazoo plant became one of the largest suppliers of coal-burning furnaces in the country.

Though he was constantly interested in new products, Roy Ingersoll was not a man to forget the farm equipment which had for so long been the backbone of his business. Under his guidance the Kalamazoo plant developed new, more efficient and economical processes, so that it became a major producer of teeth for rakes, spring harrows and weeders, and other implement parts.

In the post-war period, immediately after 1945, steel was extremely scarce and Calumet was struggling to take care of its customers. To improve this situation, Borg-Warner purchased, on May 1, 1947, the Franklin Steel Company of Franklin, Pa. whose equipment almost duplicated that of Calumet. Even with Franklin, the post-war scarcity of steel made it difficult for some of Borg-Warner's plants. Several needed large quantities of sheet steel, not produced by Calumet or Franklin, to take care of their customers, and these could be obtained only by purchasing steel at extreme premium prices. As an added measure, Roy wanted another mill that would produce light sheets for washing machine tubs, refrigerators and automobile parts. He found it might be possible to buy the Superior Sheet Steel Company at Canton, Ohio, in turn owned by the Continental Steel Corporation of Kokomo, Indiana. With Borg-Warner's backing, he entered into talks with D. A. Williams, president, and other officers of Continental Steel, at Kokomo, Indiana. After difficult negotiations a price was agreed upon, and Roy took over the general managership of the operations of Superior for Borg-Warner.

He was very fortunate to find in this company two highly efficient executives—Harry Theiss who was general works manager of the mill, and Paul Irwin, sales manager. These two men worked together as a team and soon had the plant operating at maximum capacity.

When the steel supply stabilized, late in 1949, the Superior plant was sold, but in the meantime it had not only supplied much-needed steel to Norge and other Borg-Warner plants, as well as having furnished considerable tonnage to Borg-Warner's auto and implement customers, but when sold it turned back into Borg-Warner's treasury several million dollars more than had been invested in it. Neither Ingersoll nor the other Borg-Warner officials were able to predict another steel shortage which occurred in 1951 because of the Korean conflict, that cost America so heavily in lives, men and material.

The products turned out at the Ingersoll plants play an important part in the day-to-day life of virtually every American family as well as in the defense of the nation. They range from fence posts to bathtubs, missile boosters to shovels, kitchen sinks to amphibious landing craft.

The man who had founded the Ingersoll companies and started them on the road, Stephen A. Ingersoll, did not see all of this come into being.

In the closing years of his life, having removed himself from the world of big business, he had stayed more and more with his farming interests in Montana. Proud and happy at the achievements of his sons, he could not help feeling that this whole Chicago operation, its factories mushrooming with Borg-Warner's growth, was beyond his interest; it was all too big, too vast an enterprise, too far-reaching in its implications.

In a way, his was still the world of yesterday, the days when he and Roy had stolen off for an hour or so to work in the fields at the edge of town. Or the days of Galesburg, where his children had grown, his business had reached its success, and they had been, as he put it, "big frogs in a small puddle."

On May 16, 1936, following a brief illness, Stephen A. Ingersoll died in the hospital in Galesburg at the age of 78. He was buried as he wished, by the Central Congregational Church which he and his children had attended and which he had helped in many ways to build. Relatives and friends, many who had known him in his early days at Sandoval, were there to pay their last respects.

The pastor, Niel E. Hansen, said words of high tribute. They were such as might be expected. Yet in this case, especially to those who knew him, the far-reaching achievements he had attained, and the standards of integrity he had set, the words had meaning far beyond the usual phrases of such a eulogy:

"As a man of large holdings, occupied day and night with the details of his enterprise, Mr. Ingersoll constantly fulfilled his part as the father of his family and a good citizen. His love of home, his virtuous ways, his example to his children, he has written into the very life fabric of his progeny. He was a man to whom his children's children will often refer with pride and inspiration . . .

"Steel can be a hard master. It can make a hard man. It never hardened Mr. Ingersoll. Wealth can do strange things to character and personality. It never changed Mr. Ingersoll in his relations with all other people or in the high purpose of his life."

They were words of tribute that this man's family, his widow and his children were to carry in their hearts.

12

A company nobody wanted

A CORPORATION is an entity of many parts, but its heart and soul are formed of the men, not the products; of the philosophy and stability and integrity of the people who guide its destinies. In the growth and development of Borg-Warner, the pattern was shaped by many men of high character and goals and tradition, but of all these men, two played the most dominant roles. One was Charles S. Davis, the other Roy C. Ingersoll.

Close friends and business associates over many years, Davis and Ingersoll were nevertheless a study in contrast. Their goals were the same; their methods varied greatly.

Ingersoll was a driver, who studied men and learned to lead them on to greater heights than even they believed possible; he drove himself with the same over-riding purpose. He must get there, he must drive to the top, nothing must stop the Achievement, whether it was Borg-Warner's billion-dollar destiny or winning a one-legged potato sack race.

Davis, on the other hand, was a man of almost imperturbable calm. Whatever he thought and felt, on the surface the craft was unruffled and perfectly trimmed, like his famous racing yachts. Serene and sure he sailed, certain of the course, now bending into the wind, now veering sharply to avoid danger, now scudding close to the winds and waves that washed the decks.

Davis was a man of many interests and tastes. He loved the sea and opera and society and concerts and art exhibits. He had learned to accept life on its own terms, to drink it in and enjoy it. Both men were indefatigable workers and perfectionists in their insistence on accuracy down to the last decimal point; but where Roy Ingersoll was in his office at 8:00 or 8:15, Davis arrived at 10:00; where Ingersoll ran what the Navy calls a "taut" ship, Davis was more relaxed. The job, and getting it done, were important. The hours at the desk were not. Yet each man took home his bag bulging with work, and Davis, like Ingersoll, often toiled far into the night.

Davis was a man of vast gentleness and quiet, hidden wells of strength. He was always suave, soft-spoken, and immaculately dressed—usually in dark gray suit and tie—and his entirely natural gentleness of tone and manner was in a sense his personality trademark both in business and outside.

Gentleness but not softness, for behind the soft-spoken word was the power of mind and purpose. From the start, first as chairman of the board and then as president, when he "switched jobs" with George Borg, Davis' concept was to establish on strong and unassailable foundations the worth and reputation and standards of Borg-Warner.

He had a statesman-like awareness of the new company's business responsibilities to all involved—the customers, the stockholders, the company itself and its workers, the safety and welfare of the public and the nation. In his years at the helm of the Borg-Warner Corporation, these were the primary concerns of this impeccable business leader who represented the finest flowering of industrial leadership in our country.

Borg-Warner owes a debt to Davis for his twenty-five years of service as president and chairman of the board. It was no easy task to weld into one smoothly functioning staff the highly individualistic group of men who came together in this new corporation. It was his patience, his firm and quiet wisdom in moments of stress, his deftness in the handling of individuals whose ideas did not always coincide or agree, that did much to mold these companies and these men into a co-ordinated smoothly operating team.

Roy Ingersoll believed thoroughly in the decentralized policies of Davis. Everything which his administration was to carry out furthered this policy of the independent operation at the division level. Throughout his administration he worked arduously to support and implement this policy and to provide individual divisions with every possible aid for carrying on this decentralized plan efficiently and independently.

Ingersoll's conception of the central office was not only as a place for planning and co-ordinating but also as center of service to the divisions themselves. Where he strengthened the home or central office it was to provide further service to the scattered plants, through the group vice presidents, through centralized information departments, and through a central research center that could be called on if the divisions wished to avail themselves of its diversified research facilities. The remarkably effective balance of freedom and decentralization thus maintained created a corporate structure considered by many to be unique in American industry, and executives and presidents of other firms, as well as many college and business school officials and students, have come to Chicago to study its extremely effective organization.

The decentralized pattern developed first under Davis and furthered by Ingersoll has a number of unusual aspects. A company with hundreds of products to sell, Borg-Warner has never had a central office sales force, sales manager, purchasing agent or central labor relations director. Each of these functions is handled at the division level. Many kinds of aid are available to the individual divisions—in training workers and in development of product and employment policies at the management level. Staff specialists who could not be fully utilized by individual divisions are retained by the home office and are always available when needed or desired.

At the start of the consolidation called Borg-Warner, the new giant of the auto parts industry, the task confronting Charles Davis was far more, however, than mere synchronization of operations and the establishment of sound fiscal policies, although these things were done with eminent success. Equally important was the task of getting the owners and operators of the plants which made up the new organization to work together as a team.

Perhaps never before had such a group of industrial individualists been brought together. All of the founding firms, and those that came in during the months immediately following, were headed up by men who had either founded their own companies or had been with them throughout the growing years. They were men who in many cases had worked at the benches and lathes themselves, men of strong personalities and egos. But all of the qualities which had helped them forge ahead, now had in some measure to be harnessed if each plant and mill and company was to pull together, as a team, thinking, planning and executing what was best for the over-all good of Borg-Warner, rather than for the individual divisions alone.

This was no simple assignment, for it involved not merely the owners and top-echelon management but also executives and workers all down the line. Theirs were firms with long histories of achievement. The men were proud of them and of their jobs.

They battled each other for business by every legitimate means available. One story is told of the early Borg-Warner era, when the representatives of two clutch manufacturers were locked in a struggle to obtain the contract of a major car manufacturer. Each salesman cut the price, and the profit, to the bone in an effort to get this business for his firm. Not until the battle was over, and the victor shook hands with his rival, did the buyer realize that each represented a subsidiary of Borg-Warner. (While not eliminating inter-company competition, which is considered a healthy factor for all Borg-Warner concerns, this kind of bitter rivalry did bring about changes in headquarters procedures so that competitors within the family at least know when they are treading on each other's toes—and how heavily!)

Each of the firms that had joined together for their common welfare had its history and traditions deeply welded into its being. Each had its legends and its moments of triumph.

One of the first four firms in the Borg-Warner consolidation was the Marvel-Schebler Carburetor Company, of Flint, Michigan, and later Decatur, Illinois. This company, through its development and production of carburetors, made a tremendous contribution to the automotive industry and also to the farm implement industry, for which it furnished a large percentage of carburetors used in tractors and other mechanized farm equipment. In later years, the Marvel-Schebler Division of Borg-Warner, in addition to its carburetor department, was to play an important part in the production of automatic transmissions for passenger cars and trucks and remote controlled mechanisms for use in nuclear power electric-generating plants.

The early history of this company was one of shifting patterns and fortunes. Like many other automotive parts makers, the founders of this firm, Pierce and Schebler, woodworkers and violin makers in Indianapolis, began to experiment in automotive parts around the start of the century. They developed two types of carburetors, both of which were a vast improvement on the primitive "mixing valve" used on most cars of that era.

Pierce and Schebler separated after several years, each taking one model of a carburetor and going into business for himself. The carburetors were eminently successful for both men. Schebler continued to operate in Indianapolis and this firm during its history made hundreds of thousands of carburetors, not only for cars and tractor companies but also for practically

all the fire engines in the United States. In the early 1920s, one
of their designers developed the Schebler Model B. The first
contract for this carburetor, later widely used in American cars,
came from the Chandler car people who used it in their famous
"Pike's Peak motor."

The other partner of the original team, B. N. Pierce, interested J. R. Francis, operator of a famous Indianapolis drug
store, in the carburetor product. He and Francis formed a
new company to produce what they called the Marvel Carburetor. Marvel moved in 1919 to its plant in Flint, Michigan,
and during the early 1920s the plant made carburetors for Pontiac, Oakland, Nash, Hudson, General Motors trucks, and Buick.
It supplied Buick, in fact, from 1911 to 1935, which is said to
be the longest continuous record of service by a car accessory
manufacturer to an individual customer.

In 1928, the Marvel Company purchased Schebler for $1,-
400,000, bringing together two great names of the carburetor
field. The operations were consolidated into the Marvel plant
in Flint. Not long thereafter came the Borg-Warner formation
in which Marvel-Schebler was to play a changing and revolving
role, ultimately moving into the Decatur plant and expanding
operations which, while they included carburetors, reached far
beyond into new and diversified fields.

In later years this division of Borg-Warner extended its activities into other areas, including fuel injection systems and control rod drive mechanisms for nuclear reactors. These products,
together with the carburetors, still continue their active and
successful roles under the direction of A. B. Pulliam, who became president of the division in early 1959.

Another of the original four, the Mechanics Universal Joint
Company of Rockford, Illinois, formerly known as the Mechanics Machine Company, produced the universal joints which
went into millions of automobiles and, in those early days, began
to make automotive transmissions. The company was greatly

helped at its start by a Rockford industrialist and investor, P. A. Peterson, who was to become a part owner and, in 1906, president. This company was started in 1890 by four Rockford machinists with $1,000 in capital.

In 1911, the company began to produce automobile transmissions, while at the same time experimenting with other automotive parts, including axles and differentials. In 1914 they signed an agreement to produce 25 transmissions a day for the Chevrolet Automobile Company. Eventually they were making 75 a day, but Chevrolet's needs were expanding so rapidly that the company decided to make its own transmissions.

Mechanics was also experimenting with universal joints for automobiles and had developed a "block type" in a malleable iron housing which proved to be highly efficient and was accepted by the Chevrolet Company. Very soon Chevrolet gave its entire universal joint business to Mechanics. The company was also selling to other automotive customers, and output rose to 1,000 a day. After World War I an improved model known as "Oil-Tite" with a sealed-in lubricant was introduced. This was a major development in the automotive field, since previous models of the universal joint had to be greased every 500 miles to function properly. This improvement was introduced on 1921 car models.

In 1925, under the leadership of Levin Faust, P. A. Peterson, and Eric Ekstrom, the name was changed to the Mechanics Universal Joint Company of Rockford, Illinois. It continued to grow even more rapidly after it came into the Borg-Warner consolidation in 1929. By that time it concentrated on universal joints and propeller shafts. Following its acquisition by Borg-Warner, Ekstrom became its president, treasurer, and general manager. In 1932 this subsidiary developed a roller-type bearing joint which was to become standard in the automotive industry. International Harvester tested this new development, and by 1934 Mechanics was supplying these joints for all of

Harvester's trucks as well as for Cadillac, Nash, Packard, Studebaker and other companies. By the end of the 1930s it was
supplying one half the volume of universal joints required by
Pontiac, Oldsmobile and Packard, one-third the requirements
of Chevrolet and all the requirements of Cadillac, Nash, De
Soto and International Trucks. This growth necessitated a new,
modern plant which was built on a 50-acre tract and placed in
operation in the spring of 1938.

An example of the unique relationship of Borg-Warner to
some of the automotive firms is revealed in the incident of a
contract negotiated in 1936 between General Motors and Borg-
Warner in which General Motors agreed to purchase one-half
of its requirements for universal joints from Mechanics for
use in Oldsmobile, Cadillac, LaSalle and Pontiac. After General
Motors had used the particular universal joint with certain improvements for five years, it was to have a permanent license for
this use. The contract was extremely complicated in its provi-
sions and ran fifteen pages long. However, once it was signed
and its intent fully understood, legal technicalities remained in
the background. With all specifications precisely fulfilled and
quality of production maintained at a high level, the contract
actually continued in force for many years after the official date
of its expiration. Mr. Charles Wilson, later President of General
Motors, was reported to have stated that he put this contract
away and never even looked at it again.

Over the years Mechanics continued to increase its automotive
parts production, turning out roller bearing universal joints
and propeller shafts for every type and size of passenger car, for
trucks, industrial machinery and road machinery, as well as for
farm implements and tractors, aircrafts, centrifugal pumps and
mining machinery.

Although not one of the original four, the Morse Chain Company was one of the earliest outside companies to come into
Borg-Warner, joining in 1929. Launched in the 1880s by Frank

Morse, and his brother Everett, in Trumansburg, New York, not far from Ithaca, this company originally made bicycle chains. The firm was even said to have made a strip of golden chain for a golden bicycle Diamond Jim Brady gave Lillian Russell. In their early years they were aided considerably through the interest and support given them by a great industrialist of that time, H. H. Westinghouse.

Very early in the 1890s Frank Morse had begun to experiment with new types of connecting rocker joints for his chains which were sold not only to bicycle companies but also to other industries and factories where connecting chain units were required for machinery. This was the beginning of the product that was to become, in the automotive age just ahead, the famous Morse Silent Chain.

From almost the first days of the automobile, Morse was convinced that chains could be used in connection with the timing gear of the car and thereby greatly reduce the raucous clatter of those early automobiles. But it was not until 1912 that the first Morse Silent Chain designed for automotive use was developed and installed on a Cadillac car. Previous to that the chains used in connection with the timing gears had a tendency to stretch and thereby throw off the timing and engine performance. Morse's chain with the silent-rocker joints was made so that this difficulty was eliminated. Although Morse Silent Chain was successful from the beginning, it was not until the post-war era of the 1920s that Morse's chain was almost universally used. As an example of the incredible accuracy and durability of Morse chain, one length of chain in an elevator in Ithaca was in operation for more than 25 years and showed no sign of wear, although in use constantly over that period.

Under the leadership of Frank Morse, this company carried on a kind of diversification over the years. It was briefly involved, for example, in aviation production. It had a plant in Letchworth, England, which made chain for the European mar-

kets. The Morse Company in addition was involved in such
widely diverse fields as adding machines, typewriters, battery-
powered electric clocks and coal stokers. Chains—roller chains
and rocker joint chains and sprockets—remained their chief interests, however, and the outside operations were in the main
discontinued or sold. The aircraft operation was sold to Consolidated Vultee Aircraft, for example, and the adding machine
division went to a company later purchased by the National
Cash Register Company.

The chains this company produces are made in a wide range
of sizes with a variety of application used on machines developing as much as 5,000 horsepower. Morse produces chain sprockets up to sizes of 16 feet in diameter.

By the late 1920s, when Borg-Warner became interested in
the acquisition of this company, its automotive timing chains
were used in approximately 40 per cent of America's cars. It
was also making a new type of automobile transmission. Charles
Davis, with his original interest in transmissions, became particularly interested and made a trip with Roy Ingersoll and
others to see the plant in Ithaca and look at its products, including the transmission which the Morse Company had developed.

Going through the plant, Ingersoll was particularly interested
to discover Frank Morse's rather primitive but extremely effective method of inventory control, without any IBM machine.
The small parts that made up the various sizes of chains were
kept in a series of bins. The first of each month Mr. Morse
would make a tour of the bins and put two marks on each, one
at the maximum height to which the chain parts should reach,
the other at the minimum point where they should begin to
make more of these chain parts of that size to replenish the
inventory. It was a simple and highly effective method of inventory control.

Shortly after the firm was acquired by Borg-Warner in 1929, Morse retired from active management. He died in 1935.

One of the most extraordinary developments of the early Borg-Warner years involved the company nobody wanted—a company that today is not only one of the most successful divisions of Borg-Warner but is also among the top national producers of home appliances, including refrigerators, washing machines, dryers, gas and electric stoves and other items in what is called the "white goods" field.

The Detroit Gear and Machine Company, a producer of gears and automotive transmissions since the early days of the automotive industry, had come upon hard times in the period following World War I, when competition all but wiped it out. The man who came into the leadership of the firm at that time was Howard K. Blood, young, eager and bright. In 1925 Blood and some of the younger men at Detroit Gear became interested in a refrigerator compressor unit called Rollator. Mechanical refrigeration in those days was still in an embryonic state; most of the refrigerators were nothing more than wired-up, old-fashioned ice boxes, with their compressor units located in the basement. The Rollator compressor unit—as finally designed by Detroit Gear engineers—could be built into the refrigerator itself.

Blood and some of his associates at Detroit Gear produced a few samples of this refrigerator, using ice boxes purchased from the Alaska Company of Muskegon, Michigan. When the board of directors of Detroit Gear heard of this, they ordered Blood and his cohorts to call off the whole project. Mechanical ice boxes, in their opinion, had little, if any, commercial future.

On their own, Blood and his friends organized a firm they called the Norge Company, pooled their resources, bought control of Detroit Gear and Machine, and immediately began to produce these Rollator refrigerators experimentally, while at the same time continuing to turn out gears, transmissions and other automotive parts.

Roy Ingersoll, recalling these early stages in the story of modern mechanical refrigeration, was to state, many years later, "In spite of the headaches and heartaches that this Rollator, which was brought to Blood in the late 1920s, was to create for the officers and directors of Borg-Warner as well as for Blood and his associates, his foresight in recognizing the potential of this invention, nursing it through infancy and bringing it to maturity in the middle 1930s, was a contribution to the future of Borg-Warner and the whole appliance industry for which all should be grateful."

In 1929, when Charles Davis and other Borg-Warner officials began to play with the idea of buying Detroit Gear to supplement the over-burdened production at Warner Gear, Davis also had no interest in this refrigerator company. A supplier to auto firms, Borg-Warner was not directly in the consumer business and had no experience in either consumer production or sales. Davis felt that selling to the public directly was far different from doing business with a handful of giant auto companies.

Negotiations for the purchase of Detroit Gear and its plants in Detroit, continued, however. The Borg-Warner directors wanted Detroit Gear. They had so little interest in Norge, however, that Davis put through a call from Chicago to ask one question:

"If we left Norge out of the package, how much less would Detroit Gear cost us?"

Mr. Blood's answer came back unequivocally, "The price is the same—with or without Norge."

Faced with the fact that to get one company they needed they had to buy an extra one they didn't want, Borg-Warner felt it had nothing to lose. It bought Detroit Gear and found itself also the owner of a company making Rollator refrigerators which it was supposed to sell directly to the consumer market.

Shortly after this acquisition by Borg-Warner, Blood, as head of the new subsidiary, purchased the Alaska Company in Muskegan as a source of the refrigerator boxes. When he was advised that such capital expenses had to be approved first by the Borg-Warner directors, Blood, used to running his own firm, promptly agreed to take over the purchase personally. Borg-Warner, however, decided this would not be good policy and agreed to approve the purchase already made.

Still deeper into the freezing business, and with the Muskegon plant badly in need of repairs and renovations, and new equipment, Borg-Warner spent $1,000,000—big money in depression days—getting the unwanted refrigerators into production. They would go along with Blood, the directors decided, and try to build this product into a profit-making enterprise. It was a wise decision of the board, for home appliances was one of the fields least hurt by the depression. This once unwanted refrigerator helped materially to carry Borg-Warner in those first few years, when profits from their other lines shrank perilously and in many cases disappeared altogether.

Moving swiftly as the consumer market in refrigerators showed signs of strength, Borg-Warner added a new item to the Norge list by purchasing the Detroit Vapor Stove Company in 1934, and marketing its products in conjunction with the Norge refrigerator line. In 1932 it also introduced Norge washing machines and an electric ironer and in 1933 an air conditioner.

A large factor in the extraordinary surge to success of Norge, right in the middle of the depression, was a man named John R. Knapp, who had been in the purchasing department of Detroit Gear. He arrived in Howard Blood's office one day with a request: "This new Norge Company needs a sales manager and has none." Johnny Knapp was applying for the job.

"But you're doing a job right here where you are—in Detroit Gear purchasing," Blood objected.

"I can do a better job selling Norge," Knapp insisted. "I tell you I can make this thing go."

"Based on what selling experience, Johnny?"

"None whatsoever, Mr. Blood. But on my ability to organize a sales staff and make them believe in this product because I believe in it and know what it can do. Also I understand it as well as any man involved in its development."

Blood's objections melted before Knapp's arguments and his fervor; he knew he could do the job and he got it.

Fortune continued to smile on Johnny Knapp. Grigsby-Grunow, one of the country's large producers of radios, chose this moment to go out of business. For Knapp and Norge this meant that a national distribution staff, built during the 1920s, was available, still completely intact, and Knapp quickly took advantage of the situation. As Knapp took over the sales force, rebuilt and extended it, Norge refrigerators became so popular that the Muskegon plant had to be enlarged and extra shifts put on to handle the orders.

As the depression was ending, in 1934, Norge was rolling into high gear; sales were $13,413,149 and the advertising budget for that year was $1,750,000. With Knapp's sales force going at full speed, the Norge refrigerator with its Rollator compressor had come from nowhere to become the second largest selling refrigerator in the United States in 1936, exceeded only by Frigidaire, the firm which first manufactured refrigerators and which by that time had become a division of General Motors.

In 1938 Johnny Knapp died. His death was a blow to Norge, which by that time had become, as had most of the other major companies in Borg-Warner, no longer a subsidiary but an integrated division within the corporation. (Each division is run by its own president and a supervisory board which reports to the board of directors of Borg-Warner.) Knapp had been more than the sales manager; he had been Blood's right-hand man and adviser, a spark plug of activity, a dynamo of inspiration for all the others from the president down to the newest worker in the shipping room.

With Knapp's death, they lost a power house of energy, sales-manship, and sales as well; and the profit-and-loss figures soon reflected it. Before these difficulties could be straightened out, however, the threat of war began to loom on the horizon, and everything else was pushed into the background.

After 1941 and the Pearl Harbor attack, production at Borg-Warner changed overnight, and in no place was this truer than in the Norge and Detroit Gear divisions. Howard Blood, an officer in World War I, found himself 6,000 miles from any front line—yet what he did was vital to the holding of that line.

From the Muskegon plants, even before the United States was engaged in World War II, plane-body assemblies began to come off the lines which only a few months before had been turning out refrigerators, washing machines and stoves for American housewives. Working from illegible and incomplete drawings sent over from London, Norge engineers were re-designing machine-gun turrets, and getting them into produc-tion, along with some 800 parts that went into the Curtis swivel gun turret. At other plants under Blood's supervision, engineers were developing and producing a side-twist airplane turret, gears for both Army and Navy landing craft, and a multitude of other mechanisms necessary to the conduct of modern warfare.

Refrigerators had to wait.

13

"Secretary Knox calling…"

To INDUSTRY as to the individual, the war was sudden, disruptive, often overwhelming and catastrophic. It also proved not only the personal heroism of our people, but the overpowering strength of our industrial sinews. Production in America in the war period remains one of the most stupendous achievements in the whole history of mankind. Hundreds of companies, from the greatest names of industry to the smallest and least known, combined talent and ingenuity and technological skills as never before, until the flood of machines and weapons—in the hands of fighting forces on dozens of fronts—turned into an invincible tidal wave.

President Roosevelt quickly realized that if he was to achieve the goals he had set for the production of war materials, including guns, tanks and airplanes, he must have the outstanding production man in the country. He went to the automobile industry for this man—William Knudsen, president of General Motors.

Roy Ingersoll knew and deeply respected the achievements of this great automotive leader. Some years after the war he told a reporter: "Too many have failed to appreciate the tremendous job Knudsen did for all of us and for freedom itself. He was responsible for helping thousands of plants across the nation set up efficient and economical mass production lines to meet swiftly the almost unbelievable demands of total war."

The immediacy of war and its reality can be symbolized for us sometimes in a word or phrase. Ingersoll had been aware of the gravity of the war situation for many months, yet the impact of its meaning came to him particularly strongly on a Sunday afternoon in October, 1939, as he and Lulu, driving through the fall countryside, listened to a speech over the radio: Winston Churchill's stirring "Blood, Toil, Tears, and Sweat" address to Parliament and the world.

He understood this crisis but the words of Churchill crystallized its meaning to all freedom-loving peoples as nothing he had heard before.

Yet it was still a time of peace in this country and the war seemed far away that autumn afternoon. He and Lulu had just visited their son Bob and his wife, in Middletown, Ohio, where Bob was working for the American Rolling Mill Company. The young couple were expecting their first born at almost any moment. At 4 A.M. the following day, in fact, Roy received a call that his first grandchild, a girl named Lynn, had been born. The Ingersolls were going to a meeting of the Farm Equipment Institute at French Lick that day, and they organized an impromptu party in honor of this occasion. An Ingersoll party became a tradition after that, at these meetings.

But later, despite his many diverse interests, personal matters in large measure had to be pushed to one side, as the war crisis deepened and ultimately resulted in our own full involvement.

Borg-Warner made its contribution in this story, converting its plants for the production of war matériel—transmissions, clutches, radiators for trucks and tanks, airplane turrets and many other parts vital to our fighting machine.

Just as, at Detroit Gear and Norge, turrets hurtled off the assembly lines, so it was in every other Borg-Warner plant. Borg & Beck, to help Pesco Division of Borg-Warner, undertook the manufacture of airplane pumps in addition to its clutches, now used primarily for vehicles of war. In less than ten months it had built a new factory, installed machines and was daily turning out hundreds of pumps used in propeller mechanisms. So precisely were they made, under the skillful and experienced hands of Borg & Beck experts, that though they were designed to generate only 150 pounds of pressure, they achieved up to 3000 pounds in actual use.

A hundred other Borg-Warner items could be cited. Artillery-shell casings, machine-gun-bullet links—by the hundreds of millions—helmet steel and armor plate, amphibious tractors, superchargers for aircraft engines, clutches for use in electrically-controlled gun turrets, tank tracks and pumps for airplanes, anti-aircraft gun parts, gun clips by the billions—the list is the roster of the most urgent needs of a nation at war.

Each family, too, had its part to play in war, and the Ingersolls were no exception. Roy Ingersoll served on important boards and committees, and so did his wife and daughters. Jim, the youngest boy, spent the war years on a destroyer on patrol duty in both the Atlantic and the Pacific. Bob, the older son, played another, but equally important, part.

Tall, lanky, soft-spoken, but firm, Bob had gone to work for the American Rolling Mill Company after Andover and Yale, from which he was graduated in 1937. He had specialized at college in engineering, industrial administration and business management, and in American Rolling Mill's training program had received, in effect, a post-graduate course. He had worked at the open hearths, cleaned up slag, and had learned at first hand every phase of sheet-steel manufacture up to administrative problems and control.

By 1939 he had finished this practical education and was to be transferred to Pittsburgh as assistant to the district sales manager for the American Rolling Mill Company.

On a week-end visit to his family in Winnetka, he talked with his father about his work. Roy Ingersoll wanted his son with him at Borg-Warner, and had told him so even before Bob's graduation from Yale. It was a situation not unlike that he had known with his own father: He recognized and understood Bob's desire to make good on his own. They talked it out for hours.

In the end, the father, seeing his son was uncertain, urged him not to make a quick decision.

The tall young man nodded. He had a train to catch in order to be back on the job before 8 in the morning. "Think about it, son. Think about it and let me know," the father said.

A week passed, and Bob was back for another visit. He greeted his father with a grin. "Dad, I've got news for you," he said. "If that offer's still open, I've decided I'd like to take it."

The offer was still open.

If anyone had any doubts about the independence of character of this tall son of the Ingersoll Steel Division head, they were dispelled swiftly in an incident at the West Pullman works, where Bob went in as assistant to the chief engineer, Ray Sullivan, who was later to become a vice president of Ford. Bob had been with the Steel Division a comparatively short time when Sullivan was promoted to general works manager. As his successor, he suggested Bob. The young man demurred, but Sullivan insisted. "I know what the job requires—you've got it," the older man said.

Bob, however, finally went to his father and told him, "I've got to resign. They want me to be chief engineer. I don't know enough yet to do the right job in that spot. If you insist on my taking it, I'll have to quit!"

Bob explained his reasons to his father precisely: "When you are assistant to the chief engineer," he said, "and someone comes to you with a question to which you don't know the answer, you tell him you'll find out and let him know." Bob smiled. "But when you are Chief Engineer and you don't know the answer, then you ought not to be in that position."

Although for a moment he almost doubted his own hearing, Roy Ingersoll knew Bob meant what he said. "Well, Bob," he said, after a pause, "it's up to you. It's the first time I ever heard a man threaten to quit rather than take a promotion on grounds like that, but I respect you for it, and you may be right. You go to Sullivan again and explain why you cannot accept the position and I'm sure he will understand and secure someone else to fill the position."

Bob followed the suggestion and Sullivan promptly hired a new chief engineer from outside.

Among the defense activities on which Borg-Warner embarked in the fall of 1941 was the development of an amphibious tank for the Marines, a contract Davis and Roy secured from the Navy.

Returning from Washington on the Capitol Limited, Ingersoll told Davis, "Now that we've secured this contract from the Navy to develop these amphibious tanks, we've got to do a real job for them, and for the country. Unfortunately, I can't think of any plant manager or anyone else capable of handling the project who can be spared from projects they're working on already."

Davis turned to Ingersoll and said, "Roy, we have a man who can do it and do a good job on it." When Roy asked him whom he meant, Davis said, "Your own son, Bob Ingersoll."

Roy felt that Bob was young for a job of such responsibility; Davis answered that Bob would do a job of which Borg-Warner and the Navy could be proud.

Bob Ingersoll got the job. It was decided that project headquarters would be in Rockford, Illinois, where excellent engineers were available and space could be spared.

This group was in the midst of this development, and making progress, when Bob Ingersoll, who held a reserve officer's commission in the Navy, received orders to report to the Navy in Newport News by 8:00 the next morning. Late that afternoon Bob came into his father's office, in Chicago, to tell him goodby, explaining that he was taking a 5:00 o'clock plane to Newport News. Roy was unable to go out to the airport with him and said good-by at the office.

Hardly ten minutes after Bob left, a call came to Roy Ingersoll from Secretary of the Navy Frank Knox in Washington. The Secretary's first words were, "Where is that son of yours?"

Roy told him that Bob had left ten or fifteen minutes earlier to fly to Newport and report to the Navy the next morning. Mr. Secretary's voice boomed over the long-distance wires: "Get hold of that boy some way and tell him that he is to report back immediately to the amphibious project. This is not a request; it is an order."

Roy immediately got in touch with the airport and asked them to have Robert call his father as soon as he started to check in, which Bob did. The following day, Bob was back on the project, building amphibious tanks that one day would carry U. S. Marines into the beaches of Guam, Saipan and Iwo Jima.

At the Borg-Warner Rockford Clutch Plant in Illinois, as the project developed, company designers and engineers received frequent reports relayed from the beaches on which other types of landing craft were being tried out under fire. Changes and improvements were made as a result of these combat reports. A new landing ramp was developed, so that men would never again have to climb over the sides of the craft, as they did at Tarawa, where so many hundreds lost their lives before they were able to reach the beaches.

Other plants in America, of course, were engaged in developing and producing these same vehicles, and the competition of peace times was forgotten as all worked together to achieve the incredible fleet of small landing craft and the amphibious tanks that crawled over sand and mud and rock and jagged coral reef up onto the shore, to engage and destroy the enemy.

When the project was well under way at Rockford, Bob Ingersoll was transferred to the Kalamazoo plant in Michigan to direct the building of amphibious tractors, the "Alligator" and the "Water Buffalo." After that came a craft called the LVT3— the Beach Buster, which had been designed by Bob Ingersoll's engineers at Rockford, and was used by the Marines.

Within a matter of months after final approval of the designs, the Kalamazoo plant was turning the Beach Busters out on a mass-production basis. Facilities were increased and expanded, so that as many as 12 or 14 of these amphibious monsters of steel could be turned out in a single day.

But each single day, and night, was one more frantic test. There were times, according to Rudy Wolchino, one of Bob Ingersoll's top assistants, when parts for these war machines were so desperately needed that they were flown in by private cargo plane and dropped onto the plant grounds by parachute. Even as the big planes turned and headed back to Cleveland for the next emergency load, the needed parts were being retrieved and hustled into the assembly line so that production would not be stalled.

The story of this one plant was typical of the story of all Borg-Warner. At Mechanics Universal Joint and Morse Chain and Long Manufacturing, crank shafts and clutches and gears and stabilizers now went into war planes, tanks, warships, submarines, LCTs and LSTs. Rockford Clutch, for example, supplied many thousands of the clutches used in the light and medium tanks that swept across North Africa after the Allied landings, and later lumbered over routes of victory in Sicily and Italy and France and across the Rhine into Germany.

At Warner Gear, round-the-clock production included tens

of thousands of transmissions for jeeps; gear sets for light tanks; transmissions for Army, Navy and Marine trucks of assorted sizes, shapes and purposes; 37 different kinds of airplane gears; brake hangers for trucks, bearing retainers, de-clutching units, brake drums, output shafts, axle gears and cylinder sleeves. At the same time, between 1942 and 1945 this one plant turned out more than 1,600,000 automotive transmissions, entirely for use in the war effort.

A war is fought and won in many ways and on many fronts. One important aspect was the battle for food. Donald Nelson, executive vice president of Sears Roebuck & Company, was persuaded to become head of the War Production Board. One of the problems he had to face was that many departments were headed by men without proper background and experience. It was the duty of these men to determine the products different industries were to be allowed to manufacture. To some the allotment was zero, since their regular products were considered non-essential to the war effort. This included such items as automobiles, home appliances and hundreds of other products. Under Order L-170, which went into effect on November 1, 1942, farm equipment production was cut to 20 per cent of the base period and some items were cut even further. Wheel tractors, for example, which were so vital to farm production, were cut back to 11 per cent of the 1937 to 1940 average production. There were immediate protests from the farmers across the country who had been called upon to increase production of food products. The farm equipment manufacturers and their leaders strongly protested the charge when they were accused by some Government officials of not wishing to produce farm equipment because they preferred what was said to be more lucrative war equipment contracts. This was answered by Fowler McCormick, president of International Harvester Company, for the industry and for his company, when he stated that some of their plants were shut down and were anxiously awaiting the opportunity to start again producing farm equipment. The *Farm Equipment Journal* pointed out that the Government on the one hand was crying for more food and with the other was cutting the tools by which it could be produced.

In February, 1943, a meeting of farm equipment leaders was held to see what might be done to correct this impossible situation. Roy Ingersoll was asked to set up a meeting and to head a delegation to go over this serious situation with Nelson. Ingersoll called long distance and Nelson promptly set up a meeting in his office. At 11 A.M. on Wednesday, March 3, 1943, the following were in his office: William Clark of J. I. Case, Edward S. Schiely of Massey-Harris Company, William A. Roberts of Allis-Chalmers, Frank Silloway of Deere and Company, John McCaffrey of International Harvester, Philip Knowland of B. F. Avery, W. A. McCord of Oliver and Ingersoll, and for the W.P.B. were Don Nelson and his assistant, Ed A. Locke, Jr., now president of one of Chicago's major companies, the Union Tank Car Company. The committee also called on James F. Byrnes, at that time Director of Economic Stabilization, and on Marvin Jones, United States Food Administrator.

The committee protested to Nelson that the farmers and their industry were not being treated fairly and that food production needed to win the war was being curtailed by those handling this problem on the War Production Board. Nelson agreed with them and urged that they select a man to head up a farm equipment committee of W.P.B. and he would promptly make the appointment. The group went to the Mayflower Hotel to debate this question and pick their man. Roy was delayed because he had to see Nelson on other business. When he arrived an hour later he was informed that he had been selected as chairman of the committee.

He thanked the group but stated that he was not able to accept this post because of other commitments. An International Harvester executive, Mr. Harrison, was chosen, but he declined a few days later, pointing out that it would not be proper for an executive of the largest farm equipment company to head up this committee—an opinion with which Nelson concurred.

George L. Gillette, one of the industry's best known men, a vice president of Minneapolis-Moline and a veteran of many years in the farm equipment field was then chosen for this important position. When it became necessary for Gillette to return to Minneapolis-Moline, Ingersoll, who had remained a member of the committee, though not its chairman, was asked to contact his good friend, Charles Deere Wiman, and try to persuade him to be George Gillette's successor.

Wiman had given up his position as president of Deere and Company for the duration of the war and was serving as a Colonel in the Armed Forces on duty at that time in the Pentagon. Wiman finally agreed to accept this position, which meant relinquishing his duties at the Pentagon to serve his country in an area he knew well, the farm equipment branch of W.P.B. As an assistant he secured Harry Boyle, an executive of International Harvester Company. The result of the work of George Gillette and Charles Wiman was a very considerable increase in farm equipment allocation and production. With this increase in production of farm equipment came greater production of foodstuffs which were so essential to maintain not only the fighting forces on a dozen fronts but also the working force on the home front, which turned out war materials of all kinds.

The successful effort of these industrial and farm equipment leaders in securing increased allotments made no headlines. Yet it was in its way as critical and important as many a victory on an actual battlefield of war. For without the food that these machines produced many of the other victories would not have been possible.

Another of the great contributors to final victory of the Allied forces was a company almost unknown to the general public—the Pump Engineering Service Company, otherwise called

Pesco. It was organized in 1933 to manufacture airplane pumps. By 1939, when it came into Borg-Warner, it was one of the largest manufacturer of these pumps in the country. At the start of the war it was producing 5,000 units a month; by the end, this figure had soared to more than 100,000.

Yet even in the midst of the war emergency Borg-Warner refused to budge from its well-established standard procedures. With Pesco handling dozens of war contracts, Borg-Warner directors called in the man in charge, Bill Jack, from whom they had purchased the company.

Pesco had been paying a comparatively high percentage commission to its salesmen, and while this was good for business in peace time Borg-Warner felt that with large government contracts coming in the commission should be lowered. Even while this was being discussed by the board, however, a new problem developed involving a contract Jack had been negotiating for the purchase of a firm in California headed by a man named Ralph Heintz. Since Borg-Warner officials had not been kept advised of this in advance they brought Jack to Chicago for a discussion.

Small of stature, at once rugged, smiling and imperturbable, Jack explained that what he had done was in the interests of the war effort. Patiently Davis told him that all Borg-Warner plants were pouring out an ever-mounting flood of war materials and they were still following the company's established procedures, particularly in regard to obtaining board approval in advance for any such purchases.

The inevitable result was that Jack and Borg-Warner agreed to go their separate ways. Borg-Warner called Heintz to Chicago, explained that they had not authorized the contract, and settled the whole matter by paying him a small sum sufficient to take care of his expense and trouble.

Shortly thereafter, he and Jack did get together again to form a firm which skyrocketed to headlines during the war—Jack and Heintz, producers of aircraft engine starters, also in Cleveland. Most of the headlines concerned the unusual generosity they showed to employees; in one instance they were said to have paid a secretary $39,000 a year. Not only did workers get high pay and considerable overtime but also sizable annual bonuses, all-expenses-paid vacations to Florida, Arizona, and California, and free meals.

Borg-Warner officials set to work to strengthen Pesco's management and aid it in every way possible; with the result that the firm's production and quantity reached new heights. In virtually every plane under the American flag, the Pesco pumping devices performed a host of vital services without which the planes could not have gotten off the ground.

Bill Jack's assistant replaced him at Pesco temporarily and was eventually succeeded by Robert Minshall who, before joining Borg-Warner was vice president in charge of engineering at Boeing. Under his direction at Boeing the first plans were formulated that were to culminate in the production of the B17 and the B29. Minshall, who came in as Pesco's president in July of 1941, died in 1954.

Yet often the loftiest heights are achieved not by the most famous but by the obscure. One of Borg-Warner's most dramatic contributions was performed by a company of only 40 or 50 men in Gary, Indiana, in a wood-frame plant that had once been an auto repair shop.

In a curious way, the safety of the free world depended on these men.

Originally called the Marsene Corporation and then the Marbon Company, this company was purchased by Borg-Warner in 1934, largely to put Borg-Warner into the chemical field on a small and primarily experimental basis. The firm dealt in rubber-based hydrochloride derivatives. From this experimentation this small plant began to produce on a limited scale what is called cyclo rubber, a largely synthetic crude-rubber based resin.

Experiments revealed that cyclo rubber, when combined with a chemical called polyisobutylene, made a remarkably efficient electrical wire insulating cable; the material formed easily around the wire, and because of the cyclo-molecular structure, electrical loss or seepage of power was almost nonexistent, even at incredibly high frequencies.

Robert Shattuck, a youthful scientist appointed to run the plant, under the supervision of Borg-Warner vice president George P. F. Smith, found that a number of cable companies were anxious for this product, particularly in the fall and early winter of 1940-1941. They wanted it, they said, for a new kind of cable, and they wanted all they could get as fast as they could get it. The exact purpose of the cable they were prevented from disclosing, for security reasons.

Suddenly, at this small frame building, Navy security experts showed up. So did representatives of other government agencies. They regarded the plant with dismay. It had no protection of any kind against sabotage, theft, explosion. There wasn't even a wire fence on the outside and the chemicals inside, if the mixture went wrong, could easily blow the whole plant and everybody in it to pieces.

At this point Shattuck and his staff learned the truth: The cable they were producing with their cyclo-rubber compound was being used on a thing called radar. Little known to the public then, at the height of the Battle of Britain, a network of radar screens was giving the RAF time to get into the air and thereby thwarting Hitler's attempt to conquer England. "With the high frequencies required in radar, your company at present is the only one in the world capable of producing the kind of cable required," one of the government agents declared bluntly.

Shattuck looked around him at this tiny plant and its twoscore workers. At that particular moment, when there was not even time to get another plant into production, a large measure of the world's safety lay in their hands.

They discussed ways of protecting the plant and setting up security measures without attracting attention and decided that the only protection lay in doing nothing at all, in going on precisely as before, but they were to tell anyone who asked that they were making helmets for tank drivers.

This production continued throughout the most critical months of the Battle of Britain and the early years of our own involvement in the war, until 1943, when development of new processes changed the type of radar cable needed.

Following the war, Marbon development and laboratory experimentation produced one of the finest all-around thermoplastic resins, marketed under the registered trademark, *Cycolac*. On a 330-acre plot of ground located on the Ohio River at Washington Crossing, a suburb of Parkersburg, West Virginia, a new $12,000,000 plant was completed by the middle of 1958 for production of *Cycolac* in large quantities to meet the increasing demand for this versatile material. In addition, several other plants had been built in Gary.

By 1959, *Cycolac* was being made into a number of consumer products—telephone casings for Western Electric, crash pads for General Motors and arm rests for Ford, valve fittings for Coca-Cola, pipes for plumbing, oil storage tanks, irrigation and chemical and other uses, sweeper wheels for Electro-lux, aircraft window frames and other fittings for Boeing Aircraft, food trays for Pan American Airlines, construction helmets for the building trades, football helmets for Megregot Sporting Goods and toy train parts for Lionel.

Other new products are being developed constantly by Marbon, including highly successful industrial adhesives. As the market demand mounted, still further production capacity is being added which will double production by the end of 1959.

Despite illness and the burden of leadership he had carried for many years, Charles Davis remained at the Borg-Warner helm throughout the war years, and the course he steered through that turbulent period made a brilliant industrial record. At the same time he wisely placed growing responsibility on others around him. One of those who shouldered an ever-increasing work load at the top-management level was Roy Ingersoll.

The war was in its last year when Ingersoll returned one Saturday early on a September morning to Chicago from Washington, D.C., where he had spent several days in conference after conference with government officials on various aspects of the war production program.

He was looking forward to a game of golf which he had arranged with some of his business associates and customers; since it would be only the second golf game that summer he had found time to play at the Indian Hill Golf Club where he was a member. They had planned to tee off at 10:00 o'clock. The train was late, however.

Driving on Chicago's outer drive, en route from the railroad station to the club in Winnetka, he was stopped by two traffic officers who told him that he was driving 45-miles per hour in a 35-mile zone. Roy began to tell them how he had been working all week in Washington and had been looking forward to this game of golf and a few hours' relaxation and had possibly overlooked watching the speedometer as carefully as he should. The two patrol car officers seemed to relent a little, but nevertheless asked to see his driver's license. Search as he would, he could not find it. The policemen decided he would have to go to the station house, but Ingersoll kept on talking and using his best salesmanship. What was the use of taking him to the station since he would observe the speed limit most carefully in the future, he argued. He cited other reasons, too, one after the other, until the two officers told him bluntly, "All right, all right, you win. Now get the hell out of here."

Just as he started to leave, a car swung the corner too fast and, to get out of the way, Ingersoll pulled his car in, with the result that the bumper of his car slipped neatly under the left rear fender of the police car which had been parked just in front of him, and pulled the fender off. The policemen got out of their damaged patrol car and one of them said, "You've *really* done it this time. Don't you know that everyone who even scratches a patrol car must be taken to the police station?"

But they didn't know their man. They had seen the accident and knew it was not his fault. Ingersoll argued, adding, "Look, all you have to do is go out to a garage and get yourself fitted with one of Mr. Ford's best fenders—and send me the bill. I'll pay it the day I get the invoice. And remember, I'm already an hour late for my game and have about 16 miles yet to go."

The two officers talked it over a moment and finally said, "All right, drive on—but please, Mr. Ingersoll, for heaven's sake, stay in front of us!"

In October of that year, he was leaving his office for a Northwestern-Notre Dame football game when he was once again stopped by the police. This time he had made sure he was staying within the 35-mile speed limit; in fact, all the other cars were passing him. Just then he was startled by the siren's screech and a police car directing him to the curb. He got out of the car and saw his same two uniformed friends. They asked where he was going this time.

He looked at the two friendly, smiling Irish faces before him, and loyal Northwestern supporter though he was, managed to say with a remarkable attempt at sincerity, "I'm going to the football game to watch Notre Dame beat the hell out of those Wildcats."

"Well," the police said, "seems like you're a little late. Don't you think you ought to have an escort?"

They gave him an escort at a speed faster than Roy had ever thought of going, as far as the Chicago city limits. Without further incident he reached the Northwestern stadium where Notre Dame proceeded "to beat the hell out of those Wildcats."

14

Fords go automatic

THE POST-WAR floodgates opened on a torrent of new consumer goods, especially in the automotive world with its new models, new ideas and inventions and adaptations from wartime developments to peace. America was ride-hungry and car-happy and manufacturers vied with each other to produce cars that would take people wherever they wanted to go—faster, cheaper and smoother. Out of this fierce competitive market came many new developments to make driving easier and safer. The most important of these was the automatic transmission.

Like almost every other development in automobile manufacture, the automatic transmission was no overnight invention. It was the result of painstaking research and development in automotive laboratories over the years.

Warner Gear had always been a leader in transmission development. One of its most valuable contributions was the synchronizer, by means of which the gear teeth mesh smoothly as the driver shifts from one speed to another. It was used on all standard transmissions, under licensing arrangements. Another Warner Gear development was the overdrive, which in effect gave the car four forward speeds instead of three.

Research on this important automotive contribution began about 1930. The goal was to produce a new transmission that would reduce costs and engine wear, and provide greater comfort for driver and passengers. All of these the overdrive accomplished by means of the "fourth gear" that put the car into a gear ratio where the engine had to turn only seven-tenths as fast as required by direct ratio to maintain speed.

Successful development of the overdrive is credited to Warner Gear engineers including Warner Gear's chief engineer, Palmer Orr, and to a licensor, William B. Barnes. The overdrive was sold first to the Chrysler Corporation in 1934.

During a major portion of the modern history of the automobile in which the standard form of friction clutch was generally in use, the overdrive was used as optional equipment on all major makes of cars. The total number sold and in use by 1959 had reached well over 7,000,000. Even by that date, with the widespread use of automatic transmissions, the overdrive was used by a number of leading car manufacturers, including Ford, Chrysler, General Motors, American Motors, and Studebaker.

The overdrive, in effect a semi-automatic transmission, was for Warner Gear a step in the direction of the fully automatic transmission of the future. It was Charles Davis who years before its production, had realized that his standardized type of hand shift transmission, used by most car manufacturers would be supplanted by a fully automatic model that would not only do the work of shifting gears but would also select proper time to make such shift. In the middle 1930s he started a program to develop such a transmission.

The transmission was longer in coming than even Davis had realized. An early model had been built, but was not yet in production, when World War II intervened and it was put on the shelf for the duration of the war.

At other factories, too, in those years just before the war, other engineers were experimenting and adapting and refining in an effort to produce the same thing—a practical automatic transmission. General Motors had developed its own shortly before the start of World War II. Bob Ingersoll adapted it for use in amphibious tanks and was able to suggest to the General Motors engineers several changes that had to be made if they were to operate satisfactorily. After the war, General Motors installed it in its Cadillac and later in its Pontiac. It had been installed in Oldsmobile before World War II.

Borg-Warner, with the war over and production once more concentrated on civilian needs, continued its efforts, seeking to develop a more effective transmission than any other then available.

Among the men who worked on the transmission was Harold Youngren, chief executive engineer for Borg-Warner, who had previously been chief engineer of the General Motors Oldsmobile Division. Hired away later on by Ford, which was in a period of transition and expansion, he became that company's chief engineer and vice president in charge of engineering. One of his first important jobs was to find an automatic transmission so that Ford could be in a satisfactory competitive situation with other car makers. And it was only natural that Youngren should suggest the transmission on which he himself had been working at Borg-Warner. Tested extensively for durability, performance and economy, the Borg-Warner transmission was pronounced superior to any other on the market. In the opinion of Ford engineers, this transmission was Ford's answer to their major competitors.

In the fall of 1948, long-term contracts were drawn up whereby Borg-Warner was to produce half of Ford's automatic transmission requirements for a period of years, and Ford had the privilege of making either the other half itself or of assigning the manufacture to some other firm acceptable to Borg-Warner. (It is standard Ford practice to insist on two sources for all parts and products, so that in the event of catastrophe or labor stoppage, its supply will never be cut off completely.)

A contract of this size caused a stir of activity even in such a large company as Borg-Warner. The officials of Warner Gear Division had not only participated in the negotiations but had also worked closely with Ford in the production problems made necessary by such a large scale undertaking. Within a year fifteen million dollars worth of new tools and equipment had been installed in the Warner Gear plant. The near-perfect co-ordination of hundreds of people—engineers, executives and skilled workmen and of steel mills and other suppliers—was required to get production under way.

"It was almost as hectic as the war days," one of the executives said later. "Ford wanted its new transmission immediately, and we worked around the clock to deliver."

As the first transmissions came off the assembly lines, they were rushed to a specially-constructed building in Muncie to be tested. Twenty-four hours a day, seven days a week, grueling tests went on. Cars were driven in, mud-spattered from miles in sleet and snow; hurried to the pits for transmission changes; and sent out once more. At first each transmission produced was given this extensive driving test. Other Fords undergoing tests crossed the prairie to the West, climbing hills and mountains, running for days with no stops except for gasoline.

The transmissions were put through every kind of road test conceivable, in perhaps the most exhaustive series of automobile tests ever made, before Borg-Warner was satisfied.

This was the mechanism which was to become famous as the Ford-O-Matic, known to drivers all around the world almost as an extension of drivers' own minds and hands. Shifting automatically into the correct and most economical gear, so gently that the driver had difficulty in detecting when the shift was made, it had the added advantage of an unusually effective torque converter, which helped cushion the car's start and ease it gently onto the road.

So successful were these transmissions that by 1953—three

years after Roy Ingersoll had taken over as president of Borg-Warner, they had outgrown the nearly 2,000,000 square foot plant of Warner Gear. Nor was there space available in the Cincinnati plant the Ford Motor Company had put up to produce its half of the Ford-O-Matics.

With orders piling up, Borg-Warner decided to erect a new plant, and chose Decatur, Illinois, as the site, since the company's plants in Muncie were already employing virtually every available worker in that area.

The new plant, to be operated under the auspices of the Marvel-Schebler Division, was considered one of the finest and most efficient plants in the automotive industry. In constructing this plant, Borg-Warner called on Warner Gear, with its years of experience in securing the best equipment obtainable and arranging it in the plant production line to achieve the most effective and economical production. This plant, with its 103 acres of land plus its equipment and machinery, represented an investment of $18,500,000. To staff it, a whole new force of workers was hired and trained in a highly technical and demanding operation.

Naturally, a competition developed between these two plants, Warner Gear and Decatur. Both were making the same product, yet there was a rivalry between them over the cost of each complete transmission, the maintenance of quality, and efficiency of performance of the transmissions from each plant. It was a competition that led only to better results for all.

At the same time that the Ford-O-Matic was being developed, another type of automatic transmission was being evolved at Detroit Gear. The brain child of Howard Blood, H. H. Whittingham and other Detroit Gear experts, including some outside inventors whose patents were licensed or purchased, it differed from the other Borg-Warner transmissions primarily in that it had a lock-up device which put it into direct drive once it reached a certain speed. Contracted for by Studebaker, it has been used by that company for many years, under the name Flight-O-Matic.

But it was another special customer which gave this transmission its severest test, under the most trying conditions of all—the stop-and-go traffic of the New York City streets.

Searching for new outlets for their transmission, Detroit Gear salesmen had aroused some interest by Checker Cab, one of the large fleets of taxis which operate in the crowded metropolitan area.

"Yes, we'd like to try them," one of Checker's executives said, "but automatic transmissions are supposed to use more gasoline —and in this business even one-tenth of a gallon more gas per mile can mean the difference between making a profit or winding up with a loss."

He agreed, however, to make an experiment. One hundred of the company's new cabs were fitted with the transmission and sent out on the New York streets, along with another hundred equipped with the standard gear shifts. In the hurried streets of Manhattan, through theater traffic, morning rush hours and 5:00 o'clock Friday nights, the Checker people put these transmissions through their automatic paces.

The results were overwhelming. The cars with the automatic transmission not only used less gas but required fewer repairs because of the cushioning effect of the converter in automatically shifting to different gear ratios.

As for the reaction of the drivers, Checker officials stated, "We can't get our men to take out cabs with the standard shift any more."

In the course of developing these transmissions the flexibility and versatility of the Borg-Warner setup were demonstrated. Several laboratories of the company, including the Products Development Laboratory in Detroit and the Bellwood Laboratory in Chicago, as well as experimental facilities at Warner

Gear, were employed in the development. Additional experimentation and actual production were carried out by six divisions: Borg & Beck and Long both made torque converters; Detroit Gear, Warner Gear and Marvel-Schebler were all involved in actual production; and the Spring Division in Bellwood made rollers and turbine blades for Borg & Beck, who in turn assembled them into converters for Warner Gear.

Spring Division is one of the few divisions in the Borg-Warner "family" without a past history; it was started entirely new by the parent company. In 1940 it was set up for the manufacture of springs, primarily for clutches produced by Borg-Warner's three clutch plants. It very quickly was developed for other uses as well, wrote a magnificent chapter in the company's war production record, and developed a vital part—technically a "full-phasing, one-way sprag clutch"—for use in automatic transmissions. This single development is also of use in such diverse things as aircraft cabin compressors, jet engine starters, helicopters, military trucks and power take-offs. The Spring Division also makes friction clutch plates, electric motor commutators and punch-press stampings and assemblies.

Borg-Warner soon added other customers for its transmissions. Perhaps the most important is American Motors, which in 1959 standardized on Warner Gear's transmissions, both automatic and hand-shift.

As the manufacture of foreign cars crept upward, the company expanded into that market too, and in the early 1950s the Jaguar, the Mercedes-Benz, and other European automobiles were being equipped with Detroit Gear transmissions. This business became so important, in fact, that in 1954 the home office decided to manufacture overdrives and automatic transmissions in England to take better care of its growing list of foreign customers. Morse Chain already had a subsidiary there, which was expanded by building a multi-million dollar plant to take care of the new production. The Detroit Gear equipment for producing these mechanisms was dismantled and shipped overseas, and the company began operation under the name Borg-Warner Limited. In 1956, in this new plant, located at Letchworth, 36 miles north of London, automatic transmissions soon started to roll off the line for Jaguar and others.

In Michigan, Detroit Gear was concentrating on complete transmissions, axles and hydraulic pumps for Massey-Ferguson tractors, which kept its plants operating at capacity. As labor costs continued to rise in America, however, Massey-Fergusion discovered that it could make all the parts required in their affiliated Standard Motor Company plant in Coventry, England, pay the costs of boxing and shipping, and still get them for considerably less than Detroit Gear had to charge, only a few blocks away from its Detroit assembly plant.

This bizarre economic development, coupled with the discontinuance of automatic transmission production, led eventually to the closing of the Detroit Gear plants, one of which (the Seven Mile Road plant) was bought up by the American Can Company.

Changing world conditions, including the shifting of so much of Detroit Gear's production to England, was a partial cause of this closing, but the primary reason could be found in a comment made by Roy Ingersoll regarding the shipment of Massey-Ferguson's tractor parts to Detroit from England: "The reason for this," he pointed out, "was that the labor rate over in the English factory, in American money, was approximately 60 to 70 cents an hour, while the rate paid by Detroit Gear was considerably more than $2.50 an hour. Also, these tractor parts came in as duty-free farm equipment, and could be delivered from Britain to Detroit at much less than our cost of production.

"This was heart-breaking to the management of Detroit Gear, the loss of this business, but we could not blame the customer for taking this business away from us when he could produce it much cheaper in England because of tremendous differences in labor rates."

The contract with Ford to make half its transmissions expired at the end of the 1958 model year. At this time the highly efficient Marvel-Schebler plant with its trained labor force was faced with the loss of its only product, transmissions, since this plant had been built solely to handle approximately one-fourth of the automatic transmission requirement for the Ford car.

But there was only a brief shutdown and layoff of this labor staff, because Borg-Warner had another division—York (air conditioning) which was badly in need of expansion and modernization of some of its facilities. The Decatur plant and its staff of skilled workers provided a ready-made answer. One of the most efficient producers of automatic transmissions in America shifted smoothly to production of the types of air conditioners that were mass or line produced, including hermetically-sealed compressors for air conditioned automobiles and for window units.

This series of events illustrates the resiliency of Borg-Warner and its unique industrial ability to shift with the changing conditions; developing new procedures and methods; shifting product emphasis or direction; closing down a line here and beginning another there—but always reflecting the needs of the consumer world. In a sense, it is the same pattern Stephen Ingersoll followed when he started his canning factory to supplement the coulter discs, or moved to Galesburg, or bought a steel mill to avoid a shutdown because he could not otherwise get sufficient quantities of the special steel to meet his customers' needs.

15

The saga of Norge

IN MUSKEGON, Michigan, on August 25, 1948, a group of executives were in meeting: the supervisory board of the Norge Division of Borg-Warner. All afternoon they had heard reports. Late in the afternoon Howard Blood, the Norge president, rose to present the company's overall picture. The directors leaned back contentedly as he mentioned rising sales and the continued public demand for all the Norge products—electric and gas ranges, refrigerators, home freezers, and laundry equipment, including their automatic washing machines and dryers. There was a relaxed confidence among these businessmen as he spoke of Norge's strong position in the white goods field.

Then suddenly smiles turned into looks of concern. Norge's reserve fund, Blood was saying, a fund of considerably more than $1,000,000, to be used for servicing Norge refrigerators during the 5-year guarantee period, had been used up, apparently over a period of only a few months.

They began to ask questions. Blood answered them frankly. It was the refrigerant that was causing the trouble, he said. Since the post-war shift from sulphur dioxide to *Freon* as the refrigerant, something had gone wrong with the Rollator compressor. Some of the cast-iron casings of the compressors had started to wear and failed to function properly and the entire compressor had to be replaced. "We have a 5-year guarantee on all Norge products," Blood reminded the group around the table, "and I know that Borg-Warner will live up to that guarantee—no matter what the cost."

Although neither he nor any of the others could have known it, this scene in the supervisory board meeting marked the beginning of a drama that was to continue for several years, involving an engineering miscalculation costing several million dollars, but the brand name emerged stronger than ever because the company not only corrected the error but promptly replaced the defective parts.

Norge had expanded considerably in the period after the war, and its facilities had been further increased with the purchase and construction of new plants, in Chattanooga, Tennessee, and Herrin, and Effingham, Illinois. The Herrin plant, finished in 1946, was devoted to the manufacture of washing machines, both "wringer" type and automatic. From the start, the line had been eminently successful; sales were high and increasing.

Profits from the washing machines, however, and from Norge's other successful home appliances, were being canceled out by the losses from the faulty refrigerators. The situation had grown worse; in 1948, although Norge Division sales for that year had shown an increase of $10,000,000 over the previous year, they had produced only one-third as much profit.

The directors were aware that Blood and Norge technicians were working unremittingly to correct the trouble. But what had started as a mere dribble in replacement costs became a torrent in 1949 and 1950—on a scale that few companies ever faced before and survived.

A number of the directors of Borg-Warner, who still thought of the company primarily as a supplier to the automotive business, began to urge that the corporation "unload" Norge. Roy Ingersoll, however, led another group within the board which believed firmly in Norge and in the concept of diversification.

This situation reached its climax in the fall of 1949 at a special meeting of the Borg-Warner board called to work out a solution to the Norge problem. It was obvious that something had to be done. Distributors who had been happy with Norge in the past, and appreciative of the fine name Blood and his associates had built up over the years, were nevertheless leaving Norge to take on competitive lines; the magnificent sales force which had been built up originally by Johnny Knapp was gradually being dissipated as the faulty Rollators rolled in. A crisis had arisen in the ice box; a positive and immediate way out had to be found.

The meeting was one of the grimmest since the day of the stock market crash in 1929 when Gus Shallberg, at the request of the board, had told a story that brought a gust of laughter and lifted the gloom. At this gathering over twenty years later, however, a dozen such stories would not have helped.

Yet now the need for some dramatic action and change was clear. Blood himself was aware of this. In reply to many probing questions and comments, he was able to announce that the error had been found and corrected.

However, there was a strong feeling that immediate action of some kind was required. Gus Shallberg, executive vice president, suggested the name of one of Borg-Warner's top echelon "trouble shooters," George P. F. Smith, who was later to become a vice president of Borg-Warner and who had been asked to sit in at this meeting.

Smith had formerly been with United States Rubber and later had become head of Borg-Warner's Marbon Division. He was now dividing his time between Marbon and the home office of Borg-Warner, where he was assistant to Shallberg. With Shallberg's nomination of Smith, Davis agreed. It was suggested that Smith become Blood's assistant, to work closely with him, to which Blood readily gave assent. Smith, however, stated that he did not seek this role nor did he feel that his experience or training justified his accepting it.

The directors discussed this and turned to other alternatives and Smith, believing his possible role had been put aside, returned to his own office to handle several important phone calls.

He did not realize that he was walking out just before the meeting was to reach a climax, as Blood, seeing the impasse, was to announce that he was prepared to bow out of the Norge operation, although he would continue to serve the company for some time as a director.

Long afterward, when, as vice president, he was directing Borg-Warner's Washington and New York offices, Smith recalled that decisive afternoon:

"I was gone from the meeting perhaps half an hour. When I got back into the meeting I was told I had been appointed the new president of Norge."

Smith still had grave misgivings about taking this post, for he realized fully the seriousness of the Norge situation. However, Davis, Ingersoll and others on the board all urged him to accept. It was the only immediate solution to their problem, he was told. So Smith agreed to "be a good soldier and take this job on."

Large, easy-moving, genial and ingratiating, George Smith set about his job by going into the field and talking with distributors and dealers from one end of America to the other. Many of them were about to desert the Norge ship and his plan was to hold the nucleus of a distribution staff while he improved and rebuilt the confidence of the Norge staff and distributors and the public. Losses continued throughout 1949, 1950 and 1951 as refunds and replacements mounted on the refrigerators that had been sold before the error had been corrected in the Rollator casing. The Norge division met and fulfilled every single guarantee and made good on every replacement.

Norge, meanwhile, had not stopped with correction of the faulty refrigerator. It went to work on its whole line, examining styling and materials with a view to making Norge known throughout the world for quality far above that of other refrigerators, washing machines, dryers and other such household appliances.

In 1952, as a result of these efforts, Norge showed a profit of several hundred thousand dollars, in contrast to a deficit of several million the previous year. In 1953, however, it was again in the red, although the losses were not as heavy as previously. Nevertheless, the directors of Borg-Warner now unanimously agreed, even insisted, that Borg-Warner was essentially a parts manufacturer, a supplier to other companies, and that the Norge experience proved that it had no place in the consumer field. Roy Ingersoll who had become president in 1950 was asked to begin immediately exploring the possibilities of selling the Norge division, including plants and equipment.

Almost alone in opposition to the plan, Ingersoll nevertheless advised the board, with his usual directness, that in his opinion the company not only should continue in the consumer field but should expand since many of the parts it formerly made for automotive firms were now being made by the concerns themselves, in a movement of these companies to "integrate" their plants. And he stated that Borg-Warner needed this mass consumer market.

"I believe if we can find the right man to take over the operation of Norge, it can prove in the future to be a very valuable and profit producing division of Borg-Warner," Ingersoll told the board.

However, having declared his own position, he reluctantly set about to carry out the board's wishes by finding a buyer for the Norge line. He succeeded in getting an offer from Ross Siragusa, president of the Admiral Corporation, makers of television sets and home appliances. The offer was unsatisfactory to Ingersoll, and he felt that he could get it increased. But before trying to do so he had Norge's New York City distributor, Edward L. Frohlich, meet with Siragusa to inquire about Admiral's plans for Norge. Frohlich had been a sales executive at Norge before going into the distributing side. He lunched with the head of Admiral and afterwards called Roy to protest any sale of Norge. The company could be saved and built into a profitable line, he said, and he agreed with Roy that the price offered while entirely fair from Admiral's point of view, was too low.

"Get on a plane and get out here," Ingersoll told Frohlich. "I want you to help me persuade the directors to keep Norge by telling them that."

The New York distributor was in Chicago that night. At a special meeting of the directors he painted a picture from the distributor's point of view of what Norge could do in the home-appliance field, under the right man.

No one was criticizing George Smith, who had taken the job reluctantly to pinch hit until an experienced and proven home appliance executive could be secured. Smith's performance in the emergency had been excellent, everyone agreed.

The directors listened to Frohlich and then again to Ingersoll. Suppose Mr. Ingersoll were to go out after this man, who and what would he be? Where would he find this right man for the helm?

Ingersoll asked the directors for permission to find the man that he felt could handle the situation. When the directors asked if he had any idea who the man would be, his answer was that it was an extremely difficult position to fill and that in his opinion there were probably not more than half a dozen men in the country who had the experience, personality and background to do the job properly and he did not know if any of these men would be available.

Ingersoll began his search. Within weeks he had eliminated

four of his five original possibilities. The remaining man was Judson Sayre, called "the greatest salesman in the appliance industry."

Sayre was credited with having put Bendix on its feet, after that company had been in rough seas. During the post-war period, when Ingersoll's West Pullman plant had been turning out Bendix washers, the two had become friends.

Sayre was a man of personal charm, ego, relentless drive, energy and humor and good will—with tremendous faith in himself and his product.

"I knew him," Ingersoll said, "not only as a fearless man, but as one who knew how to organize; who knew how to see that the right product was developed and then how to create such enthusiasm for it on the part of the distributors that they would go out and sell that product to the dealers throughout the country."

Mr. Sayre, however, in his brilliant career at Bendix, had become independently wealthy and except for a few advisory posts, had retired from the battleground of industry.

When Roy approached him, Sayre stated that he was not interested in this or any other job. He had retired from business and was now interested only in golf, horse racing and gin rummy. Roy told him that any man as young and active as he would soon tire of such a diet. Ingersoll never lost the chance to urge Sayre to accept this challenge, which he insisted, only a man of Sayre's special talents was capable of meeting successfully.

Rarely if ever in industry has the president of a great corporation worked so doggedly to hire one man for one job. Ingersoll's assiduous campaign was never too insistent or obvious—neither did it ever let up. So persistent was Ingersoll that when Sayre was preparing to leave for a winter vacation at his Florida home, Ingersoll and his wife who were also flying to Florida at this time to attend a meeting, urged Sayre to join them on the flight. "We'll be happy to give you a lift," Roy told Jud.

Part of the way down they talked shop, and part of the way they played gin rummy, a favorite game of both men. Ingersoll, in telling the story later, declared, "I even let him beat me at gin."

Whether that did it, or whether it was Roy's persuasive words, as they were leaving the plane in Florida, Sayre told Mrs. Ingersoll in the tone of a general about to hand over his sword, "I'm supposed to be the salesman, but Roy has sold me on taking on Norge." And added after a pause, "As he says, it's a tremendous challenge."

A short time afterward, Jud Sayre dropped in at Ingersoll's office. When he walked out, he was president and general manager of the Norge Division of Borg-Warner.

When he took over at Norge, Sayre brought with him several of the men with whom he had been associated at Bendix. One of them, Virgil Rice, who had years before been service manager and had held other important positions at the Norge plant in Muskegon, was put in charge of production, and research and development of new products at all three Norge plants.

As this new team went to work, the whole picture changed. Distributors and dealers multiplied. Production and sales leaped forward at such a rate that in seven months, from the time he took over in May, 1954, Sayre had turned the year's figures from the bleak promise of a deficit to a healthy profit, with sales 73 per cent higher than those of the previous year.

Norge's remarkable growth and accomplishments since that time could not have been achieved by Jud Sayre alone, as he himself frequently pointed out. It could be attributed to Sayres' drive, leadership and imagination, plus his ability to build a remarkable team and teamwork in every phase of the operation, culling out weakness and dead wood, bringing in replacements and new talent. This was particularly true in the building of his sales and distribution organization, the front lines in the competitive battle of the "white goods."

One of the best informed men in the appliance field, Sayre was able to determine quickly who among the dealers and on the sales staff would be able to achieve the goals he had set for Norge. Like a baseball manager, building a championship ball club, he set to work to develop a distributing force equal to, or better than, any other in the field. His own personal drive, his willingness to work to all hours, his loathing of complacency and halfway jobs—all these inspired those around him to give the best they had.

The result was an alertness and co-ordination that was an essential in reaching and holding a leading position in this industry where a carefully conceived sales plan might well be wrecked and made useless by a competitor's suddenly cutting prices on some appliances as a way of acquiring a larger percentage of the consumer market. Quick action and decisions must be made to counter such unbusinesslike practices and to develop a plan to offset them, while still enabling distributors to maintain a strong position. Only effective teamwork could make this possible. This teamwork carried Norge to a position among the top leaders in the appliance field.

The friendship of Sayre and Ingersoll became even stronger after Sayre joined Borg-Warner. Often they would talk over Norge's development, its remarkable success since Sayre took over, its problems, and their plans to make Norge a constantly larger factor in the home appliance field. On one occasion Roy asked him what he considered the basic reasons for this success, Jud answered, "It lies in qualities a lot of people still remember and use—loyalty, aggressiveness, plain honesty and integrity and the will to work, in problems handled quickly and intelligently. These are the qualities we look for in the

production line, in top management, in distributors and salesmen. We're good because they have these qualities."

The competition in the home-appliance field is bitter, and
many manufacturers will sell their products below cost on a
mass scale, to government housing projects and similar large-
scale units, just to keep their plants running and take care of
some of the overhead. Sayre and Borg-Warner have refused to
do this, still Norge production and sales continue to grow. In
1955, for example, a good sample of an average good year,
Norge's sales ran more than $129,000,000.

Even to Roy Ingersoll, who likes to win, it was well worth
losing a game of gin rummy.

16

Diversify—or die!

CHANGE IS the essence of a nation or individual, a company or group of companies. American post-war economy, in spite of the new conflict in Korea, was changing rapidly in 1950, and was to continue to change.

Missiles and missile boosters and electronics were rising out of the Aladdin's lamps of the laboratories. The automatic transmission was changing the driving habits of a nation; the clutch of yesterday was no longer the monarch of the footboard. We began to look at color television, live in air-conditioned homes, and ride in air-conditioned cars.

After twenty years of service as the head of Borg-Warner, Charles Davis resigned the presidency in 1950 but remained on as chairman of the board. His successor was a man with whom he had worked closely all these years, his friend and associate, Roy Ingersoll. He was sixty-four when he took over this new job of president. He was at an age at which men are usually set in their ideas and working habits. Yet Roy Ingersoll had to change his point of view from that required of a division director, who was used to executing orders and giving instructions as the head of all the plants and steel mills in his division, to that expected of the overseer of all the divisions of Borg-Warner, who had to deal on a far wider level of policy. The contrast was vast, for now he had to get others to carry out the policies; now he had to find new techniques of dealing with both problems and men; and now he had to convince and counsel and leave all the details to subordinates. That he was able to make this shift so successfully is one of Ingersoll's outstanding achievements, and his work in building and expanding the Borg-Warner program is one of the great triumphs of his long industrial career.

In 1950, Roy Ingersoll was sixty-four, an age when many men begin to think of retiring. More than forty years of his life had been spent in active work in industry, years filled with battles and industrial crises; with some victories and some defeats. His children now were grown and married, and had children of their own. Jim, his younger son, had come on the staff of the Ingersoll Steel and Disc Division at the end of the war in late 1945; and Bob had been vice-president in charge of manufacturing at the Chicago Works, Evansville and Kalamazoo, and that year of 1950 was to become president of the Ingersoll Products Division. In 1953, he was named an administrative vice president by the Borg-Warner board of directors, at the suggestion of Charles Davis.

Roy Ingersoll had served Borg-Warner itself many ways over these years since he first brought in the Ingersoll plants. As head of the Ingersoll Steel and Disc Division, and of related divisions that came in later, he was actually manager of seven Borg-Warner plants. These included the West Pullman plant of Ingersoll Steel Division, the two Kalamazoo plants, and the New Castle plant, plus Calumet Steel, Franklin Steel and Superior Steel.

He had made many contributions in reorganizing operations of these plants and in improving efficient methods of production and inventory control. He had developed, for example, a daily report form whereby the whole picture of a company's production, sales, inventory and similar vital statistical data could be contained on a single page.

Thus, daily, by means of these report forms, he was able to keep before him and before the other executives of the division a full picture of what was going on in these seven widely-scattered plants. This simple but highly efficient reporting technique which he developed is now used in a number of other Borg-Warner operations.

Above and beyond work, Roy Ingersoll had given a great deal of time and effort to the Chamber of Commerce, as vice president and director of the national organization and former president of the Illinois State Chamber. He was chairman of the Citizens' Advisory Committee to the Senate Committee on Banking and Currency, and first Chairman of the Advisory Committee of the Export-Import Bank, which was set up by Congress. He took part in activities of many kinds in behalf of youth; he helped build the American Cancer Society in the war against that dread disease. In a hundred different ways he served his community, with the same energetic get-it-done-now pressure that was one of his characteristic talents in business.

He continued to devote the greater part of his seemingly limitless energies to the several plants and to the overall development of the Borg-Warner Corporation, particularly through his work on the board of directors.

Perhaps no one knew better than Roy Ingersoll the needs of Borg-Warner at this time; certainly this was the attitude and belief of the directors who voted him into office. Davis himself and the other directors wanted action taken to meet the problems confronting the company if it were to continue to grow and prosper.

Roy Ingersoll was aware that the management of each division had to be strengthened wherever it was weak, wherever suitable replacements had not been made for the ability of the companies' founders who had been lost to Borg-Warner by retirement or death. Where there was deadwood among these successors it had to be cut out and replaced. In some instances, Ingersoll knew, decisions might be hard.

He was aware of the problems confronting the automotive parts business, on which the firm had been founded. More and more the motor companies were becoming more integrated and were making the major parts of their cars in their own plants.

The automatic transmissions Borg-Warner was now producing for Ford, he thought, might not represent a permanent production project; one day Ford could be producing all of its own automatic transmissions. Other parts manufacturers faced similar situations. Two of the three independent makers of automobile bodies had closed down this phase of their business and had turned to other fields, such as plumbing, for their main production.

If Borg-Warner wanted to grow, Roy Ingersoll knew, it must diversify. It must reach out into new fields to exploit its vast resources, technical knowledge and facilities to the utmost. In the changing world of mid-century America, it must find new products and new areas of production.

He was aware, too, of the snags and the possible pitfalls. In a great firm like Borg-Warner, whose annual gross sales would total slightly more than $330,000,000 in his first year as president, progress and planning for the future had to be balanced against current sales and profits and production. That $330,-000,000 figure, however, was an $80,000,000 increase over the previous year.

Ingersoll would not attempt any sudden convulsive shift in the pattern Davis had established and carried out with such great success. Every change had to be carefully considered and properly explored, planned and presented.

Yet he knew, also, beyond all doubt, that changes had to come.

In his approach to diversification the new president presented a carefully thought out plan based on sound, long-tested business principles.

It was not to be any hit or miss program. They were not going to buy any plant simply because it was up for sale. It was not to be speculation in the buying and selling of businesses. Rather it was to be a co-ordinated program built fundamentally on the policy that the Borg-Warner divisions should be diversified in their products, independent in their operations as a division, yet interrelated with other divisions through the nature of the product itself; the overall pattern would be one of an integrated diversification.

In Ingersoll's well-defined plan, a new company brought in should be able to make a contribution to Borg-Warner, and Borg-Warner should be able to make a contribution to the company and its progress through the corporation's particular skills and specialized personnel. The product should be one of which Borg-Warner had some knowledge that could be of value in the product's development and improvement. Under this policy of expanded diversification, Ingersoll also pointed out that the company brought in might be one which could use the vast financial resources of Borg-Warner to expand its productivity and sales, if its product fitted into Borg-Warner's picture and needs. Above all they were to concentrate on "growth companies"—firms with the high potential of expanding unsaturated markets.

Exploring the possibilities of new acquisitions, Ingersoll and his advisors considered more than 200 types of products in which Borg-Warner might be interested. This list was very quickly pared down to a few selective and important fields. They were interested, of course, in new automotive products and automotive parts, particularly where they could build a strong patent position. They would explore the field of home building and household equipment; this would include the entire field of home building, insulation, plumbing, every type of home appliance, winter and summer air conditioning, new light-weight building materials, especially materials designed to eliminate or reduce maintenance costs, painting and repairs and other types of upkeep in home or office. A survey was conducted of new types of construction and insulation material used in office buildings and factories, in a quest for materials Borg-Warner might be able to develop and manufacture.

Still another area of high possibility centered around oil fields and oil wells: the petroleum industry was stable and growing, not only in the United States but throughout the world. It was the type of industry Borg-Warner wished to survey and analyze to see where and if their special organization and skills could be of service.

They were interested in air conditioning and in chemicals. The chemical industry was fast growing and they found that the main problem was to determine whether they wished to purchase a chemical company or to expand into chemicals through one of their present divisions, the Marbon Division, for example. (The latter proposal was, in fact, followed with the new $12,000,000 plant built for this division's increasing role in chemical products.)

Another field in which they were interested was electronics. They considered also the recreation field because of the growing amount of leisure time, and the increasing sums spent by the public on recreational equipment.

To implement the diversification two projects were set up: one, to work with divisions and make surveys of products the divisions research and develop within the corporation; the other to explore the possibilities at growth from the acquisition of outside business.

But it was not long after taking over the office of president in 1950 that Ingersoll was aware of a serious problem that had to be resolved if he were going to put his concept of diversification into effect.

As the company had grown, so also had the number of top executives reporting to the president; when Ingersoll took over the office, there were more than 40 reporting to him, including heads of the more than 30 divisions and subsidiaries in Borg-Warner at that time. As more divisions were added, the number reporting to him would increase, unless new procedures were evolved. He could not handle both the multitude of other duties and responsibilities of the job of president and also this mass of routine and detail. He believed that a system of group vice presidents should be set up to whom a large share of this responsibility could be delegated. Each group vice president would have a number of the division heads reporting to him directly.

As a further step he asked Arthur Slade of the management consultant firm of Rogers, Slade and Hill, to aid him by carrying out a survey of personnel needs and other problems of the individual divisions. Slade's report confirmed Ingersoll's views of the need for a new organizational chart, including changes both he and Slade felt had to be made as quickly as possible. Most important of these was the establishment of the group vice president plan.

Ingersoll was determined not to change the decentralized system under which Borg-Warner had developed; he had no intention of allowing the central office to encroach on any of the prerogatives which properly belonged to the division managers. At the same time, he sought to develop a much closer liaison with all divisions of the company, by means of the group vice president plan. Through this liaison the central office could be of greater service to the divisions, consulting with them about specific problems, their plans for new products, their programs for strengthening their own divisional organization, particularly the building of management in depth at every level from the assistant foreman to the top officers of the corporation. In the incentive bonus plan, eventually developed for executives of all divisions, in fact, one of the factors in determining the size of the bonus award was the kind of job the plant manager did in training a man who could become, if required, his own successor.

It was a complex but important program which the new president presented to the board of directors. Aware of its significance to the structure and future of the company, the directors went into this project carefully, examined it in considerable detail and voted their unanimous approval.

But Ingersoll also knew that all of these plans, no matter how carefully evolved, would be less than useless without the men to carry them out, the individual leaders with the talent or vision and ability to put them into effect.

As divisional Presidents there were: at Warner Gear, Swain Russey, an astute Hoosier with a genius for production; at the Mechanics Division, Frank Richard, a human dynamo with a background as a Central Office executive; at Byron Jackson, Andrew Rose, a versatile industrial executive formerly with Warner Gear; at Borg & Beck, Harold Nutt, and at Rockford Clutch, Harry Emerson, both of whom carry on the tradition of their divisions' reputations for efficiency in manufacturing; at Calumet Steel, Howard Davis, experienced in every facet of modern steel making; and many others.

Roy had to build management in depth, at headquarters, as elsewhere in this vast company that served so many needs of the nation and beyond the nation. Certainly one of Ingersoll's most important contributions lay in the remarkable group of individuals he brought in at top management level, men who were to hold in their hands a large part of the future of the company.

17

Case history: Conditioned air

"PLANNED DIVERSIFICATION" was a business concept that allowed no rest, no time for sitting back, no complacency. Borg-Warner, to grow, to stay alive, had to be aware constantly of every new idea, every new stride forward, the changing demands of the public, and every available avenue of response to its needs.

The new world of conditioned air was a case in point.

In the investigation of an industry, a prime question at Borg-Warner is its growth potential. In air conditioning, this was found to be almost limitless.

Air conditioning had become important in America by the mid-1950s, yet the saturation of the market was only 7 or 8 per cent, in contrast to some other appliances, where the saturation figure had reached almost nine per cent.

The eventual markets and uses for air conditioning seemed equally limitless, virtually untouched, and, in some measure, unexplored. For air conditioning meant much more than air cooling. Technically, it is defined as "a process by which temperature, moisture content, movement and quality of the air in enclosed spaces are controlled simultaneously." It means, in other words, cooling, heating, purifying, eliminating noxious odors and cleansing.

These findings, the result of an investigation made at Ingersoll's urging, were presented to the officers and directors of Borg-Warner. They indicated, everyone agreed, that here was a field in which the company's vast reservoir of technical know-how could be of great importance.

The debate which followed centered not on whether the company should get into this fertile field, but on how it could. Should it gather together leading experts and authorities and build its own air-conditioning plants, or should it seek a ready-made firm already producing in this field? It was agreed, finally, that the better way would be to try to buy a company already in the business than to put another, with additional capacity, into the picture, which would take a long time for the necessary development and engineering.

After further careful survey, it was determined that the York Corporation of York, Pennsylvania, might very well be the answer.

The oldest firm in the refrigeration business in America, it had become one of the most important factors in air conditioning as well. Its products had wide public acceptance because of their high quality and their comparative freedom from service problems. And, it was also learned, York needed money for expansion and renovation of its plants to meet the increasing demands for its product. It was possible, therefore, that each company could serve the needs of the other.

There is an undercurrent of the dramatic in the story of York. The company continues to have a lasting influence on our patterns of modern living. Yet when it began—by coincidence in the same year Roy Ingersoll was born—it started, as so many of the Borg-Warner companies have, as a small enterprise with a handful of men and a product or two to manufacture. York had two patents, one on a turbine water wheel, the other on a washing machine and wringer. The plant had 17 machines and some hand tools and employed 14 workers. A few products were added from time to time, and general repair work was also done.

In 1885 this little company accepted a strange assignment. A customer in Mississippi asked it to manufacture and install an ice-making machine. After this first, it made others, but four years later, when P. H. Glatfelter bought the company, he was dubious about continuing this phase of the business.

The next year, however, brought an extremely mild winter, and in the hot summer that followed many parts of the nation began to suffer from an "ice famine." Ice-making machines were suddenly in demand, and by the following year the now enthusiastic Glatfelter had to put on a night shift to fill his orders. That warm winter marked a point of no return. Mechanical refrigeration had arrived.

As York's business in this department grew, it added new plant facilities, laboratories and branch offices. In the early 1900s it was one of the leading manufacturers of refrigeration machinery and compressors in the nation, serving ice-making and cold-storage plants, meat packers, and an occasional forward-looking restaurateur. So reliable were its machines that in 1903 all the ice-machine manufacturers of the nation met in its experimental laboratory and used its equipment to establish a standard for rating compressors.

In 1909, York battled its competition to win a contract from Eastman Kodak, which needed refrigeration for film processing in connection with another new industry that was assuming ever greater importance—motion pictures.

The company continued to pioneer in the refrigeration field. In 1914, it designed, built and installed a system of air washing, ventilating and refrigeration for the Empire Theatre in Montgomery, Alabama—officially the first air-cooling system ever used in a theater.

Ten years later, York installations heated and cooled workers in the world's first fully air-conditioned office building, a ten-story structure built by the San Joaquin Light and Power Company in Fresno, California.

In the 1930s, it won the contract to air condition the Senate Office Building in Washington, D.C., after appearing before a committee of the lawmakers with a full-fledged educational course on its process and its results. The requirements set down by the committee were rigid, but York met them, as one official put it, "with a margin of several degrees of cooling to spare."

The galaxy of "firsts" multiplied in the skies above York. In 1931, the Baltimore and Ohio's *Columbian,* running between Washington and New York, became the first fully air-conditioned train in regular service; York's newly-developed railroad air-conditioning system provided the cooling. Four years later, it installed the first successful "single-room" air conditioner in the the United States—the start of a whole new phase of the business.

In 1938, York installed a 6,000 horsepower air-conditioning plant which cooled, from one central point, the Senate Office Building, the Capitol and the old and new office buildings of the House of Representatives. It was at that time the largest such plant in the world.

Among York products was the first hermetically sealed room air conditioner, the most effective unit yet produced, which they introduced in 1948. Another product was the now world-famous "Automatic Ice Cube Maker," which turns out hundreds of pounds of ice cubes daily.

Installations of this company have ranged from atomic energy plants to the Empire State Building, from department stores and theaters to hundreds of the largest office buildings in the world's greatest cities; from Miami Beach's largest and most exclusive hotels to the 3,000 room Hilton Hotel in Chicago; from the largest heat pumps ever made, for both heating and cooling, in an industrial plant in Bensenville, Illinois, to the air-cooling system on the luxurious American liner, the *S. S. United States*.

Such was the multi-million dollar firm which Ingersoll and Borg-Warner wanted to buy. It was a company whose assets were in excess of $70,000,000, and whose annual gross income was nearly $100,000,000.

Negotiations were conducted between Stewart Lauer, the president of York, and Roy Ingersoll of Borg-Warner, together with their staff associates. There were many issues and many millions at stake. After reaching agreement on a price at which York was willing to sell, Borg-Warner obtained permission to examine all the plants and equipment. It found that while some of the plants were in excellent condition, others were old and inefficient. Despite these "spots" that needed improvement or eradication, the product York had been producing was so good and had such a tremendous reputation for being free from service trouble, that Borg-Warner's directors and officers agreed, following the investigation and report, to go ahead.

The agreement with Lauer was ultimately completed on May 9, 1956. It included the transfer to Borg-Warner of all of York's stock and assets, on the basis of one-half a Borg-Warner share plus $2 in cash in exchange for each share of York Corporation stock. President Lauer agreed to stay on for a year or two to break in whomever Borg-Warner put in as general manager, and the latter firm took over on the first of July, 1956.

Almost immediately a whole series of changes were inaugurated to improve the efficiency of the company, with Ingersoll himself directing much of the streamlining program.

An example of the care and detailed effort which he put into it can be seen in some of his own notes on this changeover:

"One of the things at that plant that I questioned was the foundry. This was a large and modern building and a very efficient foundry, with eight bays, each equipped with a ten-ton overhead crane, and I immediately saw the potential of this if it could be converted from a foundry into an efficient manufacturing plant for the production of the larger air-conditioning units, including the large units of several thousand horsepower.

"I asked the general manager of York to obtain immediately prices of castings from other foundries and discovered that we could buy them as cheaply as we could make them. This would make a fine manufacturing building available and we could move into it much of the manufacturing equipment from the old and obsolete West York plant, which could never be made into an efficiently operative plant and which I insisted must be abandoned as soon as new plant space could be provided.

"An estimate was made of the cost of converting and reconditioning this building on the inside, installing new lighting, equipment, electric power, outlets and new blowers throughout. The foundry was shut down on November 19, 1957, and the renovation of the building was immediately started. This included cleaning out approximately thirty carloads of sand and dirt on the girders, ceilings, walls and floors, and vacuum cleaning and painting every square foot of the factory. This was completed and all of the equipment moved to the plant and put into operation in the summer of 1958, and it is now probably the most modern, efficient plant in the country for manufacturing of heavy duty air-conditioning equipment. . . ."

Where personnel needed to be shifted, changed or replaced, this was done, with consideration for all parties involved, but above all with improvement of operation in mind. When Mr. Lauer retired as president, Ingersoll brought in Henry Haase, then vice president in charge of engineering and research of Borg-Warner, to head up this important new division. A graduate of the University of Wisconsin, Haase was a man of considerable experience in the refrigeration field and had actually headed a refrigeration company for several years.

The major staff that had been built over the years at York remained intact, for a personnel survey showed that it had an efficient, hard working group of employees. A new type of sales organization was launched, however, headed by the youthful but experienced new head of York's marketing services, Austin Rising, formerly general manager of the RCA air-conditioning division.

Following engineering surveys, changes were also made in products and improvements in production techniques to maintain York's high quality while reducing prices wherever they were not fully competitive.

To give the new division a complete line, including a new combination home heating and air-conditioning unit, all the heating products of Ingersoll Conditioned Air division, which had been developed to include air-conditioning units, were shifted to York, to be sold by York distributors throughout the country.

In the fall of 1957, Hasse, with the approval of Borg-Warner, bought the automotive air-conditioning unit manufactured by Lehigh Incorporated—a compressor and components for air conditioning cars which were being sold to a number of major automobile manufacturers. This operation was transferred to the Decatur plant of the Marvel-Schebler Division of Borg-Warner, where the Ford automatic transmission production was closing down with the expiration of that contract.

"When York was merged with Borg-Warner," Ingersoll wrote in his notes, "all of these changes were necessary in order to get the most efficient, economical, low-cost production on every item of air-conditioning equipment York is producing.

"Moreover, these changes were necessary in the long-range planning to make and keep York in the forefront of this large and fast-moving industry.

"In this case at least, it was better to have bought than to have built."

18

Cross section of a world

DINNER HAD BEEN pleasant in the handsome Winnetka home of the Roy Ingersolls. Now, downstairs, in the recreation room, Ingersoll and his guest chatted. Several months previous, the Borg-Warner head had written to E. S. Dulin, the man sitting opposite him, regarding the possible purchase of the company Mr. Dulin headed. There had been previous negotiations on this matter. It was an acquisition effected through an exchange of stock worth many millions of dollars. Dulin had not replied regarding the terms suggested in the letter. Now that he was in Chicago, however, he had called on Mr. Ingersoll.

Business had not been mentioned; this was apparently a purely social call. But in the downstairs recreation room after dinner, Dulin asked him suddenly, "Would Borg-Warner still be interested in going through with that purchase of our company which we talked about a few weeks back?"

Roy told him they were very much interested. He suggested they talk about it further. And there in the recreation room, in this informal way, the two men worked out and shook hands on a deal that involved the acquisition of a company whose total net sales were more than $30,000,000 a year.

Within a few hours, they had not only agreed on terms but had considered the type of press release for announcing the merger if the transaction was approved by the directors of each company. (It took their lawyers weeks of negotiation, however, and 40 pages of clauses, to put the agreement into proper legal form.)

In just such a way did a great modern firm merge with Borg-Warner: Byron Jackson, maker of industrial pumps for use deep in the earth and under the sea, in dams and pipe lines and oil fields, and in the operation of large industrial plants. Borg-Warner also secured—in Ned Dulin—one of the outstanding industrial and business leaders of the West.

Started by Jackson as a youth in the Sacramento Valley in California, in the rough and tumble days of the 1870s, the company was a pioneer in the manufacture of centrifugal pumps. From this beginning its activities ranged wide across the fields of modern industrial development—from oil-field tools to gigantic pumps for great dams and aqueducts, from electronic "fingers" for searching out oil deep in the earth to submersible pumps and others specially engineered for nuclear mechanisms.

In 1930, Byron Jackson designed and installed six 90,000-gallons-per-minute pumps for the Colorado River Aqueduct, which supplies water to Los Angeles, 457 miles away. In 1932, it built the highest "water lift" in the world, pumping a steady supply from the foot of the Grand Canyon up the cliff to the Sante Fe railroad's El Tovar at the top—a distance of 3,150 feet straight up. In 1947, it began the construction of the pumps for the Grand Coulee Dam, largest structure of this type in the world, and for the vital Trans-Arabian oil line. For Grand Coulee the Jackson Company built six enormous pumps, with suction elbows 14 feet in diameter, each lifting 720,000 gallons of water per minute and serving in the irrigation of 1,000,000 acres over an area of 4,800 square miles.

It has supplied tools for the world's deepest oil wells, and pumps for the world's first nuclear-powered submarine, the *U.S.S. Nautilus*. It has developed, engineered, built and installed pumping equipment for most of the electric powered nuclear reactors in the United States. For a commercial atomic power plant near Detroit, Michigan, operated by the Detroit Edison Company, it designed and built the world's largest "liquid sodium pump," 32 feet high and 6 feet in diameter, which delivers 11,800 gallons of liquid sodium per minute at 1,000° F. Less important on a world scale, but more important to Ingersoll in a personal sense, was an incident involving his old home town, Galesburg. The town was about to put in pumps to bring water from the Mississippi River, 36 miles away. City officials were about to place their order with a competitive firm when Ingersoll convinced them they ought to have only the best. Byron Jackson pumps now provide the pressure to bring water into Galesburg from the Mississippi.

Such was the story of one "acquisition" in the tremendous expansion program launched by Borg-Warner under Roy Ingersoll, who became, in 1955, following the death of Charles Davis, not only president but also chairman of the board. There can be no question but that at this time the Ingersoll family and name were a powerful force in Borg-Warner. When Roy Ingersoll in 1956 gave up the presidency he remained chairman of the board and the directors unanimously elected his son Bob to succeed him. Harold Ingersoll, Jr., was executive vice president of the Ingersoll Steel Division at New Castle, and Jim Ingersoll headed up the Ingersoll Products and the Kalamazoo divisions.

Nor can there be any doubt either that Roy Ingersoll put new fire and drive and potential into the Borg-Warner organization. From four auto parts companies with total assets of approximately $10,000,000, Borg-Warner had grown in 35 years to a company of more than 40 divisions and subsidiaries with more than $300,000,000 worth of net assets, working capital approaching $200,000,000 and annual net sales exceeding $600,000,000. Roy Ingersoll made no secret of his goal for the company—a yearly gross sales of $1,000,000,000.

The companies that had come in over the years, in the program of diversification, were indeed a cross section of the modern world. One was the E. C. Atkins and Company, in Indianapolis, from which Roy Ingersoll had first obtained a gleam of an idea regarding the heat treatment of his farm discs. This firm still produces the finest saws and machine knives, saw chains, band saws and similar tools and equipment in the nation. In 1956, four years after it came into Borg-Warner, it celebrated its 100th anniversary, thus becoming the first Borg-Warner division to begin its second century of production in American industry.

The kaleidoscopic pattern of these companies presented an almost fantastic array. In Mansfield, Ohio, the Ingersoll-Humphryes division produced a large variety of cast-iron and pottery bathroom and kitchen fixtures. The Humphryes products complemented the non-competing line of steel bathtubs and sinks manufactured by the Ingersoll Products Division in Chicago. "In consolidating with Humphryes," Division President Jim Ingersoll announced, "we will be carrying forward Borg-Warner's overall program of planned diversification—that is, entry into a few carefully selected industry areas, one of which is the building field."

Yet not every company purchased dated back over decades. Some were new, with their history largely still in the future. Ira Weston, for instance, founded Weston Aero Hydraulics, only in 1939 and joined Borg-Warner only in 1954. Weston was in hydraulic equipment production for use in planes during the war. When Army orders picked up during the war, and Weston lacked funds for expanding his plant, he developed an entirely new technique to meet the large military needs. Parts that were needed were fully engineered at his Los Angeles plant, then a simple but precise set of specifications was drawn up for each part and the actual production of these parts was farmed out to hundreds of small companies in the Los Angeles area, machine shops and individual machinists who might otherwise have been considered "too small" for a government contract. Weston continued to maintain its research and engineering staffs, and its assembly line where the finished product was put together.

By this unique means, Weston Aero Hydraulics not only made use of skilled machinists in these shops but also built an unusual production staff. Out of these, in 1946, Ira Weston built the production force for a new company, called simply Weston Hydraulics, Ltd., successors to Weston Aero Hydraulics. The new company produced hydraulic equipment of many kinds for many of the post-war civilian aircraft companies. Weston was skillful at bringing together an outstanding staff of hydraulic engineers, salesmen and business executives.

This firm still operated in a leased wooden plant that in no way matched the highly-precise accurate equipment Weston produced. Mr. Weston himself used to say that often he would lie awake worrying about a possible fire and destruction of the fine equipment he had installed. Yet, working in this wooden plant, this company established such a high standard of production that by 1950, only five years after the war, it was the only company of its kind in the West authorized to ship its equipment without a government inspector having to be on hand.

With the development of missiles and supersonic flight came new needs. Supersonic aircraft required tons of "muscle" or force to handle the surface controls of the plane. This was obviously beyond human strength. Weston developed what are called "servo-valves," extremely suited to control many of the flight operations through electronic mechanisms.

In 1954 this company came into Borg-Warner, following extensive negotiations conducted by one of Ingersoll's most able associates, Borg-Warner's Executive Vice President Lester Porter.

Products of this company at this time were used in the Constellation, the B47, the Northrop Flying Wing, the F8U, the B55 and many other models and missiles to come in the future.

The need for expansion had been one of the reasons that brought this firm into Borg-Warner; they were still in the wooden building. Mr. Weston at once began looking for a new location in the Los Angeles area. Ingersoll was in Europe in 1957 when he received a telegram from one of the group vice presidents asking his permission to purchase for Weston a tract of 34 acres costing $1,030,000. Ingersoll thought there must be some mistake; two zeros at least must have been added in transmitting the message. But word came back that the figure was right. Ingersoll sent word for them to hold up any action until his return.

He still remembered a little 10-acre tract his father's new company had bought on the outskirts of Galesburg at $200 an acre. On his return to America he went out to Los Angeles and found that the tract of land in North Hollywood was for the most part nothing but a large potato patch. Nevertheless its location was close to the skilled labor force Weston had built, no other similar tract was available, and Weston needed the land for new facilities, particularly in view of the excellent sales and growth of this young division.

For these reasons he gave his approval and the new plant, one of the finest and most efficient in Borg-Warner, began to emerge from the erstwhile potato patch.

In a wholly different field, that of building construction, the Reflectal Corporation, which became a part of Borg-Warner in 1952, turned out such products as *Alfol*, a top-grade aluminum-foil building insulation, *Koolshade*, a product already owned by Borg-Warner, which is a new kind of window screen that keeps out sun and heat. Acquired later and added to Refectal's construction products was a remarkable new insulating concrete known as *Betocel*.

Other new divisions operated in close support of older or

larger divisions: the Warner Automotive Division in Auburn, Indiana, supported Warner Gear in production of transmission gears and similar products, including a new kind of spin-resistant automotive differential which enables motorists to pull out of mud and sand holes, helps to prevent or minimize skidding on curves, and provides forward traction on snow and ice, even when starting up an icy hill. Another was the B-W Acceptance Corporation which was developed by Borg-Warner's executive vice president, Lester Porter, who continues as Chairmen of the Board. The corporation, now headed by James Brown, has a number of offices across the country which finance dealer inventory both for Norge and for York and which also buy consumer paper from franchised dealers.

There were very few jobs in the steel operation which Jim Ingersoll himself did not learn in these first years after the war, as he worked in various departments of the West Pullman plant of Ingersoll Steel, beginning with the Plant Engineering Department, the Industrial Engineering Department and continuing until he was in charge of the Truck Wheel and Disc Departments at the plant.

In addition, he went on the road as an agricultural salesman and then became sales manager for the Ingersoll Products Division. In many of these jobs he was reporting directly to his brother Bob, with whom he worked closely. It was an interesting and unusual "brother team operation" in industry.

In many respects Jim Ingersoll's variety of positions gave him a breadth of experience and training that paralleled the variety of positions his father had held in the beginning days at Galesburg. In 1952 this culminated in his taking over the Kalamazoo plants of the Ingersoll Products Division as vice president and works manager at a moment when these plants were working on vitally important production of the LVT amphibious tank. The Kalamazoo plants were the lead yard for this amphibious craft production for the United States Marine Corps, in charge of all procurement, design and manufacturing not only for their own plant but also for four others involved in this vital work. The program was carried out by young Jim Ingersoll with a smoothness that won praise from leaders in Washington.

In 1954 following this successful assignment, Jim Ingersoll became president of the Ingersoll Products Division in Chicago and of the Ingersoll Kalamazoo plants which also were given individual division status. He was in complete charge of production in these plants of a wide variety of products ranging from wheels and agricultural discs to bath tubs, wash tubs, giant industrial overhead cranes, airplane fuel tanks and other related items.

The variety of products manufactured by the divisions seemed almost infinite. Wherever there was something new developing in industry, Borg-Warner was concerned. The Marvel-Schebler Products Division, for example, was turning out not only carburetors for tractors, trucks, and outboard motors, but also control rod mechanisms for nuclear-powered electric generating plants. In addition, several service and sales divisions had been set up—BJ Service, Inc., of the Byron Jackson Division, the Norge Sales Corporation, and the Borg-Warner Service Parts Company.

Nor was this the full scope of the company's operations. Beyond the seas, Borg-Warner divisions were now reaching into the expanding international markets of the modern world. A division known as Borg & Beck do Brasil S.A. was turning out clutches for South American cars in Sao Paulo; the Borg-Warner International Corporation in Chicago concerned itself with overseas licensing and export of all the corporation's products; Borg-Warner, Limited, in Letchworth, England, made automatic transmissions, torque converters, one-way clutches, chains, and other parts for English automobile manufacturers. Similar items were being turned out by Borg-Warner (Australia) Limited, a Borg-Warner affiliate in Sydney, Australia.

Long Manufacturing and Morse Chain had subsidiaries which were operating in Ontario, Canada; and Byron Jackson had auxiliary plants in Toronto and Mexico City; and York-Shipley's two plants in England.

One of the chief reasons for Borg-Warner's ability to reach out in this great diversity is its highly developed patent department. Under the direction of Carl G. Stallings, its general patent counsel, it has built up a tremendous portfolio of patents in a wide variety of fields. Included in the department is a roster of outstanding patent lawyers, each specialists in particular fields—men like former assistant patent counsel, Joseph M. Gartner, later executive to Roy Ingersoll; Lyle S. Motley and Don Banner, each with the title, assistant general patent counsel with special responsibilities. Among these patents were a number of important processes and devices personally developed by Roy C. Ingersoll on which he obtained patents, which were highly profitable to the corporation.

A company is only as good as its management. This has been one cornerstone of Ingersoll's industrial philosophy. From the time he was commissioned by the board of directors to carry out his plans of growth and expansion, he had done his utmost to select and secure the best man for each post. Division heads were changed or retired or bolstered wherever needed. The rough difficult jobs were handed to tough seasoned executives who had proven themselves. Many came from inside the company, some from the outside. The important question was the job they could do for the corporation.

As Mr. Ingersoll passed more and more responsibility to the group of men he was building around him, it was his concept to select and train men who could do an even more efficient job than he himself had been doing, and he felt very strongly as he watched these men in action that he had succeeded in his plan.

"I do not know of any more capable or efficient group than these younger Borg-Warner executives," he stated in one interview. "This applies equally to the division presidents. They are hard-hitting, capably trained, understanding and dedicated men, and they are performing a tremendous job not only for this corporation but also for America, carrying on the tradition of free enterprise, initiative, vision and courage which has made our country great."

Lester Porter who came in from Calumet was one example of the type of executive Ingersoll wanted. A mid-westerner who went to the University of Illinois, Porter was first hired by Ingersoll in 1934 for the accounting department of the West Pullman plant. Porter did so outstanding a job that Ingersoll shifted him to Calumet the following year, after that plant was brought into the Borg-Warner Corporation. He performed valuable service as treasurer of Calumet, working with Ingersoll and Bruce Caldwell in re-establishing the credit high standards, and productivity of this plant which had been at low ebb at the time of its purchase.

In 1951 Porter was brought in to Borg-Warner headquarters as treasurer of the corporation to succeed Mathew Keck, who had held that position since Borg-Warner's inception but was forced to resign because of his health. Porter rose to become Borg-Warner's executive vice president as well as the president of the B-W Acceptance Corporation. Working in close association with Mr. Ingersoll, Porter helped in the development of many Borg-Warner policies and in active negotiations for many of its acquisitions. One of Porter's great values, as part of Ingersoll's top level team, is his quick grasp of even the most complex business and industrial situations, his ability to put his finger on the key factors involved, and his absolute candor in stating his views, pulling no punches. He is not only a Director of the company (elected in 1955), but he also is on more than 25 supervisory boards of directors, and is one of Ingersoll's closest advisors.

Because of his long-tested ability as a negotiator, Porter is often assigned the job of helping to reach final terms on major acquisitions. It was Porter who negotiated the Weston Hydraulics purchase. Ira Weston and Porter argued out terms for more than a week. The contract had become many pages long, and Porter finally told Weston, "There is a plane at 3 o'clock this afternoon and this deal had better be settled by then, because I am going to be on that plane."

He was on that plane, with the deal completely settled. The relationship between this division and Borg-Warner had been carried on so smoothly that no debatable point has arisen requiring them even to look at that contract since that day.

Another who has played an important role in the company is Robert Murphy, general counsel of Borg-Warner since 1948, vice president since 1955 and chairman of its executive committee since 1957. Murphy was one of the leading figures in helping to build the legal department of the corporation. Like Ingersoll, Murphy was also a graduate of Knox College in Galesburg. He was also a graduate of the Harvard Law School and a member of Phi Beta Kappa.

Murphy came into Borg-Warner through the offices of Gus Shallberg in Moline, where he went to work shortly after his graduation from law school in 1935. Shallberg had been practicing in Moline since 1902, had been city attorney and had followed a general corporation practice. Among his clients, of course, had been George Borg and this had brought Shallberg actively into the Borg-Warner picture as this firm's general counsel.

In 1935, however, he still maintained offices in Moline, in addition to those at Borg-Warner. Murphy called at the Moline office and talked with a partner of Shallberg, trial lawyer Samuel Kenworthy, about getting a job. While they were talking, Shallberg came in, learned why Murphy was there, and promptly announced that the firm needed someone fresh out of Harvard Law who would know all about this rash of New Deal legislations, the Robinson-Patman Act, the Undistributed Profits Act, the Wage and Hour Law, the National Labor Relations Act and other alphabet-agency laws and federal regulations.

Murphy was willing to work free for a time to prove himself but Shallberg insisted on paying him—$100 a month, to start. By 1937, Shallberg was in Chicago at Borg-Warner virtually all the time; Murphy was in Chicago as his aide. Murphy's role became even more important after Shallberg became Borg-Warner's executive vice president. In 1948 Murphy succeeded Shallberg as general counsel of Borg-Warner, when the latter became executive vice president.

If it can be said that Shallberg founded the legal department of this corporation, it should be added that Murphy, building on this foundation, established and shaped the department, organized its remarkable legal library, and developed its program and procedures for handling the complex problems that a corporation of this size and scope faces constantly.

In spite of the tremendous amount of work, Murphy still manages to carry on a number of civic activities, heading up the high school board of his community and being active as chairman of the Government Affairs Council of the Chicago Association of Commerce and Industry. Most of the Borg-Warner executives follow this same pattern of active interest and participation in civic affairs despite the long hours they put in at Borg-Warner.

Gus Shallberg himself, who was a part of the Borg-Warner story from the very start, epitomized the finest type of business lawyer. A man of unfailing judgment and keen wit, he refused to be frustrated by legal technicalities or bad tempers and approached every problem from the practical, human point of view. To a depth of understanding of the law he added a statesmanlike faith, not in legal jargon, but in true basic meaning of American jurisprudence.

As an attorney he helped to form Borg & Beck and had been

with them many years. He had been one of the two or three most active individuals in the formation of Borg-Warner, had been its counsel and a director of the company, and for some years, its executive vice president under Charles Davis. Over the years this man had developed a wisdom and humor combined with his experience. Admired and respected, he continued to be regarded as the elder statesmen even after his retirment on April 19, 1957.

One of the great roles Shallberg played at Borg-Warner was to form the legal department on such a solid basis that he gave the company a tremendous underlying strength in this branch. The legal problems of a large corporation such as this are fantastically diverse, involving every state in the nation, international law and all of the problems of taxation. It was Shallberg who built his department from the earliest days when Borg-Warner, like so many other companies, was only beginning to become used to the vast complex of governmental agencies, new and shifting laws and the thousand and one problems of taxation.

It was Shallberg, tall, usually quiet of tone, often with a quip or joke to lighten a dark moment, whose quiet but astute counsels played a vital role in the growth of Borg-Warner.

Also a key member of this "headquarters team" was Albert Steg, one of the most brilliant young financial and cost control executives, not only at Borg-Warner, but in the country.

Born in Buffalo, New York, in 1909, he was graduated from business school at the age of 16. He then entered public accounting and continued his education at the same time at the University of Buffalo. Following his graduation, he became, at 20, the treasurer of an investment house. In 1934, only 25 years old, he was an assistant comptroller of the Chevrolet Motor Company. Shortly after that, he became for four years an auditor for B. F. Goodrich Company, and then returned to public accounting and became a certified public accountant. In 1941, at the age of 32, he became comptroller of the American Optical Company.

Brought in by Ingersoll, Steg came to Borg-Warner from the American Optical Company in 1953 as comptroller and rose within a few years to become vice president, treasurer and a director. One of Steg's important contributions to Borg-Warner was the development of a new procedure by which divisions and subsidiaries reported not only past sales, costs, inventories and similar data, but also provided a projection of anticipated developments for the year ahead.

In conjunction with this, Steg also evolved a five-year forecast report so that the central office could have a broad picture of future plans, anticipated directions and expected results from each division and subsidiary in Borg-Warner, over both long and short-range periods. The form of these reports has been so carefully worked out that—long-range or short—all the information for an individual report can be put down on a single page.

Representing another type of Borg-Warner executive is Harry Troendly, an engineer who understands the problems, not only from the managerial but also from the technical point of view.

A native of Nebraska and a graduate in mechanical engineering from the University of Nebraska, he came into Borg-Warner in 1940 as founder and general manager of its Spring division in Bellwood, Illinois; his success in operating this division as president and general manager after 1953 resulted in his elevation five years later to group vice president at Borg-Warner.

It is this type of background and experience that Ingersoll sought most in the group vice presidents, for this position is the most important link in the relationship between the divisions and the central office.

Another of the group vice presidents is Stanley J. Roush, who also held an engineering degree—his was from Carnegie Institute—and like Troendly had a wide experience in industry, having started out as a plant and department manager of the United States Glass Company in 1938. He was president and director of the Kerotest Manufacturing Company in Pittsburgh in 1952 when Ingersoll brought him in to be head of the newly-acquired Atkins Saw Division. Two years later, after this division had been fully integrated into the Borg-Warner setup, Roush was asked to take over the presidency of another important Borg-Warner division, Morse Chain. He came in to serve the parent corporation as group vice president in 1958.

At this top management level, one of the most important people in the company was Ingersoll's son, Bob. Roy Ingersoll never spoiled his children. He wanted to help them to develop within themselves stamina and self-reliance. If they got ahead, it would have to be because of their abilities. Bob Ingersoll had risen in Borg-Warner on a basis first of all of performance.

His record in the war, in developing and producing the amphibious tank at Kalamazoo and later as head of Ingersoll Products Division at Chicago led to his becoming administrative vice president of Borg-Warner in 1953, at the urging of Davis, at that time chairman of the board.

Two years later he became a director. In 1956 Bob became president of the company, while Roy Ingersoll remained chairman of the board and chief executive officer. Later, in 1958, Bob received the added assignment of chief executive officer.

Two of the most important of the committees which help to formulate and implement policy at the top level are the Operating Committee and the Corporate Planning Committee. The Operating Committee is charged with advising the chairman of the board and the chief executive officer on general management problems. Corporate planning is concerned with long-range planning and research, technological development, product diversification developments and trends, and support and development of research at universities and by non-profit organizations for the good of industry and the public as well as Borg-Warner itself.

Both committees are responsible for exploration of new possibilities of purchase outside the company, in those circumstances where it appears that such acquisition can be valuable to the company as well as to the public interest, so that it does not in any way curtail competition or concern a product which cannot be researched and developed effectively and reasonably in one of the already operating Borg-Warner divisions. Other committees which function at the corporation's headquarters are the Executive, Finance, Compensation and Pension, Audit, and Patent Committees.

Through the work of these committees, a Policy Manual has been developed which tells much of Borg-Warner's organizational concept. There are meetings at least once a year of the Supervisory Board or Board of Directors of every division and subsidiary. A detailed and standard agenda has been prepared for these meetings which pinpoint for analysis the crucial phases of the divisions' own management. Statements as to long-range goals for operations, markets, sales and profits are required, and a five-year forecast is analyzed in detail. There are tough questions to be answered by division management as to research and development, new products and customers, and an analysis of manpower requirements over the next five years.

Roy Ingersoll recognized the importance of a favorable public acceptance of Borg-Warner, its people and its products. But he also believed that this acceptance must be deserved. Therefore the corporation itself and its top executives became prominently identified with worthy organizations and activities at state and national levels. All employees were encouraged to be good citizens by taking part in civic activities in their plant communities. And Borg-Warner's products—to quote Roy Ingersoll's maxim

—were "finely engineered, efficiently produced and sold at the lowest possible price consistent with a fair profit."

The public was kept informed of the corporation's products and activities through advertisements that today are familiar to readers of national magazines everywhere and through widely distributed communications to the world press. Roy Ingersoll personally took a deep and active interest in the development of Borg-Warner's public relations plans. At his right hand was a seasoned journalist, Donn Sutton, as Director of Public Relations and Advertising. Sutton had previously been executive editor of the worldwide Scripps-Howard newspaper feature syndicate, editor of daily newspapers, a foreign correspondent in peace and war time, a drama critic and a magazine writer.

Under his guidance, this department, through a wide variety of information media, brought home to the American public in many ways the unique story of this complex corporation and the multitude of services it renders to the public through its many diverse products.

The job of running a great company has many aspects—and headaches. From 1928 until 1955 this company, Borg-Warner, and a number of its subsidiary headquarters had been located at 310 South Michigan Avenue in Chicago. Then, because of the expansion plan of the insurance company that owned the building, they had to move. They were given only until April, 1958, to find new space. Almost at the same time that they received this information, however, the real estate firm of Collins, Tuttle and Company, of New York, came to Borg-Warner with a proposition. Collins, Tuttle wanted them to be the major tenants of a new building at 200 South Michigan that would become the Borg-Warner Building. Office space would be built to their specifications. It was an answer immediate and welcome. General Counsel Murphy was authorized at once to proceed with negotiations.

In the spring of 1958 Borg-Warner was able to move into these magnificent new quarters with modern York air-conditioned offices, handsome meeting rooms, a board of directors room, and a roof terrace with a sweeping view of Lake Michigan. There is also a large exhibition hall on the ground floor, where more than 40 divisions and subsidiaries present exhibits demonstrating Borg-Warner's variety of products and research. Connected with this hall is a small theater seating 75 people, which is available free for outside group meetings, as well as divisional meetings and special events.

Both Ingersoll and his son Robert took an active part in the planning and development of this exhibition hall, said to be one of the largest and most complete operated by a private company.

Roy Ingersoll stated that no small amount of the success of Borg-Warner must be credited to the "outside directors" who have given so unsparingly of their time and their business knowledge in developing the company's policies.

Paul H. Davis, the man who helped to put the original four companies together, was one of these. His continuous service since 1928 on the Board in many important capacities included chairmanship of the Compensation and Audit Committee as well as membership on a number of other vital committees.

In addition to Davis, there were many more of the "old timers." Among these were William P. Hemphill, director from 1929 to 1959; Philip D. Armour, director from 1936 to 1952 and chairman of the Finance Committee from 1939 to his retirement from the Board in 1952; George B. Dryden from 1932 to the present; Frank C. Ball from 1928 to 1943, succeeded by George Ball from 1943 to 1951.

The membership on the Board by a member of the Ball family was continued at the death of George A. Ball in 1951 by his nephew, Edmund F. Ball.

Although in each division, as well as at headquarters, every executive was expected to develop and train a substitute who could step into his shoes in case of emergency, in not every case was this possible. Sometimes new men had to be brought in from the outside.

In addition a steady flow of young trainees is also a part of Borg-Warner's personnel policy of building for the future. Working with universities and engineering schools, S. G. Gregory, Borg-Warner's Director of Personnel Services, and his assistant, Carl Brick, developed a highly effective recruiting program bringing in talented young graduates, engineers and young scientists from many sections of the country. They also set up a "trouble shooting" service which helped with the personnel problems as they arose in an individual plant. Management in depth calls for continuous training at all management levels.

Ingersoll had seen vast expansion, and many changes, in direction and purpose and approach. Many of the older men whom he had known and worked with in the tumultuous early days of automobiling had died, or retired or turned to other pursuits. George Borg had left the company, although he stayed on for many years as a director.

Just as World War II was beginning, in 1939, a man who owned a small radio manufacturing company came to Borg at a desperate moment. They had a chance for big government orders, he and Paul Davis, who brought him to Borg's Chicago office, explained. But they needed capital. Borg listened; the project seemed too small, actually, for him to be deeply interested. Finally, Paul Davis shrugged. "Well, I should have known better than to try to get two Swedes together in a business deal."

Borg laughed and turned to the man with Davis, "Paul didn't mention that you were a Swede."

"I am," the man said, "and a hell of a lot better Swede than you are."

Borg flushed and then, as if to disprove this, grinned, again picked up a pen, drew a checkbook from his desk and wrote out two checks—one for $25,000 which bought him a half interest in this company, and another for $10,000, which was a loan and was repaid in less than a year.

With its new financing, the firm did extraordinarily well during the war, making such items as walkie-talkies and inter-tank communication systems. By peace time it was one of the leading producers of radio electronic equipment. George was in the plant once and attended two board meetings of the company.

In the mid-1950s at a Borg-Warner board of directors' meeting, George Borg was telling about how he had sold out his interest in this company. He passed around a slip of paper showing what he had received, by way of a return on his original $25,000 investment. It was a check for $2,500,000.

They had known victories and defeats, these men who had started out at much the same time, at the dawn of a century. And they had known losses too. For Roy Ingersoll one of the heaviest had been the death of his father, in 1936, his mother, in 1944, and twelve years after that, the loss of his brother Steve. The "kid brother" of the family had done well in the world of steel and had risen through the New Castle operations to become president of the Ingersoll Steel Division, succeeding his brother Harold, who had asked for retirement. He was handling this post brilliantly when he fell ill in 1956 and died after an illness of only a few weeks. And Charles Davis, Roy's friend and predecessor, had died in Paris in 1954.

There had been many changes, and moments of grief and of loss for Roy Ingersoll, as well as moments of victory.

But the changes that had come to Ingersoll over the years, the personal tragedies and triumphs of his life, the long years of unremitting work and the success in industry that made him one of the great industrial leaders of his time—none of this changed his basic concepts, his untrammeled faith in freedom for all people, his belief in the right of a man to scale as high as his ambition and personal effort, his ability and his vision, can take him.

Never anti-labor or anti-union, he nevertheless has dared to speak out on many occasions against the corruption of some labor leaders and the fact that many unions have become so undemocratic that they have denied their workers many basic and essential rights, under the guise of protecting those very rights. He has dared to speak out against labor racketeering even when such statements were considered highly unpopular. It is true, it is something that should be said—and so, in his opinion, born of his ingrained sense of freedom and honesty, it must be said.

"Week after week, in strike after strike," he declared in one address in Los Angeles, "we see positive evidence that the Big Union Bosses do not practice the democracy that they preach. I can tell you that today the managers of scores of strike-bound plants throughout the country are receiving letters from their employees begging to return to work and for the opportunity to ballot secretly in order to demonstrate their wishes. I venture to say that in the great majority of strikes of any considerable duration, most of the striking workers, if they were permitted a secret ballot, would vote to accept their employers' offers rather than to allow their union leaders to force them into long, needless periods of idleness.

"Please let me go on record now as saying that I am no 'union baiter' . . . The present peril to our national well-being does not lie in unionism as such. The root of the trouble is un-curbed labor monopoly, which was accentuated by the Wagner Act and only slightly curbed by the Taft-Hartley Act."

They were sound and thoughtful words. But it was a con-tinuing battle and the gains were slow and hard. Early in 1959, as the Senate considered a labor reform bill to curb racketeering and unfair practices of some unions, Ingersoll wrote personally to every United States Senator, urging as a private citizen that they vote strong legislation to eliminate the corruption and unfair practices of some labor leaders and unions —practices that were proving so harmful to the American people and to the members of the unions themselves.

"I am terribly concerned," he stated, "about the possibility that the Senate of the United States may ignore the need for proper labor reform legislation. . . . This country needs now:

"1. Legislation to curb union corruption.

"2. Legislation to make unions the servants, not the masters of the American working man.

"3. Legislation to stop secondary boycotts, coercive picketing, and hot cargo clauses, which the McClellan hearings have shown to be so unfair to business and the working man and the tool of racketeers and unfair labor leaders.

"The issue before the Senate is whether any group in America shall continue to be allowed to trample on the rights of its members and engage in activities contrary to the national interest. Present union practices and conditions inside unions are completely inconsistent with the political and social traditions that are the basis of our American democratic system and way of life."

Ingersoll's sympathy for the working man is deep-rooted in his own life and ideas. He knows the hopes and ambitions of these men, not just for themselves but for their families and children. He worked with them over many years, he knows what it is to work long hours at a machine, for he did it, ten hours a day. No one was more anxious than he to see laboring conditions bettered each year. But he is against labor racketeering, secondary boycotts, labor violence, compelling men to join a union against their will; he is against featherbedding in all forms, against the employment of union funds, paid in by workers, for the benefit of any one political party, and against the un-democratic and un-American practice of preventing the union member from voting by secret ballot on all major union measures, including the calling of a strike.

He believes that the American workman is entitled to basic American freedoms.

19

Quest for tomorrow

IN THE RESIDENTIAL and commercial community of Des Plaines, some 20 miles northwest of the heart of Chicago, the laboratory arises, new and gleaming, with its test tubes and wires and electronic computers. Here are weird shaped mechanisms, modern laboratory instruments and tools, designed to probe the essence of new metal alloys and plastics, to range the whole world of physics, chemistry, aerodynamics, thermodynamics, electronics, machinery and materials to serve mankind in an age of tremendous speeds and undreamed of problems. For the array of Borg-Warner divisions and subsidiaries, this is a pioneer post, the front line of the future, assisting on specific problems and performing original research into the unknown.

This unique center of research, working in a hundred fields all at once, has been named in honor of the man who probably did most to bring it into creation—the Roy C. Ingersoll Research Center of Borg-Warner Corporation.

Few honors that he has received have meant as much to Roy Ingersoll as this one. For the laboratory is not merely a building of glass and steel; for him it looms as an enduring symbol, a memento of the past he helped to shape and a link with the future which will carry on the task, probing into areas still unexplored and into worlds unguessed.

At the bottom of the bronze plaque of Roy Ingersoll at the laboratory are words taken from one of Ingersoll's speeches:

"Tremendous as are the accomplishments of our research laboratories today in spearheading industrial growth and bettering the living standards of our people, we can be certain that these will be dwarfed by technological achievements of tomorrow. . . . May Borg-Warner, through the efforts of the dedicated men and women of this Research Center, make its full contribution to the building of an even stronger and increasingly dynamic America."

In his seventy-fifth year, he works as hard as ever, plays as hard, laughs as hard, loves the battle and the victory as much as ever.

Change has been the pattern of his life. As he walks through this laboratory in Des Plaines, he looks not at yesterday but at tomorrow. Here he finds scientists trained in the best universities and technical schools; experts in areas beyond the imagination of our forebears.

Here is the "house of hot and cold"—two air-tight rooms where air conditioning, cooling, purifying and humidifying are tested. One day the room may be freezing; the next, torrid.

Here is an electron microscope which "sees and photographs" the otherwise invisible structure of materials.

Here, in the polymer laboratory, chemists develop and test the durability, heat resistance, and adhesive qualities of new plastic compounds for new uses to which they are put today.

In another room steels and new plastics are being "fingerprinted" by means of spectroscopy, to determine and record the chemical combinations of atoms in the material. The pattern of each substance varies, it has been found, just as do the fingerprints of every individual.

Ingersoll wanders through these rooms and laboratories and testing places. Here is a chain held taut; how long will it take under given stress and vibration to pull the links apart?

Here is an automatic transmission set up to undergo the worst conditions a car could conceivably ever have to travel, over bumps, up hill and down, for days and even weeks; what has happened to it and to the individual parts after such a "journey?"

Here are scientists who have spent months on tests involving juicy tenderloin and sirloin steaks, with occasional thick lamb chops thrown in. It was their job, as scientists who happened to have especially good olfactory perception, to report on the permeation and strength of the cooking odors involved in broiling these steaks over various Norge cooking appliances.

The tests explored the effectiveness of certain air-conditioning equipment in reducing cooking, smoking and other odors. "Air conditioning is not merely getting rid of heat or humidity," laboratory officials explain. "It is also getting rid of a hundred odors, or even chemical substances, that may be irritating or harmful to humanity. One day the contamination of air in our great cities, for example, may be completely eliminated by proper air-conditioning systems. We do not know yet. We are on the edge of such discoveries."

These are the same scientists who helped Norge develop and perfect its famous vertical broiler in Norge's gas and electric stoves.

Here is the laboratory of electronics, where other scientists develop servomechanisms, remote control devices for the handling of radioactive material from points beyond the danger zone, mechanically or electronically controlled "slave" fingers made of steel or plastics. Here are instruments that dig into the earth and report back the nature of the strata a mile or more below.

In the "furnace room" of this laboratory materials are worked under heat and vacuum conditions. In the heat treatment area of the metallurgical laboratory are low-temperature drying ovens, and a furnace which reaches a temperature of

5,000° F. In the "materials analysis and research" laboratories are facilities for probing metals, polymers, protective coatings and organic and inorganic mixtures. Utilizing the electron microscope to obtain photographs magnified 100,000 times, this laboratory is one of the most complete in the world for the examination of basic matter.

Many of the new and only partially developed products first discovered in these laboratories are carried to successful completion by the expert engineering and development departments of the individual divisions.

The incredible variety of the laboratory reflects the incredible variety of the company it serves. These scientists, who at times work in the realm of abstract investigation, ranging beyond the borders of fact or accepted theory, are nevertheless working for a corporation which produces materials to fill the needs of millions of people. Their investigations deal with the materials that will produce for tomorrow better and more difficult materials that go into and improve airplanes, homes and automobiles and nuclear power plants and electronic tubes, missiles, and bathtubs, refrigerators and clothes washers, tractors and fence posts and giant pumps.

These, and other things as yet undiscovered and undreamed of, merge and form and take shape in the "Roy C. Ingersoll Research Center of Borg-Warner Corporation" in Des Plaines, Illinois.

Important honors and tributes came to him. In 1958, on the 50th anniversary of his beginning his full-time work at the Galesburg plant, he had been given a celebration at the Borg-Warner offices. Leaders of many fields gathered to pay him tribute.

In 1959, in his seventy-fifth year, the things he remembered and appreciated most were extraordinarily simple as he looked back over those three-quarters of a century. They were his family, the friendships that he had built and his associates with whom he had worked and with whom he had shared so much in the years at Borg-Warner. These were the important and worthwhile things. These were the warm realities that gave unusual meaning to the long years of work.

He was also deeply proud of the success of his sons, of the fact that both Bob and Jim were recognized and respected for their capabilities and accomplishments. In many ways in his sons he saw life repeating its pattern. Both took an active role in many civic groups, Bob was president of Winnetka's Board of Education, helped direct the Sunday school and is a trustee of the Congregational Church and of Chicago University. He was proud of all his children and of the fourteen grandchildren they had given to Mrs. Ingersoll and him. They were leading worthwhile lives and were carrying on the work that had been started by their grandfather.

Perhaps the deepest realization that came to him was the span of change through which he had lived, from the era when he had watched the oxen and Conestoga wagons to these days of missiles and jets. Jets literally have annihilated space. He and his son Bob and other Borg-Warner executives fly to Europe now in approximately the same time it used to take to fly to California.

Roy had lived through an almost unbelievable number of changes, had seen so many new developments come into being: airplanes, radio, television, mechanized farming, almost magical new home appliances, television and turbojets, electronics, atomic power, the beginnings of the exploration of space, plus fantastic new developments in the fields of communication and transportation, thermo-plastics and other new materials.

He had seen whole techniques of production and agriculture change. He had seen this country put on wheels. He was aware both of the promise and the dangers that lay in the future. Perhaps never before, he believed, had mankind had such opportunity, in so many diverse directions, to advance beyond the frontiers of present knowledge, to explore the unknown and to lift the standards for all human beings.

Yet he also saw the dangers of weakness and possible disaster in the growth of ideas alien to our traditions and freedom: the welfare state, cradle-to-grave security programs, the danger of destroying the individual's initiative by too much reliance on government instead of on himself for all his needs and protection. He saw the future as a great still-unopened book of promise—and his prayer was that mankind would not lose the opportunities by turning instead to the shopworn but still dangerous socialist theories of those who would forfeit our freedom.

Ahead he saw peril and hope. "The next seventy-five years," he told an interviewer in the spring of 1959, "will depend on and be shaped by the course we follow as individuals. If we surrender to the lines of communism, to the false doctrines of socialism and welfare-stateism we will plunge ourselves as a nation over the cliffs. In that way lies only ruin for our country and our ideals, ourselves and our families. If the government continues to spend far beyond its revenue and labor continues to demand and secure wage increases far beyond increases in productivity, then I am fearful that savings, pensions and insurance will be destroyed by the flames of inflation which would be a disaster second only to being swallowed up by communism as Krushchev has predicted."

But he stated that he has confidence in America and the American people, once they are given the facts on the dangers that lie ahead. "If we cling instead to the tested ideals of freedom, these years can be the most fruitful and exciting of history. Untold wonders lie ahead in every field of endeavor. It can be a magnificent adventure for mankind—these next seventy-five years—if we hold to our belief in independence, in the individual and his worth and his responsibility in the tried and tested ways of freedom."

This is Ingersoll's view of the future—in his seventy-fifth year. At the same time he remains as practical and realistic as always in his outlook toward business, society and our economic life.

"We must all realize and appreciate our interdependence on each other," was the way he said it at a recent annual stockholders' meeting. "It is industry's obligation to make profits which can and should be used to pay its shareholders a proper return for the use of their money, and to continue to improve its productivity.

"It is industry's obligation to its employees to pay fair wages and to provide clean, safe and well-lighted factories, equipped with the most efficient machinery that can be justified. In addition, it is industry's obligation to plan for new products and for the improvement of the present ones so that they may merit the greater confidence of customers, who in turn will use more of those products.

"There is the obligation of the workman to use these tools efficiently and to give an honest day's work for an honest day's pay; to co-operate with his fellow employees and his supervisors to effect all savings possible, thereby helping to insure the continuation of the company's business and the security of the employees' jobs.

"And it is the obligation of the community to provide the very best educational and recreational and other facilities that make for better and more pleasant living conditions—and also for the community to plan, just as industry must, for future growth. . . ."

There are good years, and bad, in all industrial activity. The year 1958 was one of recession, and Borg-Warner's earnings reflected the drop in general business levels. Yet diversification kept this company strong even through a period of somewhat curtailed national income, and by the end of the first half of 1959, Ingersoll was delighted to be able to report to the stockholders that the corporation in the first six months of this year had the highest sales and profits ever achieved in any comparable six months in the corporation's history.*

The information was particularly welcome to Ingersoll in this anniversary year.

But he gives the full credit for this outstanding achievement to the younger executives and to the division presidents and their staffs who are shaping and carrying out the sound and forward-looking policies which he had so considerable a part in developing. He has high praise, too, for the thousands of Borg-Warner supervisors and loyal employees who have made great individual and collective contributions to the success of Borg-Warner.

The remarkable rebounding strength of the company was a high tribute to the policy of diversification, to the development of new products, to the ability to shift emphasis from one field to another.

To Roy Ingersoll as chairman of the board this was the application also of a philosophy that he had never forgotten in the long years of his rise in American industry. It was his basic fundamental faith in action which he had learned half a century before from the bearded banker of Norwalk, Ohio, John Gardiner: "Don't cry over spilt milk. Go out and get yourself another cow."

---

* For the first six months of 1959: net sales, $327,803,597; earnings after taxes, $18,290,376. Projected capital expenditures in 1959: $23,000,000.

APPENDICES

BORG-WARNER CORPORATION
Chicago, Illinois

Founder & Successor Presidents	Dates of Incumbency	Name at Founding	Changes in Name & Date
**Founded by Merger		Motor Units Corporation (5/10/28–6/5/28)	Borg-Warner Corporation June 5, 1928
George W. Borg	6/5/28 to 3/22/29		
Charles S. Davis	3/22/29 to 4/28/50		
Roy C. Ingersoll	4/28/50 to 4/27/56		
Robert S. Ingersoll	4/27/56 to Present		

**Group of Companies Merged at Founding

BORG-WARNER CORPORATION—CORPORATE HISTORY AND GROWTH

Name	Date Acquired or Date of Change in Name	Products	1st Pres. or Mgr. Before and after Acquisition or Change (A) Indicates President Prior to Acquisition Only	Sales Full Year Prior to Change
**Borg & Beck Company (Became Borg & Beck Division 1/1/35)	June 5, 1928	Auto Clutches	George W. Borg	$3,838,494
**Warner Gear Company (Became Warner Gear Division 1/1/35)	June 5, 1928	Auto Transmissions	R. P. Johnson, Sr.	4,975,102
**Marvel Carburetor Company (Became Marvel-Schebler Products Division 8/1/36)	June 5, 1928	Auto Carburetors	J. R. Francis	4,381,295

Company	Date	Products	Name	Sales Figure
**Mechanics Machine Company (Became Mechanics Universal Joint Division 1/1/35)	June 5, 1928	Auto Universal Joints	E. S. Ekstrom	4,542,504
Galesburg Coulter-Disc Company (Became Ingersoll Products Division 11-21-50)	Jan. 10, 1929	Farm Implement Discs		6,004,804
(Galesburg Coulter-Disc Company was the successor to the Sandoval Manufacturing Company which was founded by S. A. Ingersoll in 1884 in Sandoval, Illinois. The business was moved to Galesburg, Illinois in 1904 and the name was changed to the Galesburg Coulter-Disc Company.)				
Long Manufacturing Co. (Became Long Manufacturing Division 1/1/35)	Feb. 13, 1929	Auto Clutches and Radiators	J. L. Dryden	5,885,301
Morse Chain Co.	April 10, 1929	Auto Timing Chains, Sprockets, Industrial Chain	Frank L. Morse	5,708,607
Rockford Drilling Machine Company (Became Rockford Clutch Division 1/1/35)	May 17, 1929	Industrial Clutches, Machine Tools	E. C. Traner A) Levin Faust	1,121,800
Borg-Warner Service Parts Company	July 31, 1929	Auto Parts Sales Organization	Mathew Keck	(Created Company)
Norge Corporation and Subsidiary, Detroit Gear & Machine Co. (Norge Corp. became Norge Division 1/1/35)	Aug. 22, 1929	Refrigerators, Gears and Transmissions	H. E. Blood	3,762,000
(Detroit Gear merged with Long Manufacturing Division July 1, 1956)				
Chicago Rolling Mills, Inc.	Feb. 11, 1930	Rolled Steel Products	R. C. Ingersoll (A) Stephen L. Ingersoll	(No Sales Figure Available)

277

Name	Date Acquired or Date of Change in Name	Products	1st Pres. or Mgr. Before and after Acquisition or Change (A) Indicates President Prior to Acquisition Only	Sales Full Year Prior to Change
(Purchased by Borg-Warner Corp. for Galesburg Coulter-Disc Co. so it could serve some of its customers more economically than at Galesburg.)			(Minutes of a special directors meeting of the Galesburg Coulter-Disc Co., Feb. 11, 1930 state that: "said rolling mill has never been operated except for test purposes and is not now engaged in the manufacture of steel products for any customers..")	
Ingersoll Steel & Disc Co. (The Galesburg Coulter Disc Co. and the Indiana Rolling Mill Co. which had been family owned, were consolidated Dec. 17, 1927 under the name of Galesburg Coulter-Disc Co. Ingersoll plants at Galesburg, New Castle and Chicago were combined under the name of Ingersoll Steel & Disc Co.)	Feb. 27, 1930	Farm Implement Discs, Specialty Steels	R. C. Ingersoll	(Created Division)
Detroit Vapor Stove Company (Consolidated with Norge Division)	Aug. 29, 1934	Gas Ranges	H. E. Blood (A) A. G. Sherman	$2,146,117
Borg-Warner International Corporation	Oct. 5, 1934	Foreign Licensing and Export for Borg-Warner Products	R. W. Gifford	(Created Company)
Marsene Corp. (Purchased from the George W. Borg Corp. became Marbon Chemical Division 1/1/54)	Oct. 16, 1934	Transparent Film	W. P. Hemphill (A) G. W. Borg	(No sales figures reported until 1936)
Calumet Steel Company (Became Calumet Steel Division 1/1/37)	June 10, 1935	Rolled Frame & Reinforcing Bars	R. C. Ingersoll (A) J. H. Porter	1,140,950

278

Name	Date	Product	Officers	Value
Norge Heating & Conditioning Div. (After World War II this division was reorganized and renamed Norge Heat Div. with C. S. Davis, Jr. as President and consolidated with Ingersoll Conditioned Air Div. 1/1/54.)	Aug. 30, 1935	Domestic Heating & Air Conditioning Equipment	H. E. Blood	(Created Division)
Long Manufacturing Company Limited	Dec. 31, 1936	Auto Clutches	J. L. Dryden	(Created Company) 972,672
United States Pressed Steel Products Co. (Was immediately consolidated with Ingersoll Steel & Disc Div.)	Jan. 11, 1937	Automotive and Farm Implement Parts and Furnaces	R. C. Ingersoll (A) C. V. Brown	
Warner Automotive Parts Division (Became Warner Automotive Parts Division 2/3/38 and Warner Automotive Division 1/1/58)	Dec. 31, 1938	Auto Replacement Gears and Other Parts	R. L. Allison	(Created Division)
Warner Gear Company Limited	Dec. 31, 1938	Synchronizer Units for Passenger Cars and Trucks	C. S. Davis	(Created Company)
Pump Engineering Service Corp. (Became Pesco Products Div. 1/1/47)	April 18, 1939	Hydraulic, Fuel and Air Pumps and Electric Motors for Aircraft	D. E. Gamble (A) W. S. Jack	2,001,334
Spring Division	Dec. 31, 1940	Automotive Springs	D. E. Gamble	(Created Division)
Superior Sheet Steel Division — Formerly a Subsidiary of Continental Steel Corp., Kokomo, Indiana (Operations ceased July 15, 1949 and plant was sold)	Dec. 2, 1946	Steel Sheets	R. C. Ingersoll (A) D. A. Williams	5,453,000
Franklin Steel Company (Became Franklin Steel Div. 5/1/47)	July 30, 1947	Rolled Steel, Flats, Rounds, Angles, Fence Posts, Concrete Reinforcing Bars	R. C. Ingersoll (A) S. J. Walker	1,191,329

BORG-WARNER CORPORATION—CORPORATE HISTORY AND GROWTH (CONTINUED)

Name	Date Acquired or Date of Change in Name	Products	1st Pres. or Mgr. before and after Acquisition or Change (A) Indicates President Prior to Acquisition Only	Sales Full Year Prior to Change
Ingersoll Products Division (Formed out of Ingersoll Steel & Disc Division to operate Ingersoll plants in Chicago, Illinois and Kalamazoo, Michigan.)	Nov. 21, 1950	Auto & Farm Implement Parts, Washing Machine Tubs, Sinks and Bathtubs	R. S. Ingersoll	$30,300,171 (Total Sales, 1950, for Ingersoll plants in Chicago and Kalamazoo)
Ingersoll Steel Division (Formed out of Ingersoll Steel & Disc Division to operate the Ingersoll Steel mill at New Castle, Indiana)	Nov. 21, 1950	Specialty Steels, Saw Steel, Forging Ingots, Shovels, Steel Sheets & Plates	H. G. Ingersoll, Sr.	7,494,956 (Total sales, 1950, of Ingersoll Steel mill in New Castle, Indiana)
Reflectal Corp.	April 1, 1952	Insulation	Robert S. Ingersoll (A) J. D. Giles	1,232,903
E. C. Atkins & Company (Became Atkins Saw Division 9/1/52)	Sept. 1, 1952	Saws for Industrial and Home Use	Stanley J. Roush (A) Elias C. Atkins	9,992,874
Wooster Division	Oct. 15, 1952	Hydraulic Fuel & Air Pumps & Electric Motors for Aircraft	Robert J. Minshall	(Created Division)
B-W Acceptance Corporation	Sept. 3, 1953	For the Purpose of Financing Norge Appliances	L. G. Porter	(Created Division)

Marver-Schebler Transmission Dept. (Transmission production was completed in September 1958 and the plant became the Decatur Works of York Division after being converted to the manufacture of air conditioning equipment.)	July 1, 1954	Automatic Transmissions	R. C. Ingersoll	
Weston Hydraulics, Ltd.	Aug. 1, 1954	Hydraulic and Pneumatic Equipment for Aircraft and Missiles	Ira E. Weston	5,770,948
Ingersoll Kalamazoo Division	Dec. 7, 1954	Amphibious Landing Vehicles, Boosters for Guided Missiles, Materials Handling Equipment	J. H. Ingersoll	(Created Division)
Ingersoll Conditioned Air Division (Ingersoll Kalamazoo and Ingersoll Conditioned Air Divisions were created to operate the Kalamazoo Plants of Ingersoll Products Div. Ingersoll Conditioned Air was transferred to York Div. Dec. 31, 1958)	Dec. 7, 1954	Heating & Air Conditioning Equipment for Homes, Water Heaters, Incinerators	J. H. Ingersoll	(Created Division)
Borg-Warner Limited (Successor to the Morse Chain Company Limited which was founded in 1919 and was acquired May 10, 1929 as part of the assets of Morse Chain Company)	Dec. 17, 1954	Automatic Transmissions, Overdrives, Automotive Timing Chains & Sprockets, Roller Chain & Sprockets, One-Way Clutches, Torque Converters	F. S. Mitman (A) Noel Mostyn	(Created Division)
Norge Sales Corp.	Dec. 24, 1954	Sales Organization for Norge Appliances	J. S. Sayre	(Created Company)

BORG-WARNER CORPORATION—CORPORATE HISTORY AND GROWTH (CONTINUED)

Name	Date Acquired or Date of Change in Name	Products	1st Pres. or Mgr. before and after Acquisition or Change (A) Indicates President Prior to Acquisition Only	Sales Full Year Prior to Change
Brooks Equipment & Manufacturing Company (Company liquidated Sept. 9, 1955 and operations consolidated with Ingersoll Kalamazoo Division)	Mar. 14, 1955	Materials Handling Equipment	James H. Ingersoll (A) E. N. Brooks	$1,156,256
Byron Jackson Company and Subsidiaries: Byron Jackson of Canada Ltd. Byron Jackson Co. S.A. BJ Service, Inc. (Became Byron Jackson Div. 9/1/55)	Sept. 1, 1955	Pumps, Oil Tools, Rubber Products, Oil Field Services, Electronic Instruments	E. S. Dulin E. S. Dulin E. S. Dulin E. S. Dulin	30,978,665
Primor Products, Inc. (Consolidated with York Division 12/31/58)	Dec. 31, 1955	Air Conditioning Systems	James H. Ingersoll (A) Gorton F. Price	1,797,489
Eberhardt-Denver Co. (Consolidated with Morse Chain Co.)	Feb. 6, 1956	Speed Reducers	Stanley J. Roush (A) F. R. Eberhardt	2,026,676
Morse Chain of Canada, Ltd.	March 15, 1956	Automotive Timing Products	Stanley J. Roush	(Created Company)
Industrial Crane and Hoist Company (Consolidated with Ingersoll Products Div.)	May 31, 1956	Industrial Cranes and Hoists	James H. Ingersoll (A) Paul W. Pearson	2,708,482
Borg & Beck do Brasil, S.A.	June 7, 1956	Automotive Clutches	M. W. Simonsen	(Created Company)

Company	Date	Products/Services	Officers	Sales
...R Corporation (Became York Division 7/1/56) and subsidiary: York Shipley, Limited	July 1, 1956	Air Conditioning & Refrigeration Equipment	Henry M. Haase (A) S. E. Lauer Rowland Burnstan (A) C. B. Morrison	82,713,623 (Includes sales of York-Shipley Ltd., English subsidiary)
Humphryes Manufacturing Company (Became Ingersoll-Humphryes Division Aug. 1, 1956)	Aug. 1, 1956	Bathroom and Kitchen Fixtures	James H. Ingersoll (A) D. J. Jones	6,577,753
Chemical Process Co. (Consolidated with BJ Service, Inc.)	Oct. 1, 1956	Oil Field Services	John B. Merritt (A) C. K. West	7,583,611
Coote & Jorgensen Ltd. (Became Borg-Warner (Australia) Limited)	April 1, 1957	Automotive and Tractor Transmisssions and other Automotive Industrial Parts	G. V. Patrick (A) B. O. Smith	3,859,000
Cello Products Limited	Sept. 25, 1957	Plumbing Fittings	T. J. Ault (A) H. W. Lee	1,239,046
BJ Service of Canada, Ltd.	May 29, 1958	Oil Well Cementing and Formation Testing	G. M. Davis	(Created Company)
Byron Jackson N.V. (A subsidiary in Etten en Leur, Holland. Construction of plant is to be completed in 1959.)	Feb. 16, 1959	Oil Tools	E. M. Rees	(Created Company)

BORG-WARNER CORPORATION—FINANCIAL DATA

	1929	1930	1940	1950	1955	1958
Sales	$54,175,818	$37,360,000	$75,163,241	$330,924,422	$552,192,430	$533,033,188
Capital Employed	34,233,222	33,004,065	43,601,008	146,029,804	244,715,812	330,035,067
Net Worth	31,839,887	30,724,536	41,745,128	143,491,134	235,284,562	307,876,800
Profits A/T	6,684,504	2,318,120	6,730,462	29,027,224	41,075,784	21,135,260

TEN YEAR SUMMARY

BORG-WARNER CORPORATION

Financial Statistics:

(Millions of Dollars)										
	1958	1957	1956	1955	1954	1953	1952	1951	1950	1949
Net Sales	$533.0	$608.5	$598.6	$552.1	$380.3	$407.3	$353.9	$369.1	$330.9	$252.3
Net Income	21.1	34.0	35.8	41.0	24.4	23.9	22.9	21.2	29.0	22.0

Appendix B

AMERICAN MOTORS CORPORATION
Detroit, Michigan

Founder & Successor Presidents	Dates of Incumbency	Date of Founding	Name at Founding	Changes in Name & Date
Charles W. Nash (F)*		1916	**Nash Motors Co.	Nash-Kelvinator (Jan. 1, 1937)
Charles W. Nash	1916-1930			

American Motors Corp.
(May 1, 1954)

Earl H. McCarty	1930–1937
George W. Mason	1937–1954
George W. Romney	1954–Present

*Founder

**HISTORICAL SUMMARY: Incorporated in Maryland, July 29, 1916, under the name of Nash Motors Company; successor to Thomas B. Jeffery Company, founded by Thomas B. Jeffery (1845-1910), which first built two experimental Rambler automobiles in 1901 designed by Charles T Jeffery, son of the founder. These first two Ramblers underwent months of tests but were never marketed because Jeffery considered them too radical. However, in 1902 the first Rambler offered for sale was a one-cylinder model known as the "runabout" and 1,500 of these cars were sold in the first year. After twelve years of building automobiles and trucks under the name Rambler, the Thomas B. Jeffery Company in 1914 renamed their product "Jeffery," to honor the founder, who had died four years earlier.

In August of 1916, Charles W. Nash resigned as president of General Motors to purchase the Thomas B. Jeffery Company and bring out a car under his own name. In the summer of 1917, Nash changed the nameplate on the Jeffery car to bear his name for the first time but this was not a Nash-designed car. The first Nash-designed car with a six-cylinder valve-in-head engine was introduced in the fall of 1917. In 1918 Nash built more trucks than automobiles, 11,000 trucks being built for the U.S. Army.

1920—June, Nash Motors Company expanded its assembly operations to include Milwaukee. Previously, Kenosha, Wisconsin, operations had been the sole producer.

1928—138,138 units produced; considered up until that time a record production year in the 26-year history of Nash Motors Company. This record was not surpassed until 21 years later.

1934—Nash produced its 1,000,000th car and at that time Charles W. Nash was chairman of the board and Earl H. McCarty was president.

1937—January 4, Nash Motors Company merged with the Kelvinator Corp. of Detroit to form Nash-Kelvinator Corp. George W. Mason became president and Charles W. Nash was chairman of the board.

1948—Charles W. Nash died on June 6 at eighty-four and on June 30 George W. Mason became chairman of the board and president of Nash-Kelvinator Corp.

1950—On April 18, the two-millionth Nash came off the Kenosha assembly line.

1954—On May 1, 1954, Nash-Kelvinator Corp. and Hudson Motor Car Company were merged to form American Motors Corp., with George W. Mason as chairman of the board and president. A. E. Barit, retiring Hudson president, became a director and consultant. George Romney was named executive vice-president. At the time of the merger Nash and Hudson had built more than 6,000,000 passenger cars.

Upon the untimely death in October, 1954, of Mr. Mason, George Romney became chairman of the board and president on October 19, 1954. George Romney joined Nash-Kelvinator Corp. in 1948 as assistant to the president; in 1950, he became a vice-president; in 1954, the executive vice-president and a member of the board of directors.

NOTE: Before the formation of American Motors on May 1, 1954, the predecessor companies built 6,300,000 cars and approximately 25,000 trucks. Since May 1, 1954 and through the end of the 1959 model year (which will be in August) American Motors will have built 925,780 cars and no trucks.

AMERICAN MOTORS CORPORATION—CORPORATE HISTORY AND GROWTH

Name	Date Acquired	Products	President or Manager at Time	Sales Full Year Prior to Change
Nash Motors***	Jan. 1, 1937	Autos	—	—
Kelvinator Corp.***	Jan. 1, 1937	Home Appliances	—	—
Kalamazoo Stove & Furnace Co. (Stove & Range Business)	Jan. 26, 1952	Stoves and Ranges	—	—
Altorfer Bros. Co. (Controlling Interest)	Sept. 1952	Laundry Equipment		
Hudson Motor Car Co.	May 1954	Autos	A. E. Barit	$192,846,000

***Merged into Nash-Kelvinator Corporation

AMERICAN MOTORS CORPORATION—FINANCIAL DATA

	1917	1920	1930	1940	1950	1955	1958
Cars Produced in U.S.	6,561	35,084	54,729	52,995	189,543	161,790	217,332
Sales	$16,761,795	$57,185,766	$52,140,109	$73,489,574	$427,203,107	$441,127,272	$470,349,420
Capital Employed	—	—	—	—	134,550,014	157,998,138	147,514,024
Net Worth	7,466,134	17,531,837	47,609,126	40,006,531	114,550,014	143,998,138	137,514,024
Profits A/T (Loss)	2,027,784	7,007,471	7,601,164	1,505,151	28,836,326	(6,956,425)	26,085,134

AMERICAN MOTORS CORPORATION

Financial Statistics:
Source: Moody's

	1958	1957	1956	1955	1954	1953	1952	1951	1950	1949
					(Millions of Dollars)					
Net Sales	$470.3	$362.2	$408.4	$441.1	$400.3 B	$478.6	$358.4	$401.1	$427.2	$364.1
Net Income	26.0	(11.8)	(19.7)	(6.9)	11.0	14.1	12.6	16.2	28.8	26.2

Unit Sales of Cars:
Source: Ward's

	1958	1957	1956	1955	1954	1953	1952	1951	1950	1949
Nash	0	3,561	17,842	51,315	29,371 A	135,394	152,141	161,209	189,543	142,592
Hudson	0	1,345	7,182	26,623	28,840 A	76,331	76,348	93,327	143,006	142,462
Rambler	217,332	109,178	79,166	83,852	37,779	(Rambler introduced in 1954)				
Total	217,332	114,084	104,190	161,790	95,990					

A. Hudson Motor Car Company merged into Nash-Kelvinator 5/1/54 to form American Motors and production shown of Hudson for years 1949 thru 1953 is for Hudson Motor Car Company only; production shown for Nash for years 1949 through 1953 is for Nash-Kelvinator Corporation only.

B. May 1, 1954 through 1958 includes Hudson Motor Car Co. sales and net income; years 1949 to May 1, 1954 Nash-Kelvinator Corporation sales and net income.

CHRYSLER CORPORATION
Detroit, Michigan

Founder & Successor Presidents	Dates of Incumbency	Date of Founding	Name at Founding	Changes in Name & Date
Dodge Bros. Mfg. Co.				
John Dodge F*	1901–1920	1901	Dodge Bros. Mfg. Co.	Dodge Division of Chrysler Corp. (1928)
Horace Dodge (F)*	1901–1920			

CHRYSLER CORPORATION (CONTINUED)

Founder & Successor Presidents	Dates of Incumbency	Date of Founding	Name at Founding	Changes in Name & Date
Dodge Bros. (Cont'd)				
Operated by Heirs of Dodge Bros.	1920–1925		Note: Manufactured Auto Parts until 1914 when First Dodge Car was Produced	
Sold to Dillon, Read & Co. for $146,000,000	1925–1928			
Sold to Chrysler Corp. (See Historical Note)	1928			
Chrysler Corp.				
Walter P. Chrysler (F)*		June 6, 1925 as a Delaware Corporation to acquire properties and business of Maxwell Motor Corp., a West Virginia corporation, organized in 1921 which previously had acquired properties of Maxwell Motor Company, Inc., and stock of Chalmers Motor Corporation.	Chrysler Corp.	
Walter P. Chrysler	1925–1935			
K. T. Keller	1935–1950			
L. L. Colbert	1950–Present			

*Founder

HISTORICAL NOTE: Walter P. Chrysler started as a journeyman machinist in 1895 and later became a superintendent of motive power of the Chicago Great Western Railway until 1910; a works manager of Buick Motor Car Company from 1910; within five years was president and general manager until 1917; vice president in charge of manufacturing of General Motors which brought him into contact with William C. Durant then president of General Motors, and an attempt to retire at 45 years of age in 1919. Chrysler had chafed under the inactive life of retirement and while he was still actively reorganizing Willys-Overland in 1920, at a salary of $1,000,000 per year, various interests joined in bringing out a plan for reorganizing Maxwell-Chalmers, which company had failed through over-extension of production during the period immediately after World War I and for other reasons. Walter P. Chrysler was appointed Chairman of the Maxwell-Chalmers Managing and Reorganization Committee, and the new Maxwell, a West Virginia corporation, took over operations.

At this time Walter P. Chrysler had an idea for a new car with a high compression engine and worked with three automotive engineers named Fred M. Zeder, Owen Skelton and Carl Breer who later formed the nucleus around which Chrysler Corporation eventually built its engineering division. These engineers and their assistants moved into the vacant Chalmers plant early in 1923 (production of Chalmers cars had been discontinued shortly after the first of that year) and went to work in utmost secrecy. The car was ready to show in January 1924 but was not yet in production; 32,000 Chrysler Sixes were sold in 1924—then a record first year's sales for a new car.

In 1925 under a voluntary plan, the Maxwell Motor Corporation transferred its business and property to a new company, the present Chrysler Corporation, which was founded in June 1925, and the Maxwell car was superseded by a new four-cylinder Chrysler and by the fall of 1925 both the old Chalmers plant on East Jefferson Avenue in Detroit and the Maxwell plant in Highland Park were turning out Chrysler cars. That year, too, the new company bought plant facilities (later known as the Kercheval plant) just across the way from the East Jefferson plant for making auto bodies.

On May 6, 1928 De Soto was introduced.
In June 1928 Plymouth was introduced.

On July 2, 1928 Chrysler Corporation purchased Dodge Brothers Manufacturing Company and its properties with 1,253,557 shares of Chrysler common stock, then at about $80.00 per share in the market, and also assumed the Dodge notes amounting to $59,000,000.

Late in 1953 Chrysler Corporation purchased principal automotive plants, machinery and equipment of the Briggs Manufacturing Company, auto body manufacturers, for $35,000,000 and $27,000,000 for inventory. More than 30,000 Briggs employees transferred to Chrysler Corporation payrolls and the organization was called the Automotive Body Division of Chrysler Corporation.

1925–1958—Chrysler U. S. Unit sales of cars and trucks totaled 24,746,276; U. S. truck production for years 1928–1958 totaled 2,514,420.

CHRYSLER CORPORATION—CORPORATE HISTORY AND GROWTH

	Name	Date Acquired	Products	President or Manager at the Time	Sales Full Year Prior to Change
Chrysler Corp. {	Dodge Bros. Mfg. Co.	1928	Autos	Dillon, Reed & Co.	NA
	Switzer-Cummings Co.	1945	Heating & Cooling Equipment	—	—
	Briggs Mfg. Co.	1953	Auto Bodies		

CHRYSLER CORPORATION—FINANCIAL DATA

	1910	1925	1930	1940	1950	1955	1958
Autos & Trucks Produced in U.S.	—	137,668	269,023	1,044,290	1,441,423	1,579,215	696,819
Sales	—			$744,561,239	$2,190,693,425	$3,466,222,350	$2,165,381,754
Capital Employed	—				514,281,849	777,073,402	945,280,066
Net Worth	—				514,281,849	652,073,402	691,280,066
Profits A/T (Loss)	—			37,802,279	127,876,791	100,063,330	(33,824,565)

TEN YEAR SUMMARY

CHRYSLER CORPORATION AND ALL WHOLLY-OWNED SUBSIDIARIES

Financial Statistics:	1958	1957	1956	1955	1954	A 1953	1952	1951	1950	1949
						(Millions of dollars)				
Net Sales	$2,165	$3,565	$2,676	$3,466	$2,072	$3,348	$2,600	$2,546	$2,190	$2,084
Net Earnings	(33.8)	120	20	100	18	75	78.6	71.9	127.8	132.1
Unit Sales of Cars and Trucks:										
Plymouth	387,617	684,475	495,285	814,578	426,888	650,509	474,836	621,013	569,871	574,447
Dodge	134,627	326,732	251,835	332,484	171,015	298,544	422,390	488,360	454,418	444,746
De Soto	38,043	117,179	105,823	134,305	73,321	128,418	97,558	120,412	126,664	105,846
Chrysler	54,237	122,980	102,178	168,901	99,727	149,944	120,678	162,916	164,697	141,241
Imperial	13,488	37,916	12,351	13,393	5,456	9,304	(Included with Chrysler)			
Dodge & Fargo Trucks	68,807	92,669	110,405	115,554	107,362	107,864	162,871	169,115	125,773	151,513
Sub-Total Cars and Trucks	696,819	1,381,951	1,077,877	1,579,215	883,769	1,344,583	1,278,333	1,561,816	1,441,423	1,417,793

B Simca Cars and Trucks   7,280

Grand Total   704,099

A-Excludes sales of wholly-owned foreign subsidiaries
B-Sold subsequent to September 30, 1958
Sources: Chrysler Annual Reports; Moody's; Ward's

FORD MOTOR COMPANY
Dearborn, Michigan

Date of Founding	Name at Founding	Changes in Name & Date
July 16, 1903	Ford Motor Co. (Incorporated in Michigan)	Ford Motor Company (Incorporated in Delaware July 9, 1919)*

Founder & Successor Presidents	Dates of Incumbency
Henry Ford (F)*	
Alexander Malcomson (F)*	
John S. Gray (F)*	
John F. Dodge (F)*	
Horace E. Dodge (F)*	
James Couzens (F)* and six other men (F)*	
John S. Gray	1902–1906
Henry Ford I	1906–1919
Edsel B. Ford	1919–1943
Henry Ford I	1943–1945
Henry Ford II	1945–Present

*Founders

HISTORICAL NOTE: Henry Ford, born July 30, 1863 at Springwells township farm, Wayne County, Michigan, began experiments in 1889 on an internal combustion engine and worked through 1893, at which time he developed a two-cylinder gasoline engine and completed his first car at 58 Bagley Avenue, Detroit, Michigan in 1896. On August 20, 1902 an agreement for partnership was signed by Henry Ford I and Alexander Malcomson, a Detroit coal dealer, under the style of Ford and Malcomson to bring an auto upon the mar-

FORD MOTOR COMPANY (CONTINUED)

ket. This partnership was the predecessor of the Ford Motor Company incorporated on June 6, 1903 having $150,000 in capital stock; $100,000 issued; $28,000 paid, twelve stockholders; Mr. Ford being named vice president and chief engineer, received one-quarter of stock for the car design. The first car, a two-cylinder Model A, sold July 23, 1903 and in 1904 Ford was the first manufacturer to mount engine longitudinally with frame; also first to use torque tube drive. In 1906 Henry Ford I succeeded John S. Gray as president of the company and acquired 58-1/2% of the stock and in 1908 the Model T was introduced, the first production model with left side steering.

1915—December 10th, first 1,000,000th Ford car was built.
1919—January 1st, Edsel B. Ford succeeded Henry Ford I as president.
1919—July 9, Ford Motor Company reorganized as a Delaware corporation with capitalization of $100 million.
1919—July 11, Henry Ford I and Edsel B. Ford became sole owners of the company. The total cost of the transaction to Ford was:

Holder	No. of Shares	Purchase Price
Dodge Brothers	2000	$ 25,000,000
John W. Anderson	1000	12,500,000
Gray Heirs	2100	26,250,000
H. H. Rackham	1000	12,500,000
James Couzens	2180	29,308,857.90
Rosetta Hauss	20	262,036.67
Total	8300	$105,820,894.57

This transaction would make the total value of all shares, with Ford's, about $255 million, which most stockholders regarded as considerably less than their actual worth.

1927—May 26, 15,000,000th Ford car built—last Model T—Model A introduced.
1931—April 14, 20,000,000th Ford car built.
1932—March 9, first Ford V-8 built.
1938—October 8 Mercury production started.
1943—May 26th Edsel B. Ford died and Henry Ford I re-elected president on June 1st.
1945—September 21 Henry Ford II named as president.
1947—April 7 Henry Ford I, 83, died at his home in Dearborn, Michigan.
1954—Thunderbird added to line.

292

1955—June 24th, 20,000,000th V-8 engine built by company since 1932.
1956—January 17th Ford Foundation sold 10,200,000 shares of the 53,461,470 outstanding shares of stock to the public at $64.50 per share for a total price of $657,900,000. Total amount of Ford shares held by the Ford Foundation after the public sale was 36,148,620.

1956—July 21st the Lincoln and Continental Divisions consolidated.
1956—On November 19 new Edsel car announced.
1957—September 4 new Edsel car introduced to the public.
1957—December 15th, 25,000,000th V-8 engine produced.
1958–1903—Produced 40,709,126 passenger cars and 8,562,647 trucks; total 49,271,773 units in U. S.

FORD MOTOR COMPANY—CORPORATE HISTORY AND GROWTH

Name	Date Acquired	Products
Lincoln Motor Co.	2/4/22	Autos
Fordson Coal Co.	Organized 2/7/23	Coal Mines
Ford International Division	Organized 1949	Technical Advice to Foreign Affiliates
12 European & Egyptian Companies formerly held by Ford of England	1950	Autos
Dearborn Motors, Inc. (Farm & Tractor Section)	July 1953	Farm Equipment
Aeronutronic Systems, Inc.	Organized 5/10/56	Weapons Systems

10 YEAR SUMMARY OF FACTORY SALES FROM U.S. PLANTS
FORD MOTOR COMPANY

	1958	1957	1956	1955	1954	1953	1952	1951	1950	1949
Ford car**	1,038,492	1,522,196	1,373,135	1,763,659	1,395,576	1,180,552	775,307	902,343	1,185,823	841,623
Edsel car	28,953	50,393	—	—	—	—	—	—	—	—
Mercury car	129,304	274,908	246,540	435,012	256,429	318,693	195,322	238,613	333,663	203,846

10 YEAR SUMMARY OF FACTORY SALES FROM U.S. PLANTS (CONTINUED)

	1958	1957	1956	1955	1954	1953	1952	1951	1950	1949
Lincoln car***	27,147	37,308	48,665	40,885	35,794	41,865	32,215	25,188	35,536	32,987
Passenger cars, total	1,223,896	1,884,805	1,668,340	2,239,556	1,687,799	1,541,110	1,002,844	1,166,144	1,555,022	1,078,456
Trucks, total	242,906	339,400	295,517	373,639	303,380	315,398	235,450	319,848	342,220	245,372
Passenger cars and trucks	1,466,802	2,224,205	1,963,857	2,613,195	1,991,179	1,856,508	1,238,294	1,485,992	1,897,242	1,323,828

**Includes the Thunderbird.
***Includes the Continental.

10 YEAR SUMMARY OF PRODUCTION FOR FOREIGN MARKETS
FORD MOTOR COMPANY AND FOREIGN SUBSIDIARIES

	1958	1957	1956	1955	1954	1953	1952	1951	1950	1949
Passenger cars										
U.S. exports	29,602	38,986	38,969	58,366	46,401	40,038	38,819	39,453	24,719	27,047
England	284,081	241,260	227,236	241,502	210,155	160,575	93,499	93,381	98,972	78,725
Canada	90,151	109,889	119,598	137,644	102,540	124,185	82,913	79,371	94,161	72,868
Germany****	111,976	67,254	64,872	58,456	42,631	35,888	30,693	27,065	24,443	11,109
Total passenger cars	515,810	457,389	450,675	495,968	401,727	360,686	245,924	239,270	242,295	189,749
Trucks										
U.S. exports	36,753	46,867	46,198	43,030	43,470	33,745	37,991	45,619	37,474	26,653
England	74,485	55,248	57,064	65,398	41,946	43,474	38,671	41,551	43,891	39,693
Canada	15,348	24,258	29,268	28,066	20,041	31,441	49,277	39,485	34,865	39,262
Germany****	16,556	20,035	21,274	21,924	15,839	8,121	9,704	8,095	5,373	6,248
Total trucks	143,142	146,408	153,804	158,418	121,296	116,781	135,643	134,750	121,603	111,856
Tractors										
U.S. exports	1,319	2,788	3,051	5,856	6,845	6,372	7,663	13,324	11,241	16,205

England	58,518	46,114	40,991	48,872	45,689	29,575	30,444	35,868	42,275	33,375
Total tractors	59,837	48,902	44,042	54,728	52,534	35,947	38,107	49,192	53,516	49,580
Total passenger cars, trucks and tractors	718,789	652,699	648,521	709,114	575,557	513,414	419,674	423,212	417,414	351,185

****Adjusted. Taunus station wagons on passenger car chassis reclassified as passenger cars.

FORD MOTOR COMPANY — FINANCIAL DATA

	1910	1920	1930	1946	1950	1955	1958
Sales	—	—	—	$894,500,000	$3,029,500,000	$5,594,000,000	$4,130,339,499
Capital Employed	—	—	—	723,000,000	1,213,200,000	1,941,700,000	2,430,132,032
Net Worth	—	—	—	714,400,000	1,155,300,000	1,868,200,000	2,141,634,576
Profits A/T (Loss)	—	—	—	($8,100,000)	260,300,000	437,000,000	95,742,238
Unit Sales in U.S. Including Export							
Passenger Cars	32,053	419,517	1,158,677	705,966	1,555,022	2,239,556	1,223,896
Ford Trucks	—	43,934	272,897	203,097	342,220	373,639	242,906
Total	32,053	463,451	1,431,574	909,063	1,897,242	2,613,195	1,466,802
**Tractors	—	67,329	—	35,742	97,956	66,656	46,315
Production for Foreign Markets, Including Export							
Passenger Cars	—	—	—	102,193	242,295	495,968	515,810
Trucks	—	—	—	118,362	121,603	158,418	143,142
**Tractors	—	—	—	25,290	53,516	54,728	59,837
Total	—	—	—	245,845	417,414	709,114	718,789

Sources: Ford Annual Reports; Moody's; Ward's.

TEN YEAR FINANCIAL SUMMARY

FORD MOTOR COMPANY AND CONSOLIDATED SUBSIDIARIES

Financial Statistics:

	1958	1957	1956	1955	1954	1953	1952	1951	1950	1949
					(Dollar amounts in millions)					
Net Sales	$4,130.3	5,771.3	4,647.0	5,594.0	4,062.3	4,211.3	2,640.2	2,741.8	3,029.5	2,249.4
Net Income	$ 95.7	282.8	236.6	437.0	227.8	165.8	116.9	126.1	260.3	177.1

**Tractor production began in 1917 when 254 Fordsons were produced; rose to 67,329 in 1920, dropped to 36,783 in the depression of 1920–1921 (during this period also there was the move to the Rouge, when tractor production was suspended for six months) but rose to 68,985 in 1922 and climbed to a peak of 101,898 in 1923. In February, 1928, tractor manufacture in the United States was abandoned and the greater part of the production machinery at the Rouge was shipped overseas; however, tractor production was resumed in the United States, in 1939.

GENERAL MOTORS CORPORATION
Detroit, Michigan

Founder & Successor Presidents	Dates of Incumbency	Date of Founding	Name at Founding	Changes in Name & Date
(See Historical Notes)		1897	Olds Motor Vehicle Company	General Motors Co. Sept. 16, 1908
George E. Daniels	Sept. 1908–Oct. 1908			General Motors Corporation
William M. Eaton	Oct. 1908–Nov. 1910			(Incorp. October 13, 1916)
James J. Storrow	Nov. 1910–Jan. 1911			
Thomas Neal	Jan. 1911–Nov. 1912			
C. W. Nash	Nov. 1912–June 1916			
W. C. Durant	June 1916–Nov. 1920			
Pierre S. DuPont	Nov. 1920–May 1923			
Alfred P. Sloan, Jr.	May 1923–May 1937			
Wm. S. Knudson	May 1937–Sept. 1940			

C. E. Wilson   Jan. 1941–Jan. 1953

Harlow H. Curtice   Feb. 1953–Sept. 1958

John F. Gordon   Sept. 1958–Present

HISTORICAL NOTE: R. E. Olds completed his first successful Oldsmobile in 1897. Five years later Henry M. Leland founded Cadillac, and in 1903 Buick Motor Company was formed from a predecessor firm established by David Buick. In 1907 Edward M. Murphy organized the Oakland Motor Car Company in Pontiac, the four firms, which joined G. M. within months after its incorporation on Sept. 16, 1908, became the nucleus of the company later known as General Motor Corporation.

1902—Cadillac Automobile Company organized.

1903—Buick Motor Company organized.

1907—Oakland Motor Company (predecessor of Pontiac Motor Division) organized.

1908—Fisher Body Company organized and Buick and Oldsmobile joined G.M.

1909—Oakland and Cadillac joined G.M.

The first exclusive parts manufacturing unit to join G.M. (in 1910) was Jackson-Church-Wilcox—forerunner of the Saginaw Steering Gear Division. It was followed in the same year by the Champion Ignition Company, now A.C. Spark Plug Division.

1911—Chevrolet Motor Company organized. Acquired by G.M. in 1918.

1916—G.M. organized as a Delaware corporation.

1918—United Motors Corporation became affiliated with G.M. and included the Dayton Engineering Laboratories, Remy Electric, Klaxon, Harrison Radiator, Jaxon Steel Products, Hyatt Roller Bearing, New Departure and United Motors Service companies.

Fisher Body joined General Motors in 1919 and other parts supplier units were added in subsequent years including what are now the Delco Appliance, Guide Lamp, Inland Manufacturing, Moraine Products and Packard Electric Divisions.

Other major fields in which G.M. acquired or developed companies producing non-automotive products are, as follows: household appliances, Diesel engines and locomotives, and aircraft engines and propellers.

1925—Yellow Truck and Coach Manufacturing Company organized, with General Motors Truck as a subsidiary and General Motors Corporation holding a large interest.

1926—Pontiac car introduced by Oakland.

1930—Electro-Motive Company of Cleveland acquired by G. M.

1940—25,000,000th G.M. United States made vehicle produced.

1954—50,000,000th G.M. United States made vehicle produced.

1908-1958—General Motors Corporation produced in the United States a total of 60,104,704 passenger automobiles and 12,530,231 commercial vehicles (trucks and coaches) in the United States.

297

GENERAL MOTORS CORPORATION—CORPORATE HISTORY AND GROWTH

Name	Date Acquired	Products
Chevrolet Motor Co.	May 2, 1918	Autos
*United Motors Corp.	Dec. 31, 1918	Auto Parts
Fisher Body Corp. (Majority Interest)	1919	Bodies
Fisher Body Corp. (All Assets)	June 30, 1926	Bodies
Vauxhall Motors, Ltd.	1925	Autos
Yellow Truck & Coach Co.	9/30/43	Trucks & Coaches
Adam Opel A.G. (Majority Interest)	March 1929	Autos
Allison Eng. Co.	May 1929	Auto Parts
Fokker Aircraft Corp.	1929	Airplanes
(Later changed to North American Aviation Corp.)		
North East Electric Co.	Oct. 1929	—
Winton Engine Co.	June 1930	Engines
Adam Opel Co. (Minority Interest)	1931	Autos
Sunlight Electrical Mfg. Co.	April 1, 1933	Electric Motors
Electro-Motive Corp.	Organized 1935	Diesel Locomotives
Engineering Projects, Inc.	1940	Airplane Propellers
Euclid Road Machinery Co.	Sept. 1953	Road Machinery

*United Motors Included the following:
Dayton Engineering Laboratories
Remy Electric
Harrison Radiator
Klaxon
Jaxon Steel Products
Hyatt Roller Bearing
New Departure
United Motors Service Companies

GENERAL MOTORS CORPORATION—FINANCIAL DATA

	1917	1920	1930	1940	1950	1955	1958
Sales in Dollars	$96,295,741	$567,320,603	$983,375,137	$1,794,936,642	$7,531,086,846	$12,443,277,420	$9,521,965,629
Capital Employed					2,670,898,529	5,010,455,043	5,751,326,392
Net Worth	14,294,482	37,750,375	151,098,992		2,387,379,115	4,255,055,724	5,016,839,689
Profits A/T				195,621,721	834,044,039	1,189,477,082	633,628,076
Unit Sales to Dealers in U.S. Canada Including Overseas Shipments	1919						
Passenger Cars	368,338	353,033	997,937	(see tables below)			
Trucks	23,400	40,042	160,356	" " "			
Total	391,738	393,075	1,158,293	2,025,213	3,992,298	5,030,994	3,310,493
Unit Sales United States							
Passenger cars	(Included in Table Above)			—	3,046,593	3,977,686	2,179,847
Trucks & Coaches	" " "			—	606,765	498,986	346,398
Total					3,653,358	4,476,672	2,526,245
Unit Sales Canada & Overseas Cars & Trucks	(Included in Table Above)			55,353	338,940	554,322	784,248
Total Unit Sales All Sources	391,738	393,075	1,174,115	2,080,566	3,992,298	5,030,994	3,310,493

299

GENERAL MOTORS CORPORATION AND CONSOLIDATED SUBSIDIARIES

TEN YEAR SUMMARY

Financial Statistics:

	1958	1957	1956	1955	1954	1953	1952	1951	1950	1949
	(Millions of dollars)									
Net Sales	$9,521.9	10,989.8	10,796.4	12,443.2	9,823.5	10,027.9	7,549.1	7,465.5	7,531.0	5,700.8
Net Income	633.6	843.5	847.3	1,189.4	805.9	598.1	558.7	506.1	834.0	656.4

Sources: G. M. Annual Reports; Moody's; Ward's

UNIT SALES OF CARS AND TRUCKS TO DEALERS AND OVERSEAS SHIPMENTS

TEN YEAR SUMMARY

Sales of Cars and Trucks
Manufactured in the United States

PASSENGER CARS	1958	1957	1956	1955	1954	1953	1952	1951	1950	1949
Buick	258,394	407,546	535,315	780,237	536,894	481,557	315,301	405,880	554,326	397,978
Cadillac	126,087	152,660	140,340	153,134	122,144	104,999	95,420	104,601	109,515	82,043
Chevrolet	1,263,690	1,519,340	1,619,578	1,821,695	1,421,476	1,477,382	871,503	1,124,846	1,517,609	1,106,051
Oldsmobile	310,909	390,305	433,061	642,156	431,462	323,361	224,684	286,452	397,884	282,734
Pontiac	220,767	341,875	334,628	580,464	372,051	413,060	274,177	345,234	467,259	333,398
TOTAL passenger cars	2,179,847	2,811,726	3,062,922	3,977,686	2,884,027	2,800,359	1,781,085	2,267,013	3,046,593	2,202,204

TRUCKS AND COACHES

Chevrolet	280,302	352,562	351,032	392,193	328,102	361,848	329,086	431,010	492,002	381,591
GMC	66,096	72,890	93,787	106,793	83,823	113,026	123,258	129,644	112,557	86,677
Other	—	—	—	—	4	1,353	968	1,823	2,206	2,422
TOTAL trucks and coaches	346,398	425,452	444,819	498,986	411,929	476,227	453,312	562,477	606,765	470,690
TOTAL U.S.	2,526,245	3,237,178	3,507,741	4,476,672	3,295,956	3,276,586	2,234,397	2,829,490	3,653,358	2,672,894
Sales of Cars and Trucks Manufactured in:										
Canadian Plants	186,625	181,322	184,981	161,374	153,808	219,413	199,763	186,996	158,805	91,503
Overseas Plants:										
Holden	110,626	94,557	68,893	63,800	54,796	44,175	31,945	25,177	20,113	7,725
Opel	312,873	228,736	205,605	186,999	164,117	110,164	83,282	77,594	72,568	40,058
Vauxhall	174,124	143,573	123,643	142,149	130,951	110,141	79,813	77,877	87,454	84,168
TOTAL Overseas Plants	597,623	466,866	398,141	392,948	349,864	264,480	195,040	180,648	180,135	131,951
TOTAL Canada and Overseas	784,248	648,188	583,122	554,322	503,672	483,893	394,803	367,644	338,940	223,454
TOTAL SALES all sources	3,310,493	3,885,366	4,090,863	5,030,994	3,799,628	3,760,479	2,629,200	3,197,134	3,992,298	2,896,348

STUDEBAKER-PACKARD CORPORATION
South Bend, Indiana

Founder & Successor Presidents		Dates of Incumbency	Name at Founding	Date of Founding	Changes in Name & Date
(See Historical Note)					
Henry Studebaker F*			Feb. 1852 H. and C. Studebaker	Feb. 1852	Studebaker Bros. Mfg. Co. (1868)
Clement Studebaker F*					Studebaker Corp. (1911)
Henry Studebaker	Partnership	1852–1858	Manufactured wagons, buggies		Studebaker-Packard Corporation October 1, 1954
Clement Studebaker			and parts therefor		
Clement Studebaker	Partnership	1858–1868			
John M. Studebaker					
Clement Studebaker		1868–1902			
John M. Studebaker		1902–1911			
Frederick Fish		1911–1915			
A. R. Erskine		1915–1933			
H. S. Vance					
P. G. Hoffman	Receivers	1933–1935			
A. G. Bean					
Paul G. Hoffman		1935–1948			
Harold S. Vance		1948–1954			

STUDEBAKER

HISTORICAL NOTE, STUDEBAKER: Henry and Clement Studebaker founded the company as a partnership in February 1852 building wagons and operating a blacksmith shop. In 1868 the Studebaker Brothers Manufacturing Company was organized from H and C Studebaker with three stockholders: Clement E., John M. and Peter E. Studebaker. In March 1911, when the company entered the automobile business, the Studebaker Corporation was formed and acquired the Studebaker Brothers Manufacturing Company and the Everitt-Metzer-Flanders Auto Manufacturing Company. In 1928 Studebaker acquired an interest in Pierce-Arrow Motor Car Co. In 1932 an attempt to obtain new working capital by a merger with White Motor Company was blocked by minority stockholders of that company after Studebaker had obtained 95% of the stock. In 1933 Studebaker went into receivership and during that time sold their controlling interest in Pierce-Arrow. The Studebaker Corporation reorganized and came out of receivership on March 8, 1935.

(See Historical Note)

	Years	Company
J. W. Packard (F)*	1899 (First Auto Produced)	Packard & Weiss Ohio Auto Co.
W. D. Packard (F)*		Packard Motor Car Co. (1903) Incorporated in Michigan in 1909
J. W. Packard	1903–1908	Studebaker-Packard Corporation Oct. 1, 1954
H. B. Joy	1908–1916	
Alvan Macauley	1916–1939	
M. M. Gilman	1937–1942	
George J. Christopher	1942–1949	
Hugh J. Ferry	1949–1952	
James J. Nance	1952–1954	

PACKARD

	Years
James J. Nance	1954–1956
Harold E. Churchill	1956–Present

*Founders

STUDEBAKER-PACKARD CORP.

HISTORICAL NOTE, PACKARD: Packard Motor Car Company was incorporated in Michigan on September 1, 1909 to take over a company of similar name organized under West Virginia laws in 1903, which in turn had succeeded to businesses carried on by Packard & Weiss and by the Ohio Automobile Co. In 1899 J. W. Packard built the first Packard car. Effective October 1, 1954 Packard Motor Car Company purchased the business and assets of The Studebaker Corporation in exchange for the stock and assumption of the liabilities of The Studebaker Corporation. At this time the name of Packard Motor Car Company was changed to Studebaker-Packard Corporation.

NOTE: Up to the date of the merger with Packard (Oct. 1, 1954) Studebaker manufactured 3,845,000 passenger cars and 750,000 trucks. After the merger and through the year 1958 Studebaker-Packard Corp. manufactured 469,000 passenger cars and 66,000 trucks.

303

STUDEBAKER-PACKARD CORPORATION—CORPORATE HISTORY AND GROWTH

	Name	Date Acquired	Products	President or Manager at the Time	Sales Full Year Prior to Change
PACKARD STUDEBAKER	Studebaker Bros. Mfg. Co.**	1911	Wagons	—	—
	Everett-Metzer-Flanders Auto Mfg. Co.**	1911	Autos	—	—
	Pierce-Arrow Motor Car Co.	1928	Autos	—	—
	**Merged to form Studebaker Corporation				
STUDEBAKER	Studebaker Corp. (see Above)	Oct. 1, 1954	Autos	Harold S. Vance	$594,249,552 Studebaker 335,800,000 Packard $930,049,552 Combined Total

STUDEBAKER-PACKARD CORPORATION—FINANCIAL DATA

	1914	1920	1930	1940	1950	1953	1954
Cars Produced in U.S.	35,923 1910	53,675	56,190	120,256	333,718	230,170	Merged with Packard Motor Car Co. to Form Studebaker-Packard Corp.
Sales	$9,603,661 1911	$90,652,363	$86,083,940	$84,164,224	$477,066,365	$594,249,552	
Capital Invested	41,431,600	69,800,000	82,951,800	19,499,865	20,511,310	20,706,310	
Net Worth	42,376,432	83,267,048	101,464,295	23,809,315	99,872,345	108,460,360	
Profits A/T	1,653,582	9,822,054	1,540,202	2,124,628	22,506,829	2,687,973	

STUDEBAKER

		1910	1920	1930	1940	1950	Studebaker-Packard Corporation 1955	1958
PACKARD	Cars Prod. in U.S.	3,084	6,236	28,177	76,927	72,138	209,991	71,997
	Sales	$14,967,852	$58,894,525	$57,690,021	$69,235,169	$173,410,107	$480,006,110	$180,657,592
	Capital Invested	—	27,108,600	50,000,000	40,766,721	41,513,743	62,974,418	51,158,113
	Net Worth	—	47,866,272	64,877,333	44,222,950	75,331,072	118,928,189	60,436,203
	Profits A/T (Loss)	2,312,787	6,276,863	9,034,220	774,147	5,162,348	(29,705,093)	(13,390,937)

TEN YEAR SUMMARY

STUDEBAKER-PACKARD CORPORATION

(Millions of Dollars)

Financial Statistics:

	1958	1957	1956	1955	1954	1953	1952	1951	1950	1949
Combined Sales	$180.6	$213.2	$303.0	$480.0	$222.3					
Combined Net Income (Loss)	(13.3)	(11.1)	(103.3)	(29.7)	(26.1)					
Packard										
Sales						$335.8	$233.7	$178.1	$173.4	$212.5
Net Income						5.4	5.6	5.5	5.1	7.7
Studebaker										
Sales						$594.2	$585.3	$503.3	$477.0	$473.1
Net Income						2.6	14.2	12.6	22.5	27.5

305

TEN YEAR SUMMARY (CONTINUED)

STUDEBAKER-PACKARD CORPORATION

(Millions of Dollars)

Financial Statistics:

Unit Sales of Cars & Trucks

Studebaker	56,924	73,468	95,323	121,172	107,240	197,459	172,004	232,528	281,572	239,900
Packard	3,510	5,543	13,193	68,770	27,337	80,341	62,988	76,075	72,138	104,593
					B					
Subtotal	60,434	79,011	108,516	189,942	134,577	277,800	234,992	308,603	353,710	344,493
Studebaker Trucks	11,563	14,220	11,467	20,049	15,877	32,711	59,833	53,360	52,146	64,971
					B					
Grand Total	71,997	93,231	119,983	209,991	150,454	310,511	294,825	361,963	405,856	409,464

B—Studebaker Corporation merged with Packard Motor Car Company Oct. 1, 1954; production figures 1954–1958 indicate combined production Studebaker-Packard Corporation; figures for 1949 thru 1953 indicate separate production of these companies.

Sources: Studebaker-Packard Annual Reports; Moody's; Ward's

APPENDIX C

ALLIS-CHALMERS MANUFACTURING COMPANY
Milwaukee, Wisconsin

Founder & Successor Presidents	Dates of Incumbency	Date of Founding	Name at Founding	Changes in Name & Date
Charles S. Decker (F)*		1847	Decker & Seville	Edward P. Allis & Co. (1861)
James Seville (F)*				

Edward P. Allis   1861 - 1889   Incorporated as E. P. Allis Co.
William W. Allis   1889 - 1901   (1890)
Stuart Lyman   1901 -   Allis-Chalmers Co.
Charles Allis   1901 - 1904   (1901)
B. H. Warren   1904 - 1905   Allis-Chalmers Mfg. Co.
W. H. Whiteside   1905 - 1911   (1913)
C. W. Call   1911 - 1912
Otto H. Falk   1912 - 1913
(Receiver)
Otto H. Falk   1913 - 1932
Max W. Babb   1932 - 1942
W. C. Buchanan   1942 -
Walter Geist   1942 - 1951
W. A. Roberts   1951 - 1955
R. S. Stevenson   1955 - Present
*Founders

ALLIS-CHALMERS MFG. CO.—CORPORATE HISTORY AND GROWTH

Name	Date Acquired	Products	President or Manager at the Time	Sales Full Year Prior to Change
E. P. Allis Co.**	1901	Farm Equipment	Wm. W. Allis	NA
Fraser & Chalmers Co. **	1901	" "	W. J. Chalmers	NA
Gates Iron Works**	1901	" "	P. W. Gates	NA
Dickson Mfg. Co.**	1901	" "	Thomas Dickson	NA
Monarch Tractors Corp.	1928	Crawler Type Tractors	R. W. Gotshall	$1,400,000

307

ALLIS-CHALMERS MFG. CO.—CORPORATE HISTORY AND GROWTH (CONTINUED)

Name	Date Acquired	Products	President or Manager at the Time	Sales Full Year Prior to Change
LaCrosse Plow Co.	1929	Plows, Harrows, Tillage Tools	H. J. Hirshheimer	NA
Advance-Rumely Corp.	1931	Harvesters & Threshing Machinery	Finley P. Mount	$10,000,000
Brenneis Mfg. Co.	1938	Deep Tillage Tools	Louis Brenneis	$100,000
LaPlant-Choate Mfg. Co.	1952	Motor Scrapers, Motor Wagons	A. D. Dennis	$10,400,000
The Buda Company	1953	Diesel Engines, Material Handling Equipment	R. K. Mangan	$40,500,000
Gleaner Harvester Corp.	1955	Harvesters	George Reuland	$5,900,000
Baker Mfg. Co.	1955	Bulldozers & Snow Plows	W. C. Staley	$4,100,000
Allis-Chalmers Credit Corp.	1956	Financing	—	—
Allis-Chalmers International Div.	1957	Export Sales	—	—

**Group of Companies in original merger

ALLIS-CHALMERS MANUFACTURING COMPANY—FINANCIAL DATA

	1900	1914	1920	1930	1940	1950	1958
Sales	—	$10,300,000	$31,500,000	$41,500,000	$87,100,000	$343,700,000	$532,000,000
Capital Employed	—	43,200,000	54,400,000	68,500,000	96,400,000	208,500,000	399,700,000
Net Worth	—	43,200,000	54,400,000	53,500,000	71,100,000	175,500,000	307,800,000
Profits A/T (Loss)	—	(300,000)	3,600,000	3,600,000	6,200,000	23,100,000	19,700,000

ALLIS-CHALMERS MANUFACTURING COMPANY

Financial Statistics:

	1958	1957	1956	1955	1954	1953	1952	1951	1950	1949
	(Millions of Dollars)									
Sales	$532.0	$534.1	$547.4	$535.0	$492.9	$514.4	$513.6	$457.0	$343.7	$351.0
Net Income	19.7	17.8	20.3	24.8	26.1	21.9	24.4	22.4	23.1	18.7

ATHENS PLOW COMPANY
Athens, Tennessee

Date of Founding	Name at Founding	Changes in Name & Date
May 1921	Athens Plow Company	Athens Plow Co., Inc. May 1923

Founder & Successor Presidents	Dates of Incumbency
E. L. Willson (F)*	May 1921–1/14/31
R. J. Fisher	1/14/31–4/9/49
E. L. Willson	
James H. Willson	Aug. 1949–Present

ATHENS PLOW COMPANY—CORPORATE HISTORY AND GROWTH

Name	Date Acquired	Products	President or Manager at the Time	Sales Full Year Prior to Change
Taylor Plow Co.	April 1928	Disc Plows	J. H. Taylor	—

ATHENS PLOW COMPANY—FINANCIAL DATA

	1900	1910	1920	1930	1940	1950	1958
Sales	Not Available						
Capital Invested	" "						
Net Worth	" "						
Profits A/T	" "						

J. I. CASE COMPANY
Racine, Wisconsin

Founder & Successor Presidents	Dates of Incumbency	Date of Founding	Name at Founding	Changes in Name & Date
Jerome I. Case (F)* (See Historical Note)	1880–1892	Feb. 25, 1880	J. I. Case Threshing Machine Company of Wisconsin (Successor to J. I. Case & Co., originally established in 1842 by Jerome I. Case.)	J. I. Case Company June 1, 1929
Stephen Bull	1892–1897			
Frank K. Bull	1897–1916			
Warren J. Davis	1916–1924			
Leon R. Clausen	1924–1948			
Theodore Johnson	1948–1953			
John T. Brown	1953–1958			
Marc B. Rojtman	1958–Present			

Historical Note: Other co-founders included
Stephen Bull, Massena B. Erskine and Robert H. Baker

310

J. I. CASE COMPANY—CORPORATE HISTORY AND GROWTH

Name	Date Acquired	Products	President or Manager at the Time	Sales Full Year Prior to Change
Pierce Motor Co.	Sept. 1912	Automobiles	James Cowling	NA
Grand Detour Co.	1919	Steel Plows	Col. W. D. Brinton	NA
Emerson-Brantingham Corporation	1928	Farm Implements	C. S. Brantingham	NA
American Tractor Co.	Jan. 10, 1957	Tractors, Bulldozers	Marc B. Rojtman	$10,250,000

J. I. CASE COMPANY—FINANCIAL DATA

	1900	1910	1920	1930	1940	1950	1958
Sales	$3,306,000	$6,947,000	$34,550,000	$32,547,000	$25,613,000	$142,280,000	$177,893,000
Capital Invested	1,000,000		26,000,000	33,043,000	32,954,000	34,907,000	62,305,000
Net Worth	3,310,000		29,816,000	45,024,000	40,557,000	73,602,000	111,402,000
Profit After Taxes	524,000		1,937,000	2,600,000	1,378,000	15,136,000	4,314,000

TEN YEAR SUMMARY
J. I. CASE COMPANY

Financial Statistics:

(Millions of Dollars)

	1958	1957	1956	1955	1954	1953	1952	1951	1950	1949
Sales	$177.8	$117.7	$81.5	$88.8	$87.1	$104.4	$142.9	$153.5	$132.6	$156.0
Net Income (Loss)	4.3	1.3	(.98)	.90	(.54)	.78	7.0	9.7	15.1	17.6

311

Peoria, Illinois

Founder & Successor Presidents	Dates of Incumbency	Name at Founding	Date of Founding	Changes in Name & Date
(See Note)		Caterpillar Tractor Company	April 15, 1925	None
B. S. Shuman	4/16/25-5/14/25			
R. C. Force	5/14/25-6/24/30			
B. C. Heacock	6/24/30-9/23/41			
L. B. Neumiller	9/23/41-3/30/54			
H. S. Eberhard	3/30/54-Present			

NOTE: Founded by a group headed by H. H. Fair of San Francisco. B. S. Shuman, employee of law firm which handled legal steps in incorporation of Company.

CATERPILLAR TRACTOR COMPANY — CORPORATE HISTORY AND GROWTH

Name	Date Acquired	Products	President or Manager at the Time	Sales Full Year Prior to Change
C. L. Best Tractor Co.	May 1925	Crawler Tractors	C. L. Best	$5,191,000
The Holt Mfg. Co.	May 1925	Crawler Tractors, etc.	C. L. Neumiller	8,623,000
Russell Grader Mfg. Co.	Dec. 1928	Earth Moving Equipment	R. E. Ellertson	3,802,000
Trackson Company	Dec. 1951	Auxiliary Equipment, Shovels, etc.	W. H. Stiemke	5,785,000
Englehart Mfg. Co.	Aug. 1956	Machine Parts	C. E. Murray	2,365,000

CATERPILLAR TRACTOR COMPANY — FINANCIAL DATA

	1900	1910	1926	1930	1940	1950	1958
Sales			$20,699,000	$45,355,000	$73,063,000	$337,285,000	$585,164,000
Capital Employed			19,516,612	52,321,487	50,863,130	156,334,490	403,667,253

312

TEN YEAR SUMMARY

CATERPILLAR TRACTOR COMPANY

	1949	1950	1951	1952	1953	1954	1955	1956	1957	1958
Net Worth				—	—	19,516,612	42,321,487	46,863,130	138,244,490	303,667,253
Profit After Taxes				—	—	4,318,000	9,094,000	7,827,000	29,239,000	32,240,000

Financial Statistics:

(Millions of Dollars)

	1949	1950	1951	1952	1953	1954	1955	1956	1957	1958
Sales	$254.8	$337.2	$393.7	$477.5	$433.8	$401.0	$523.9	$685.9	$649.9	$585.1
Net Income	18.8	29.2	15.7	22.1	20.2	25.1	34.7	55.4	39.7	32.2

HISTORICAL SUMMARY
Caterpillar Tractor Company

Predecessor firms were C. L. Best Tractor Co. (San Leandro, Calif.) and the Holt Manufacturing Company (Stockton, Calif. and Peoria, Ill.), both of whom began building combined harvesters in 1885 and 1886 respectively. In 1925, the Best and Holt firms—by then leading builders of track-type tractors—merged to form Caterpillar Tractor Co., thus using an old and familiar Holt trademark, "Caterpillar," in their new corporate name. Soon after formation of Caterpillar Tractor Co., six city blocks of Holt facilities in Stockton became a subsidiary, the Western Harvester Company. Caterpillar entered the road machinery business in 1928 when it acquired the Russell Grader Manufacturing Company (Minneapolis).

Caterpillar operates nine domestic plants and five overseas. One plant stands today on the site of the 1886 Best plant in San Leandro. The Peoria, Illinois, plant, which occupied only 124,000 square feet when it was acquired in 1909 by the Holt firm, today is a large industrial complex of 5,900,000 square feet with highly efficient manufacturing facilities. With the exception of those two factories, all of Caterpillar's plants in the United States have been built or acquired since 1949. The locations of the other seven plants and the dates of the beginning of their operations are: Joliet, Illinois, 1951; Milwaukee, 1951; York, Pa., 1953; Decatur, Illinois, 1955; Davenport, Iowa, 1956; Aurora, Illinois, 1958; and Mossville, Illinois, 1959. Caterpillar also operates plants in Leicester and Newcastle, England, and Glasgow, Scotland; Caterpillar Brasil S. A. in Sao Paulo; and Caterpillar of Australia Pty. Ltd. in Melbourne. Caterpillar reported export sales of $276,000,000 in 1957 and $227,000,000 in 1958.

Caterpillar has experienced its greatest period of growth since World War II (see foregoing tables) and under the leadership of two men—Louis B. Neumiller and Harmon S. Eberhard. Neumiller began his career in Peoria as a clerk-stenographer in 1915, served in the U. S. Ordnance Corps in World War I, returned to the Peoria plant as an engineer, became parts manager in 1925, then service manager of the diesel line in 1931. Advancing through sales and industrial relations, he was elected President in 1941. Eberhard succeeded him 12½ years later. Eberhard had joined Holt in California in 1916 as a draftsman, became Chief Engineer in 1933, rose to Vice President in charge of research, engineering and manufacturing in 1942 and was promoted to Executive Vice President in 1950.

The story of Caterpillar's post-war growth is illustrated by the fact that of its $423,000,000 of capital expenditures since 1925, $366,000,000 has been expended since 1945—and that the net worth of the company increased from $12,400,000 in 1925, to $138,200,000 a quarter of a century later, to $202,700,000 in 1955, and to $303,700,000 in 1958.

In mid-1959, Neumiller and Eberhard were able to report to their stockholders the largest six-months sales ($404,500,000) and earnings ($28,900,000) in Caterpillar's history.

COLUMBUS IRON WORKS COMPANY
Columbus, Georgia

Founder & Successor Presidents	Dates of Incumbency	Date of Founding	Name at Founding	Changes in Name & Date
William R. Brown and Joseph W. Thomas } (F)*		1853 Incorporated on Feb. 18, 1856	Columbus Iron Works Company	
Joseph W. Thomas	1856–1858			
William R. Brown	1859–1901			

314

George B. Whiteside — 1902 (2 Mos)
George W. Brown — 1902–1903
George B. Whiteside — 1904
W. M. Teague — 1905
A. J. Teague — 1906–1910
W. M. Teague — 1911–1914
A. J. Teague — 1915–1918
F. W. Teague — 1919–1924
W. C. Bradley — 1925–1932
D. A. Turner — 1933–1947
E. S. Waddell — 1948–1955
T. Howard — 1956–Present
*Founders

COLUMBUS IRON WORKS COMPANY—CORPORATE HISTORY AND GROWTH

Name	Date Acquired	Products	President or Manager at the Time	Sales Full Year Prior to Change
Southern Plow Co.	June 22, 1881	Sweeps and Plow Stocks	Elias Haimann	

COLUMBUS IRON WORKS COMPANY—FINANCIAL DATA

	1900	1910	1920	1930	1940	1950	1958
Sales	—	—	$1,261,163	$1,023,594	$1,478,713	$3,382,692	$3,459,757
Capital Invested	$120,000	$600,000	600,000	750,000	750,000	750,000	1,000,000
Net Worth	—	822,123	963,003	960,023	694,950	1,494,949	2,014,505
Profits After Taxes (Loss)	—	81,330	85,487	(31,587)	26,542	39,560	12,126

315

DEERE & COMPANY
Moline, Illinois

Founder & Successor Presidents	Dates of Incumbency	Name at Founding	Date of Founding	Changes in Name & Date
John Deere (F)* (See Historical Note)		Deere, Tate & Gould	1837	John Deere & Company 1852
John Deere	1869 - 1886			Deere & Company 1858
Charles Deere	1886 - 1907			Incorporated on August 15, 1868
William Butterworth	1907 - 1928			Re-incorporated on March 6, 1911
Charles Deere Wiman	1928 - 1942			Re-organized 1958 under laws of Delaware
Burton F. Peek	1942 - 1944			
Charles Deere Wiman	1944 - 1955			
William A. Hewitt	1955 - Present			

*Founder

**On March 6, 1911, a new Illinois corporation also named Deere & Company acquired assets of these companies in a series of stock transactions.

HISTORICAL NOTE: John Deere produced his first steel plow in 1837, generally considered the date for the founding of John Deere & Co. Originally a sole proprietorship, the firm operated as a partnership under various names including Andrus and Deere in Grand Detour, Illinois, between 1843 and 1847. In that year John Deere moved to Moline, Illinois and formed a new partnership on May 25, 1847 under the name Deere, Tate and Gould. That partnership was dissolved and the firm name changed to John Deere & Company in 1852, to be followed in turn by a change to the name Deere & Company in 1858. On August 15, 1868, Deere & Company was incorporated in Illinois.

JOHN DEERE & COMPANY—CORPORATE HISTORY AND GROWTH

Name	Date Acquired	Products	President or Manager at the Time	Sales Full Year Prior to Change
Deere, Mansur & Co., Kansas	1869	—	—	—
Deere, Mansur & Co.-St. Louis	1874	—	—	—

Name	Date Acquired	Products	President or Manager at the Time	Sales First Year Prior to Change
Deere, Wells & Co.	1881	—	—	—
Deere & Webber Co.	1882	—	—	—
Hawley Bros. Hardware Co.	1889	—	—	—
Fairchild & Co., Ltd.	1907	—	—	—
Moline Wagon Co.	1910	—	W. A. Rosenfeld	—
**Deere & Co. (1868 Corp.)	1911	Plows & Tillage Tools	Wm. Butterworth	—
**Deere & Mansur Co.	1911	Corn Planters, Disc Harrows	Wm. Butterworth	$2,506,000
**Marseilles Co.	1911	Farm Elevators, Corn Shellers	George Peek	304,000
**Dain Mfg. Co.	1911	Hay Tools	Joseph Dain	1,278,000
**Union Malleable Iron Co.	1911	Malleable Iron Castings	Ralph Day	—
**Fort Smith Wagon Co.	1911	Farm Wagons	—	420,000
**Davenport Wagon Co.	1911	Farm Wagons	—	187,000
**Syracuse Chilled Plow Co.	1911	Chilled Cast Plows	J. L. Hecht	$1,494,000
**Van Brunt Mfg. Co.	1911	Grain Drills	Carleton A. Chase	1,822,000
**Kemp & Burpee Co.	1911	Manure Spreaders	W. A. Van Brunt	—
Waterloo Gas Engine Co.	1918	Farm Tractors	Warren C. Brayton	—
Hoover Mfg. Co.	1926	Potato Harvesters	George B. Miller	—
Sester Mfg. Co.	1928	Endgate Seeders	I. W. Hoover	—
Wagner-Langemo Co.	1930	Threshers	Charles P. Sester	—
Killefer Mfg. Corp.	1937	Heavy Tillage Tools	O. P. Robb	—
Vermilion Malleable Works	1946	Malleable Iron Castings	—	—
Lindeman Power Equipment Co.	1947	Special Tillage Tools	J. G. Lindeman	—

DEERE & COMPANY—FINANCIAL DATA

	1900	1912	1920	1930	1940	1950	1958
Sales	—	$28,954,000	$58,137,000	$63,390,000	$77,874,000	$304,071,000	$464,767,000
Capital Employed	—	68,546,000	80,342,000	82,005,000	105,229,000	244,897,000	431,105,000

DEERE & COMPANY—FINANCIAL DATA (CONTINUED)

	1900	1912	1920	1930	1940	1950	1958
Net Worth	—	62,448,000	80,202,000	82,005,000	105,229,000	225,397,000	313,985,000
Profits A/T	—	4,366,000	13,326,000	7,635,000	13,873,000	42,757,000	42,067,000

TEN YEAR SUMMARY
DEERE & COMPANY

Financial Statistics:

(Millions of Dollars)

	1958	1957	1956	1955	1954	1953	1952	1951	1950	1949
Sales	$464.7	$393.5	$321.0	$359.9	$319.9	$378.4	$383.1	$433.0	$304.0	$361.6
Net Income	42.0	28.6	20.0	28.3	20.6	24.7	35.1	35.6	42.7	39.4

INTERNATIONAL HARVESTER COMPANY
Chicago, Illinois

Founder & Successor Presidents	Dates of Incumbency	Date of Founding	Name at Founding	Changes in Name & Date
		Aug. 12, 1902	International Harvester Company	
**Founded by Consolidation				
C. H. McCormick	1902–1918			
H. F. McCormick	1918–1922			
Alexander Legge	1922–1929			
H. F. Perkins	1929–1931			
Alexander Legge	1931–1933			
A. E. McKinstry	1933–1935			

318

Sidney McAllister   1935–1941

Fowler McCormick   1941–1946

J. L. McCaffrey   1946–1956

P. V. Moulder   1956–1957

F. W. Jenks   1957–Present

**Group of Companies Merged at Founding

HISTORICAL NOTE: International Harvester Company was formed in 1902 through the consolidation of five companies which produced harvesting machinery. They were the McCormick Harvesting Machinery Company, Chicago; Deering Harvester Company, Chicago; Plano Manufacturing Company, West Pullman, Illinois; Warder, Bushnell and Glessner, Springfield, Ohio; and Milwaukee Harvester Company, Milwaukee.

The principal firms in this group were the McCormick and Deering companies. The McCormick business dates back to July 1831, when young 22 year old Cyrus Hall McCormick demonstrated the first successful reaper in a small field near Steele's tavern, Virginia.

The McCormick business grew slowly but steadily. In 1843, for example, the young proprietor sold 29 machines and in 1844 the figure climbed to 50. On August 30, 1847 Cyrus Hall McCormick and Charles M. Gray formed a partnership, purchased three lots on the north bank of the Chicago river, and immediately began construction of a factory in which to build 500 reapers for the 1848 harvest. From this time growth was much faster than in the earlier years.

By 1856, the McCormick Reaper Works had a capacity of 40 reapers a day and 4,000 were actually made that year.

In keeping with Mr. McCormick's policy of constant improvements on his machine, the late 50's and early 60's were marked by important advances in reaper design and the addition of a machine to cut hay. Anything that would conserve manpower was, of course, important—especially during the War Between the States in the first half of the 1860's.

Along with much of Chicago, McCormick was burned out by the Great Chicago Fire of 1871 but he rebuilt anew on a much larger scale in 1872.

In 1879 Mr. McCormick reorganized the company, dissolving the partnership contracts and forming a corporation with himself as president. On his death in 1884, he was succeeded as president by his eldest son, Cyrus H. McCormick. It was only a few years after the death of the elder McCormick that occurred what was called the "harvester war" of the 1890's. So costly and ruinous was this fierce competition that the harvester manufacturers soon sought to arrange a truce of some kind. It was in such a setting as this that the International Harvester consolidation of 1902 took place.

319

Name	Date Acquired	Products	President or Manager at the Time	Sales Full Year Prior to Change
**McCormick Harvesting Machinery Co.	Aug. 12, 1902	Harvesting Machinery	Cyrus H. McCormick	NA
**Deering Harvester Co.	Aug. 12, 1902	Harvesting Machinery	William Deering	NA
**Plano Manufacturing Co.	Aug. 12, 1902	Harvesting Machinery	William H. Jones	NA
**Warder Bushnell & Glessner	Aug. 12, 1902	Harvesting Machinery	John J. Glessner	NA
**Milwaukee Harvester Company	Aug. 12, 1902	Harvesting Machinery	NA	NA
D. M. Osborne & Co.	January 1903	Harvesting Machinery, Tillage Tools, Twine	NA	NA
Weber Wagon Co.	November 1904	Farm Wagons	W. H. Weber	NA
Minnie Harvester Co.	September 1905	Harvesting Machines & Twine	NA	NA
Aultman-Miller Co.	November 1905	Harvesting Machines & Mowers	NA	NA
Keystone Co.	November 1905	Hay Machines, Corn Shellers, Tillage Tools	NA	NA
Accurate Engineering Co.	October 1917	Artillery Wheels During World War I	NA	NA
Chattanooga Plow Works	May 1919	Chilled Plows	NA	NA
Parlin & Orendorff	July 1919	Full Line of Plows	U. G. Orendorff	NA
Springfield Spring Co.	June 1920	Implement Springs	NA	NA
Dyrr Manufacturing Co.	October 1937	Hay & Deep Tillage Tools	J. V. Dyrr	NA
Frank G. Hough Company	October 1952	Construction Equipment	Frank G. Hough	NA

320

INTERNATIONAL HARVESTER COMPANY—FINANCIAL DATA

	1910	1920	1930	1940	1950	1958
Sales	$101,166,359	$225,044,046	$279,299,843	$274,682,399	$942,601,961	$1,098,389,954
Capital Employed	162,557,853	241,964,683	352,159,272	400,344,252	614,551,359	882,961,387
Net Worth	$162,557,853	$241,964,683	$352,159,272	$400,344,252	$614,551,359	$782,961,387
Profits A/T	16,084,819	16,655,353	25,703,192	23,161,109	66,714,716	42,987,435

Prior to 1940 the Company presented its annual financial statements on a consolidated basis.
Since 1939 these statements have been presented on an unconsolidated basis.

TEN YEAR SUMMARY
INTERNATIONAL HARVESTER COMPANY

Financial Statistics

	1958	1957	1956	1955	1954	1953	1952	1951	1950	1949
					(Millions of Dollars)					
Sales	$1,098.3	$1,171.3	$1,252.0	$1,165.7	$994.0	$1,256.1	$1,204.0	$1,277.3	$942.6	$908.9
Net Income	42.9	45.6	49.6	55.5	36.3	52.0	55.6	63.0	66.7	33.0

KEWANEE MACHINERY & CONVEYOR COMPANY
Kewanee, Illinois

Founder & Successor Presidents	Dates of Incumbency	Date of Founding	Name at Founding	Changes in Name & Date
B. F. Baker and W. D. Glidden } (F)*		1912	Kewanee Corn Hanger Company	Kewanee Implement Company (1916) Kewanee Machinery & Conveyor Company (1930)

KEWANEE MACHINERY & CONVEYOR COMPANY (CONTINUED)
Kewanee, Illinois

Founder & Successor Presidents	Dates of Incumbency	Name at Founding	Date of Founding	Changes in Name & Date
B. F. Baker	1915–1939			
R. B. Glidden	1939–1950			
R. L. Glidden	1951–Present			

KEWANEE MACHINERY & CONVEYOR COMPANY—CORPORATE HISTORY AND GROWTH

Name	Date Acquired	Products	President or Manager at the Time	Sales Full Year Prior to Change
Hart Grain Weigher Co.	1922	Bucket Elevators	—	—
National Coal Conveyor Co.	1930	Conveyors	—	—

KEWANEE MACHINERY & CONVEYOR COMPANY—FINANCIAL DATA

	1900	1910	1920	1930	1940	1950	1958
Sales	Not Available						
Capital Invested	"	"					
Net Worth	"	"					
Profits A/T	"	"					

KRAUSE CORPORATION
Hutchinson, Kansas

Founder & Successor Presidents	Dates of Incumbency	Name at Founding	Date of Founding	Changes in Name & Date
Henry Krause (F)*	1924–1948	Krause Mfg. Co.	1924	Krause Plow Corporation, Inc. (1946)
Norman L. Krause	1948–Present			Krause Corporation (1955)

322

KRAUSE CORPORATION—FINANCIAL DATA

	1900	1910	1920	1930	1940	1950	1958
Sales	—	—	NA	NA	$45,000	$2,433,000	$3,279,000
Capital Invested	—	—	—	—	—	—	—
Net Worth	—	—	—	—	60,000	1,406,000***	1,762,000
Profits A/T	—	—	—	—	5,000	191,000	218,000

***1946—At time of Incorporation $147,000

MASSEY-FERGUSON LIMITED
Toronto, Canada

Founder & Successor Presidents	Dates of Incumbency	Date of Founding	Name at Founding	Changes in Name & Date
Daniel Massey (F)*	1847 - 1855	1847	Daniel Massey, Founder	Newcastle Foundry and Machine Manufactory C.W. 1849
Hart A. Massey (F)*	1855 - 1891			Newcastle Agricultural Works 1862
Hart A. Massey	1891 - 1896			
Walter E. H. Massey	1896 - 1901			Massey Manufacturing Company 1870
Chester D. Massey	1901 - 1903			
Sir Lyman Melvin-Jones	1903 - 1917			Massey-Harris Company, Limited 1891
Thomas Findley	1917 - 1921			
Vincent Massey	1922 - 1925			Massey-Harris-Ferguson Limited 1953
Joseph N. Shenstone	1925 - 1930			

323

MASSEY-FERGUSON LIMITED (CONTINUED)
Toronto, Canada

Founder & Successor Presidents	Dates of Incumbency	Name at Founding	Date of Founding	Change in Name & Date
Thomas Bradshaw	1930			Massey-Ferguson Limited
T. A. Russell	1930 - 1940			1958
James S. Duncan	1940 - 1956			
Albert A. Thornbrough	1956 - Present			

*Founders
**Merged to form Massey-Harris Company, Ltd. 1891

MASSEY-FERGUSON LIMITED—CORPORATE HISTORY AND GROWTH

Name	Date Acquired	Products	President or Manager at the Time	Sales Full Year Prior to Change
Toronto Reaper & Mower Company	1881	Mowers, Reapers, Binder		NA
**Massey Manufacturing Co.	1891	Mowers, Reapers, Binders		NA
**A. Harris, Son and Company Limited	1891	Mowers, Reapers, Binders		NA
**Patterson and Brothers Company Limited	1891	Full line or Implements	John D. Patterson	NA
**J. O. Wisner Son and Company	1891	Tillage and Seeding	Wareham S. Wisner	NA
Verity Plow Company	1892	Plows	W. H. Verity	NA
Corbin Disc Harrow Co.	1893	Disc Harrows	NA	NA
Bain Wagon Company Limited	1896	Wagons, Sleighs	John A. Bain	NA
Kemp Manure Spreader Company	1904	Manure Spreader	NA	NA
Deyo-Macey Engine Co.	1913	Gasoline Engines	NA	NA

Company	Year	Products	Executive
Johnston Harvester Company	1917	Binders, Harrows, Reapers, Spreader, Mowers, Loaders	NA
J. I. Case Plow Company	1928	Tractors and Implements	Harry M. Wallis, Sr.
Goble Disc Works	1949	Disc Harrows	NA
Harry Ferguson Companies	1953	Tractors and 3-point hitch Mounted Implements	Harry Ferguson
H. V. McKay Massey Harris Proprietary Limited	1955	Full line of Implements	Cecil N. McKay
Mid-Western Industries, Inc.	1957	Front end loaders, back hoe and other light industrial equipment	Charles J. Davis
F. Perkins Limited	1959	Diesel Engines	Frank Perkins

MASSEY-FERGUSON LIMITED—FINANCIAL DATA

	1900	1910	1920	1930	1940	1950	1958
Sales	$5,990,838	$13,026,000	$25,570,000	$37,263,000	$24,267,022	$196,025,391	$440,109,455
Capital Invested	5,000,000	12,000,000	18,131,700	38,788,055	38,864,653	15,461,989	56,539,296
Net Worth	8,566,690	16,710,750	280,098,391	39,035,441	17,599,965	50,740,256	153,258,850
Profits A/T (Loss)	NA	2,264,373	1,817,021	(2,247,440)	805,568	17,540,803	13,025,282

TEN YEAR SUMMARY
MASSEY-FERGUSON LIMITED

Financial Statistics:

	1958	1957	1956	1955	1954	1953	1952	1951	1950	1949
					(Millions of Dollars)					
Sales	$440.1	$412.4	$372.1	$367.3	$297.7	$189.1	$224.8	$197.3	$196.0	$160.0
Net Income	13.0	(4.7)	3.1	12.1	7.1	7.3	10.8	13.1	17.5	16.1

Hopkins, Minnesota

Founder & Successor Presidents	Dates of Incumbency	Name at Founding	Date of Founding	Changes in Name & Date
W. C. MacFarlane (F)*	}	Minneapolis-Moline Power Implement Company	March 30, 1929	Minneapolis-Moline Company Feb. 21, 1949
G. L. Gillette				
W. S. Peddie				
W. C. Rich				
W. C. MacFarlane	1929–1957			
H. S. Reddig	1957			
J. R. Duncan	1957–Present			

*Founders

HISTORICAL NOTE: As a result of a financial reorganization, Minneapolis-Moline Power Implement Company was merged into and became a part of Minneapolis-Moline Company on February 21, 1949.

On March 30, 1929 Minneapolis-Moline Power Implement Company was formed by merger of Minneapolis Steel and Machinery Company founded by James L. Record, associates—Ralph P. Gillette, Otis P. Briggs; The Minneapolis Threshing Machine Company founded by John S. McDonald, associates—Levi Longfellow, J. B. Bushnell, G. H. Rust; and Moline Implement Company (formerly Moline Plow Company) founded by Hugh S. Johnson, associates—Robert W. Lea, Harold B. Dinneen.

MINNEAPOLIS-MOLINE COMPANY—CORPORATE HISTORY AND GROWTH

Name	Date Acquired	Products	President or Manager at the Time	Sales Full Year Prior to Change
Minneapolis Steel & Machinery Co.**	March 30, 1929	—	W. C. MacFarlane	$8,885,000
The Minneapolis Threshing Machine Co.**	March 30, 1929	—	Nelson A. Wiff	5,741,057
Moline Implement Co.**	March 30, 1929	—	R. W. Lea	3,685,328
B. F. Avery & Sons Co.	March 1, 1951	Tractors & Tillage Tools	P. H. Noland	5,361,455

**Group of Companies Merged at Founding

326

MINNEAPOLIS-MOLINE COMPANY—FINANCIAL DATA

	1900	1910	1920	1930	1940	1950	1958
Sales	—	—	—	$13,487,558	$16,367,627	$79,175,356	$53,601,782
Capital Invested	—	—	—	18,849,096	14,250,926	15,978,175	11,640,751
Net Worth	—	—	—	20,723,857	15,567,123	39,367,870	33,775,061
Profits A/T (Loss)	—	—	—	1,043,940	1,165,736	7,001,711	(1,729,883)

TEN YEAR SUMMARY

MINNEAPOLIS-MOLINE COMPANY

Financial Statistics: (Millions of Dollars)

	1958	1957	1956	1955	1954	1953	1952	1951	1950	1949
Sales	$53.6	$57.4	$66.2	$72.2	$77.4	$105.6	$92.5	$91.0	$79.1	$73.5
Net Income (Loss)	(1.7)	(5.0)	.534	.679	(.044)	4.4	2.1	5.3	7.0	6.3

OLIVER CORPORATION
Chicago, Illinois

Founder & Successor Presidents	Dates of Incumbency	Date of Founding	Name at Founding	Changes in Name & Date
Founded by Merger** (See Historical Note)		Feb. 13, 1929	Oliver Agricultural Equipment Co.	Oliver Farm Equipment Co. Feb. 26, 1929 / The Oliver Corporation Oct. 4, 1944
M. W. Ellis	1929–1930			
C. R. Messinger	1930–1933			
M. H. Pettit	1934–1935			
C. R. Messinger	1936–1937			

327

OLIVER CORPORATION (CONTINUED)
Chicago, Illinois

Founder & Successor Presidents	Dates of Incumbency	Date of Founding	Name at Founding	Changes in Name & Date
Cal Sivright	1937–1944			
Alva W. Phelps	1944–1950			
A. King McCord	1950–1956			
Alva W. Phelps	1956–1958			
Carl L. Hecker	1958–Present			

HISTORICAL NOTE: The Oliver Corporation was formed in 1929 by the merger of Oliver Chilled Plow Works, plow and tillage tool manufacturer, of South Bend, Indiana; Hart-Parr Company, wheel tractor manufacturer, of Charles City, Iowa; Nichols & Shepard Company, threshing and harvesting machinery manufacturer, of Battle Creek, Michigan; and American Seeding Machine Company, grain drill, planter, and seeding machine manufacturer, of Springfield, Ohio,

Oliver Chilled Plow Works had its beginning in 1855, when James Oliver established a foundry in South Bend, Indiana. Hart-Parr Company was organized in 1901 by Charles W. Hart and Charles H. Parr. Nichols & Shepard Company had its beginning in a business started by John Nichols in 1848. The American Seeding Machine Company was the product of a number of mergers of different seeding machine companies, one of which (Bickford & Huffman Co.) was started in 1842 in Macedon, New York.

OLIVER CORPORATION—CORPORATE HISTORY AND GROWTH

Name	Date Acquired	Products	President or Manager at the Time	Sales Full Year Prior to Change
Oliver Chilled Plow Works**	Feb. 13, 1929	Plow & Tillage Tools	Joseph D. Oliver	$11,227,000
Hart-Parr Co.**	Feb. 13, 1929	Wheel Tractors	M. W. Ellis	7,158,000
Nichols & Sheppard Co.**	Feb. 13, 1929	Threshing & Harvesting	Louis Brown	6,109,000
American Seeding Machine Co.**	Feb. 13, 1929	Grain Drill, Planters Seeders	W. H. Stackhouse	2,944,000

The Cleveland Tractor Co.	Nov. 1, 1944	Crawler Tractors	W. King White
A. B. Farquhar Co.	Jan. 1, 1952	Sprayers, Conveyors, etc.	W. J. Fisher
Be-Ge Mfg. Co.	Nov. 10, 1953	Hydraulics, Farm Equipment	Albert Gurries

**Group of Companies Merged at Founding

OLIVER CORPORATION—FINANCIAL DATA

	1900	1910	1920	1930	1940	1950	1958
Sales	—	—	—	$24,934,000	$19,107,000	$98,836,000	$113,328,000
Capital Invested	—	—	—	30,744,000	16,878,000	29,171,000	38,018,000
Net Worth	—	—	—	34,369,000	20,692,000	53,904,000	76,491,000
Profits A/T (Loss)	—	—	—	(4,835,000)	866,000	6,241,000	2,594,000

TEN YEAR SUMMARY

OLIVER CORPORATION

ROME PLOW COMPANY
Cedar Town, Georgia

Financial Statistics:

	1958	1957	1956	1955	1954	1953	1952	1951	1950	1949
Sales	$113.3	$101.6	$107.8	$133.5	$128.3	$136.6	$134.4	$119.5	$98.8	$101.3
Net Income	2.5	.6	1.9	4.7	3.7	2.8	6.0	6.0	6.2	6.1

Founder & Successor Presidents	Dates of Incumbency	Name at Founding	Date of Founding	Changes in Name & Date
A. P. McKay (F)*	1932–1944	Rome Plow Company	Feb. 22, 1932	—
A. P. McKay				

ROME PLOW COMPANY (CONTINUED)
Cedar Town, Georgia

Founder & Successor Presidents	Dates of Incumbency	Date of Founding	Name at Founding	Changes in Name & Date
Tom Mullen	1944–1945			
Jack Lemann	1945–1953			
C. C. Mullen	1954–Present			
*Founder				

ROME PLOW COMPANY—FINANCIAL DATA

	1900	1910	1920	1932	1940	1950	1958
Sales	—	—	—	$2,123	$162,525	$1,731,452	$3,320,097
Capital Invested	—	—	—	7,500	60,000	250,000	786,400
Net Worth	—	—	—	4,074	68,768	518,999	1,106,546
Profits A/T	—	—	—	(3,425)	7,516	87,718	63,377
(Loss)							(See Note)

NOTE: A bonus arrangement of $60,000 and an Employees' Stock Bonus Fund of $117,000 would have boosted the net after taxes to $152,000, if net after taxes were figured on the same basis as for 1950 and prior years.

330

SCHAFER PLOW, INC.
Pratt, Kansas

Founder & Successor Presidents	Dates of Incumbency	Name at Founding	Date of Founding	Changes in Name & Date
W. G. Schafer (F)*	1945–Present	Schafer Plow, Inc.	1945	—

SCHAFER PLOW, INC.—FINANCIAL DATA

	1900	1910	1920	1930	1940	1950	1958
Sales	—	—	—	—	—	$532,124	$944,801
Capital Employed	—	—	—	—	—	104,937	88,776
Net Worth	—	—	—	—	—	104,937	88,776
Profits A/T	—	—	—	—	—	–NA	NA

TAYLOR IMPLEMENT MANUFACTURING COMPANY
Athens, Tennessee

Founder & Successor Presidents	Dates of Incumbency	Name at Founding	Date of Founding	Changes in Name & Date
Joseph H. Taylor (F)*	1947–Present	Taylor Implement Mfg. Co.	1947	—
Joseph H. Taylor				

TAYLOR IMPLEMENT MANUFACTURING COMPANY — FINANCIAL DATA

	1900	1910	1920	1930	1947	1950	1958
Sales	—	—	—	—	NA	NA	NA
Capital Invested	—	—	—	—	$75,000	$100,000	$100,000
Net Worth	—	—	—	—	85,000	230,000	391,000
Profits A/T	—	—	—	—	NA	NA	NA

TOWNER MANUFACTURING COMPANY
Santa Ana, California

Founder & Successor Presidents	Dates of Incumbency	Date of Founding	Name at Founding	Changes in Name & Date
Fred Towner (F)* (See Historical Note)		1915	Towner Mfg. Co.	—
Fred Towner	1915–1935			
Howard Rapp	1935–1942			
Howard Rapp George A. Sattler }**	1942–1957			
George A. Sattler	1957–1958			
B. R. Twist	1958–Present			

*Founder
**Partnership

HISTORICAL NOTE: Howard Rapp acquired ownership in the '30's. In 1942 George A. Sattler bought one-half interest and the company was operated as a partnership until February 1, 1957. Howard Rapp passed away November, 1954. George Sattler was elected President of the newly formed corporation, same name as partnership, and served until his death, September, 1958. B. R. Twist succeeded him as President at that time.

Presently manufacturers of offset disc harrows.

TOWNER MANUFACTURING COMPANY—FINANCIAL DATA

	1900	1910	1920	1930	1940	1950	1958
Sales	—	—	—	—	$300,000	$1,615,000	$1,597,000
Capital Invested	—	—	—	—	100,000	689,000	450,000
Net Worth	—	—	—	—	100,000	689,000	(Note)450,000
Profits A/T	—	—	—	—	—	141,000	14,000

NOTE: Does not include the value of the buildings and equipment which were retained by the old partnership and leased to the Corporation.

Appendix D

MANUFACTURERS' SHIPMENTS OF FARM MACHINES AND EQUIPMENT, 1947–1958

(In Millions of Dollars)

Year	Total Manufacturers' Shipments*	Total Shipped for Export*	Total* Domestic Shipments	Shipments for Use in the United States					
				Plows and Listers	Planting, Seeding, and Fertilizing Machinery	Harvesting Machinery	Haying Machinery	Harrows, Rollers Pulverizers & Stalk Cutters	Other
1947	1,294.7	162.0	1,132.7	73.5	69.9	174.7	87.9	42.7	684.0
1948	1,733.7	220.1	1,513.6	87.6	104.9	226.4	142.2	67.6	884.9
1949	997.8	84.9	912.8	82.4	109.4	266.0	140.4	69.8	244.8
1950	1,001.8	78.5	923.2	86.5	107.5	263.4	146.6	70.8	248.4
1951	1,219.0	95.0	1,123.9	96.0	127.2	313.1	196.6	86.9	304.1
1952	1,104.1	91.5	1,012.6	80.1	121.6	272.3	191.3	78.3	269.0
1953	1,003.3	94.6	908.7	59.3	103.1	248.0	179.1	73.0	246.2
1954	883.3	n.a.	n.a.	57.4	89.7	219.7	137.2	63.8	n.a.
1955	912.1	67.8	844.3	58.4	84.0	223.6	158.6	67.0	252.7
1956	854.6	75.3	779.2	54.5	75.1	202.4	130.3	66.7	249.9
1957	897.6	69.5	828.1	54.9	82.7	233.8	130.3	69.6	256.8
1958	**1,074.5	57.8	1,016.6	68.7	96.3	294.9	165.7	85.0	306.0

*Includes tractor production for years 1947 and 1948 only. See separate table for tractor production.

**Subject to Revision

Sources: Bureau of the Census
Economic Almanac—1958
Economic Almanac—1953–1954

Appendix E

PRODUCTION OF TRACTORS
Number Produced*

Year	Wheel-type	Tracklaying	Garden Tractors & Motor Tillers	Total
1948	529,587	39,412	184,624	753,623
1949	555,523	44,613	126,839	726,975
1950	498,768	43,680	151,198	693,646
1951	567,446	49,614	177,169	794,229
1952	418,669	48,651	199,321	666,641
1953	393,426	51,862	245,609	690,897
1954	248,626	39,404	191,235	479,265
1955	330,141	46,973**	185,696	562,810
1956	214,654	57,611**	200,997	473,262
1957	229,050	36,802**	178,097	443,949
1958	241,269	24,231**	n.a.	n.a.

*Includes domestic farm and non-farm use, and export.
**Excludes contractors' off-highway type.
n.a. Not Available
Source: Farm Equipment Institute
    U.S. Department of Commerce
    Bureau of the Census

335

Index